THE

PUBLICATIONS

OF THE

Northamptonshire Record Society

FOUNDED IN DECEMBER, 1920

VOLUME XXXII

FOR THE YEAR ENDED 31 DECEMBER 1982

A
NORTHAMPTONSHIRE
MISCELLANY

Edited by
EDMUND KING

Northampton
1983

© Northamptonshire Record Society 1983

ISBN 0 901275 47 6

Published by the Northamptonshire Record Society,
Delapre Abbey, Northampton NN4 9AW

Printed by Butler & Tanner Ltd., Frome, Somerset

CONTENTS

ILLUSTRATIONS

Between pages 58 and 59

Plates 1, 2, 3 and 4 are reproduced by permission of the British Library; plates 5, 7 and 8 by permission of the Northamptonshire Record Office

ACKNOWLEDGEMENTS

Volume 32 of the Society's record series is the first to take the form of a *Miscellany*. The Hotot estate records comprise BL Add. MS 54228, reproduced by permission of the British Library Board, and extracts from Bodleian Library MS top. Northants c. 19, reproduced by permission of the Bodleian Library, Oxford. Both the Daventry Tithing Book and the Militia Lists are in the Northamptonshire Record Office, and are reproduced by permission of the Chief Archivist, Mr Patrick King. Each of the editors wishes to thank Mr King and the staff of the Record Office for their assistance.

The Society and myself must thank the British Academy for a generous grant from its Small Grants Research Fund in the Humanities towards my research expenses in pursuing the Hotots. We must also thank Dr Marjorie Chibnall for reading my text, and for making many valuable suggestions for its improvement. Dr Sandra Raban, Mr James Campbell, Mr David Hall and Dr David Crook were kind enough to help with individual queries.

Mr Greenall wishes to thank the following for advice, help and information: his colleague, Mr A. E. Brown; the Librarian and Deputy Archivist at Christ Church, Oxford; the Rev K. A. Ward, formerly rector of Daventry; and the County Archivists and their staffs at Derby and Shrewsbury.

Mr Hatley and Mr Statham wish to thank Mrs Jenny King for making the index of names to the Militia Lists, Mrs Jacqueline Minchinton for reading the section in the introduction relating to the family and associates of John Clare, and Dr Diana Sutherland for information about the geology of the Peterborough district.

EDMUND KING

1

ESTATE RECORDS OF THE HOTOT FAMILY

EDITED BY

EDMUND KING

INTRODUCTION

The first of the documents here edited has come to rest at the British Library, where it is Additional Manuscript 54228, after an interesting career. It was seen by the Northamptonshire historian John Bridges, when he was collecting material for his history of the county, between 1718 and his death in 1742. The Hotot family had continued in the male line until c 1400, when the heiress to the estate married Richard Dudley. It was his descendant, Sir Matthew Dudley (died 1721), who showed the Hotot records to John Bridges. There were then two books, the volume which survives, and a later volume, since lost and for which the only evidence survives in Bridges' transcripts.[1] Extracts from both books, particularly the information on family history, were published when Bridges' history finally appeared in 1791.[2] Bridges referred to the two manuscripts simply as MS A and MS B. These identifications have been retained. MS A is the surviving manuscript, which contains the earliest material: MS B survives only in part, in Bridges' transcripts.

The later history of MS A can be established as follows. It came into the possession of George Paton (1721-1807), a Scottish antiquary, and a man of great learning in English as well as Scottish topography.[3] His manuscripts were dispersed in 1811, and the Hotot volume was picked up on an Edinburgh bookstall by John Caley, secretary to the first record commission between 1801 and 1834.[4] The volume returned to Northamptonshire when Caley presented it to George Baker (1781-1851), whose own history of the county was published between 1822 and 1841.[5] But only briefly, for in 1844 Baker sold his Northamptonshire collections to the legendary Sir Thomas Phillipps.[6] The volume's history thereafter can be followed in one of the classics of modern bibliographical literature, A. N. L. Munby's *Phillipps Studies*. The individual manuscript though was lost to view. It was recorded as untraced in Dr Davis's invaluable list of cartularies published in 1958.[7] But then in one of the regular series of Phillipps sales, held on 28 November 1967, there appeared lot 91: Cartulary of the Hotot family of Clopton, Northants. 'This is a rare example of a family cartulary, similar in nature to the cartularies of the great monastic houses but briefer and more roughly put together.'[8]

---

[1] Bodleian Library MS top. Northants c. 19, pp. 28-68; on these transcripts see F. Madan, *Summary Catalogue of Western Manuscripts in the Bodleian Library*, iii (Oxford, 1895), pp. 642-51.

[2] J. Bridges, *The History and Antiquities of Northamptonshire* (1791), ii. 367-72.

[3] See *DNB*.

[4] See *DNB* for information on Caley's important but far from distinguished career. For his acquisition of the Hotot volume see *Catalogus Manuscriptorum in Bibliotheca Phillippica* (1968 repr), p. 210, sub MS 12025.

[5] See *DNB*; see also Sotheby & Co, *Bibliotheca Phillippica, Medieval Manuscripts: New Ser. Pt III*, catalogue of sale on 26 June 1967, pp. 70-80.

[6] A. N. L. Munby, *Phillipps Studies, no 4: The Formation of the Phillipps Library from 1841 to 1872* (Cambridge, 1956), pp. 20-2; cf *ibid.*, no 2, p. 36; no 3, p. 107n.

[7] G. R. C. Davis, *Medieval Cartularies of Great Britain* (1958), no 1256.

[8] Sotheby & Co, *Bibliotheca Phillippica, Medieval Manuscripts: New Ser. Pt III*, catalogue of sale on 28 November 1967, no 91, pp. 33-4; from which the provenance given here.

Documents of this kind are indeed rare. Dr Davis's list shows 1185 cartularies made by religious houses, but only 159 cartularies of secular provenance. Many of these secular cartularies are magnate records. The majority date from the fourteenth and fifteenth centuries. The interest of the Hotot book is that it is early, from the thirteenth century, and that it contains the records of a knightly family. Northamptonshire is particularly rich in early records of lay estates. Two cartularies, one of which appeared in another Phillipps sale in 1976, show the acquisitions of the Braybrooke family.[9] The Braybrookes are notable for their active trade in property that had been mortgaged to the Jews, and as such they have been studied by H. G. Richardson.[10] There is a valuable file of Basset rolls, contemporary with the Hotot records and containing material of a similar kind. It includes a roll of charters, a feodary, and miscellaneous memoranda.[11] They are particularly concerned to trace the holding of fees and their fragmentation; they re-count the descent of holdings in a manner reminiscent of pleadings in the contemporary royal court. The Bassets held a barony though, and the Braybrookes grew to a similar rank. Nearer in substance to Hotot was Henry de Bray, lord of Harlestone, who copied out his own estate book in 1322.[12] This also is based on charters of the acquisition of land and the record of tenures. But it has a great deal of material which we would regard as miscellaneous but Henry de Bray did not. There are lists—of counties, of bishops, of kings, of weights and measures. And not least, as he wrote to instruct his son, there is the history of his family. The Hotot records also start with a family history.

The Clapton family

The estate book begins with the establishment of a knightly tenancy centred upon Clapton shortly after the Norman Conquest.[13]

> Turold abbot of Peterborough gave Roger of Lovetot baron of Southoe a fee of two knights in Clapton, Polebrook and Catworth, to hold of the said abbot and his successors. Roger of Lovetot gave Alfred de Grauntcourt his knight the whole fee which he had by gift of the abbot in Clapton, namely four hides as one knight's fee. And Roger gave Alfred in the vill of Clapton one hide and one virgate for a quarter fee, and this was of Roger of Southoe's own barony, not pertaining to Peterborough in any way, save only that it was in the liberty of the abbot.

Bridges surmised that Roger of Lovetot's grant was made 'about the third year of William Rufus'.[14] The establishment of Alfred at Clapton must, however, be looked for a little earlier, for he is recorded as the Domesday holder of the estate under Eustace the sheriff of Huntingdon.[15] There can be little question as to the Norman origin of the family thus established on

[9] Sotheby & Co, *ibid.*, *Pt XI*, sale of 30 November 1976, no 874, pp. 51–2; BL Sloane MS 986 (=Davis, no 1206).
[10] H. G. Richardson, *The English Jewry under Angevin Kings* (1960), pp. 100–2, 270–80.
[11] BL Sloane MS 31 nos 3–7. The charter roll is no 4 (=Davis, no 1188A), and is to be edited by Prof. William T. Reedy for the Pipe Roll Society.
[12] Dorothy Willis (ed.), *The Estate Book of Henry de Bray* (Camden Soc. 3rd Ser. xxvii, 1916).
[13] These are the opening words of MS A.
[14] Bodleian Lib. MS top. Northants c. 19, p. 57; thence in Bridges, ii. 367.
[15] *Domesday Book*, i, fo 228a.

the heavy claylands on the borders of Northamptonshire and Hunting-donshire.[16]

This is a small knightly estate, and for the century which followed its establishment the information on it is not great. In the Northamptonshire Survey, from some time in the reign of Henry I, the tenant is Walter.[17] According to the family history, Walter was Alfred's son, and succeeded to all his father's estates. It is likely the same Walter who appears as witness to a charter for St Neot's priory dated 1149.[18] Before 1155 he had been succeeded by William of Clapton,[19] who was the Lovetot tenant in 1166,[20] and whose later activities are well recorded. After the revolt of 1173-4 he owed 20s for forest pleas, and the more substantial sum of 40 marks as one of a group of Peterborough tenants purchasing the freedom of Jordan of Waterville.[21] Another indication of his connection with the local men of the honour is provided by his marriage. According to the later family history, William married twice. The first wife was Ivetta de Muskham; and there is a little story about her. It says that she was the sister of Geoffrey de Muskham, bishop of Chester, and was born in the neighbourhood of Newark.[22]

After his marriage, returning home with his wife from the place of her birth, on the road beyond Wittering, at a distance William saw his mansion house of Clapton in flames; and on his arrival found it, with the preparations and provisions for celebrating the wedding-feast, de-stroyed by fire. This accident, our author says, was a judgement from heaven; as, in the reign of King Stephen, he had converted more than a third part of the churchyard to a profane use, and had cut down a noble grove of ash-trees which grew in it, for the purpose of building his said manor-house.

Geoffrey de Muschamp was bishop of Coventry and Litchfield (or Chester) between 1198 and 1208.[23] This passage allows him to be identified with Muskham near Newark on Trent.[24] The connection of this part of Not-tinghamshire with Clapton in Northamptonshire is most obviously the existence of a Peterborough abbey fee in each place.[25] The honour can be seen here as a marriage-market, and something of the marriage customs glimpsed also.

The greater part of the surviving records for William of Clapton, as well as his secure place in the history of the Hotots, arise from his alienation of land. It was given, in smallish parcels, to the church; and in larger parcels

[16] It is more difficult to identify the Norman town from which they originated. Loyd's survey shows a Grandcourt and a Graincourt: L. C. Loyd, *The Origins of some Anglo-Norman Families* (Harleian Soc. ciii, 1951), pp. 47-8.

[17] *VCH Northants,* i. 366.

[18] F. M. Stenton (ed.), *Facsimiles of Early Charters from Northamptonshire Collections* (NRS, iv, 1930), p. 62. Mellows was in error in stating that William of Clapton occurs in 1146; the reference is to William of Lovetot: *Pytchley,* pp. 93-4nn.

[19] W. H. Hart and P. A. Lyons (eds.), *Cartularium Monasterii de Rameseia,* i (Rolls Ser. 79, 1884), p. 79, a charter of abbot Martin of Bec (1133-55).

[20] *Red Book of the Exchequer,* i. 372.

[21] *Pipe Roll 22 Henry II,* p. 52; *Pipe Roll 23 Henry II,* p. 95.

[22] **B 4 no 3**; in the version of Bridges, ii. 368.

[23] *DNB,* sub *Geoffrey* de Muschamp.

[24] A. M. Oliver, 'The family of Muschamp, barons of Wooler', *Arch. Aeliana,* 4th ser. xiv (1937), pp. 243-4 suggests that both the Northumberland Muschamps and the Derbyshire Muschamps derived from Muskham. He further suggested that the two families were related, an idea seemingly discounted by C. J. Holdsworth in *Rufford Charters,* i (Thoroton Soc. xxix, 1973), pp. cii-cvi.

[25] *Pytchley,* pp. 138-9.

to members of his family. The grants to the church will be considered first of all. The largest grants went to Peterborough abbey. King John in 1199 confirmed to the almonry, 'of the gift of William of Clapton 27 acres of land, and the meadow of Sineswald, and a virgate of land; and besides this a large virgate of land'.[26] The first of these gifts was confirmed to the abbey in an early fine made in 1190, in return for which William was given 10 marks and his wife Emma 12 bezants.[27] Another virgate in Clapton had been granted to the Templars before 1185.[28] He gave 24 acres of demesne land to the nuns of Chicksand, Bedfordshire.[29] And when his daughter Emma entered the nunnery at Stamford, he gave them two virgates of land, one in villeinage and the other of demesne.[30] When this is taken with the grant of the *personatus* of Clapton church to St Neot's priory,[31] the range of ecclesiastical foundations which could make an appeal to men of this rank appears very clearly. It provides a further example of the range of his horizons.

The range is extended further when we come to consider William's relations, for William was a man who had a lot of relations. William's grant of land to the Templars was made jointly with (or at least warranted by) his brothers Robert and Richard.[32] Robert seems to have controlled the Polebrook estate,[33] while Richard had some land at Kingsthorpe.[34] Another brother, Reginald, was priest of the family church (A3). And William had three sisters, two of whom have an important part to play in the story of the alienation of his land. Dionisia married Robert of Ufford, to whom no story attaches, but who is likely a member of a family holding of Peterborough abbey in the Soke.[35] The elder sister was Alice, who married Robert Hotot.

The Hotot family

There is no family history to vouch for the eleventh century origins of the Hotot family. In 1162-3 Robert Hotot owed 6s 8d for a forest offence.[36] In 1166 the return of knights fees made by William d'Aubigny showed Ralph Hotot owing half a knight's fee.[37] In 1175-6 the heavy forest eyre showed Thomas Hotot owing 20s for a forest offence.[38] According to the Clapton family history, Robert Hotot of Carlton married Alice the daughter of Walter de Grauntcourt, and their son and heir was Thomas Hotot. It can be established from this that the family came from East Carlton, near Rockingham Castle, and that they held of the barony of Belvoir. To establish a succession is more difficult. If Clapton seems to have too few twelfth century generations, the Hotots are in danger of having too many.

[26] Stenton, *Early Charters*, p. 46.
[27] C. N. L. Brooke and M. M. Postan (eds.), *Carte Nativorum* (NRS, xx, 1960), no 502; and cf E. King, *Peterborough Abbey 1086-1310* (Cambridge, 1973), pp. 90-1.
[28] **B 4 no 4**; B. A. Lees (ed.), *Records of the Templars in England in the Twelfth Century* (1935), p. 116 and note 10.
[29] **B 4 no 7**; cf **A 2**.
[30] **B 4 no 3**.
[31] Stenton, *Early Charters*, p. 68 (charter of 1182).
[32] Lees, *Records of Templars*, p. 116.
[33] *Curia Regis Rolls*, i. 117, 119-20.
[34] Doris M. Stenton (ed.), *The Earliest Northamptonshire Assise Rolls, A.D. 1202 and 1203* (NRS, v, 1930), pp. 46-7.
[35] *ibid.* p. 1.
[36] *Pipe Roll 9 Henry II*, p. 40.
[37] *Red Book of the Exchequer*, i. 328.
[38] *Pipe Roll 22 Henry II*, p. 51.

It would simplify the descent, and reconcile the generations, if the 1163 Robert was the husband of Alice, and their son succeeded shortly before 1175-6, and had an active career of nearly forty years.

For the latter part of that career the information is abundant. The early *Curia Regis Rolls*, from 1196 and up to 1211, show Thomas Hotot as an active and senior member of the gentry of northern Northamptonshire and adjacent parts of Rutland.[39] The activity is proved by the range of grand assises on which he served, from Luffenham in Rutland to Barnack in the Soke of Peterborough, from Stanion in Corby hundred to Raunds in Higham Ferrers hundred. His seniority is suggested by the fact that in which ever part of the region he served, he was one of the first two or three knights named. A man of this rank needs to be seen in terms of lordship as well as of geography. In 1196 William d'Aubigny named Thomas Hotot or *magister* Albert as his attorneys in a plea of land in Rutland.[40] If d'Aubigny lordship was important in this area so also was that of Mauduit, for East Carlton lay in the shadow of Rockingham Castle, which the Mauduits had controlled from the early twelfth century. The survival of a good range of Mauduit charters, both originals and cartulary copies, show this other side of Thomas's activity.[41] These relate to the acquisitions of Robert II Mauduit in Luffenham, Rutland. In them Thomas Hotot is usually the first, and otherwise the second witness. The charters suggest a close contact with Mauduit lordship, and may reveal the holding of some administrative position from them.

The material examined so far shows that East Carlton remained the base of the Hotots until the end of Thomas Hotot's life. His death must have occurred shortly after 1212, and his son occurs in 1218.[42] To show how this son's estate records, which are printed here, are the records of lordship in Clapton, Northamptonshire and Turvey, Bedfordshire reference needs to be made to the marriages of Robert Hotot and his son. William of Clapton, the uncle of Thomas Hotot, 'gave Thomas 60 acres of his demesne along with the virgate which Albricus the son of Quene used to hold and the virgate which Walter the archer used to hold'. The charter granting this land is preserved in the estate book **(A 20)**, and it shows that the grant was substantial.[43] Thomas Hotot married twice. To quote the family history again: 'Thomas begat Robert, Thomas and Reginald from Alice of Oleby, and from the second namely Alice of Eyri he begat William, Richard, Walter, Roger and Fulk. Thomas the father of these eight brothers gave Richard his son the whole tenement which he had of the gift of his uncle in Clapton, in the year in which King John mustered his army upon Barham Down.'[44] The first wife was Alice of Welby, in the northern

---

[39] *Curia Regis Rolls*, i. 16, 31; ii. 138, 220, 252; iii. 106, 159, 195, 227-8, 290-1, 322; iv. 83, 183, 298; v. 29, 112, 254; vi. 31, 59, 131; vii. 337.

[40] R. Allen Brown (ed.), *Memoranda Roll 10 John* (Pipe Roll Soc. NS 31, 1957), p. 86.

[41] Emma Mason (ed.), *The Beauchamp Cartulary* (Pipe Roll Soc. NS 43, 1980), pp. xxxv, lvii (map), nos 219-20, 222-3, 227-9, 231 (nos 227 and 229 are also printed in Stenton, *Early Charters*, pp. 34-5, 30-1).

[42] He last appears in the pipe roll of 1211-12: *Pipe Roll 14 John*, p. 134; *Excerpta e Rotulis Finium*, i (Rec. Com. 1835), pp. 20-1.

[43] The service owed was one-tenth of a knight's fee, and the sixty acres would seem to represent one-tenth of a five-hide holding. The parcels are given, however, and they total 113 acres.

[44] Bridges, ii. 368; A. L. Poole, *From Domesday Book to Magna Carta*, 2nd edn (Oxford, 1955), p. 459.

tip of Leicestershire, an area which lay in the shadow of Belvoir Castle.[45] On Thomas's death his eldest son by Alice of Welby obtained the ancestral property at East Carlton, and it may be presumed that the younger sons of the same marriage were supported from it in some way. The sons of the second marriage obtained their father's acquisitions. The eldest of these sons entered Peterborough abbey as a monk.[46] And so it is as a second son of a second marriage, hardly the best start in life, that Richard Hotot enters the scene. A family acquisition of 120 acres was quite as much as he could expect. I believe though that he probably had more than this, and that to his grandfather's acquisition he added the portion of his mother.

The estate book shows the acquisitions of Richard Hotot in Clapton, but it also shows his activity in the land market of Turvey, Bedfordshire. His interest in this village, eighteen miles away from Clapton, in a different county and in a different area of lordship, is hard to explain, unless he started with some property there. According to the Hundred Rolls, the prior of St Neot's possessed the advowson of the church of Turvey, 'of the gift of William le Heyr in the time of King Richard'.[47] There are three charters of William le Heyr or le Heir noted in the index to the twelfth century Turvey charters in the St Neot's cartulary, but this section of the cartulary is missing, so their texts do not survive.[48] There is no mention of later members of the Eyr family in later charters from Turvey, which, as will be seen, are abundant. It seems likely that Alice of Eyri was a member of this family, possibly the daughter and the heiress of William. The Eyr family seem to have been the tenants of the Belvoir holding in Turvey,[49] and so this marriage also is to be explained in terms of lordship.

These two acquisitions provided the base upon which Richard Hotot built. For build he did very vigorously, as his estate records show. I will examine first his acquisitions in Clapton, and then those in Turvey. In Clapton the story must be taken back to another of the daughters of Walter of Clapton. This was Dionisia, a formidable lady.[50]

> Of Dionisia the second daughter of Walter de Grauntcourt it is recorded that when a maiden, clad in a tunic, with a hat upon her head and armed only with a hollow shield, about the seventeenth year of King Stephen she attacked a certain knight, with one blow of her spear bringing him to the ground, and carried off his horse.

[45] Alice was the daughter of Gilbert of Welby. This was a Basset fee: *Book of Fees*, p. 949. In the Basset memoranda there is a note that Gilbert gave the homage and service from a carucate in Harby, Leics, to Thomas of Hotot with his daughter in free marriage: BL Sloane MS 31 no 7, rot. 12r. This Gilbert occurs in a charter for Garendon Abbey in the Belvoir muniments, which Round dated 1162 × 1170. The witness list concludes: '... Gilleberto de Alebi et Thoma fratre eius et omni comitatu Legrecestrie.' *HMC Rutland*, iv (1905), p. 5.

[46] William Hotot, abbot of Peterborough 1246 × 1249, was born at Carlton. He built a new chapel and a new hall at the neighbouring abbey manor of Cottingham, the only substantial building of his pontificate; and when he was forced to resign office in 1249 he was granted for a time the manor of Cottingham for his support: BL Add. MS 39758, fos 84v–86r; *Matthaei Parisiensis Chronica Majora*, ed. H. R. Luard, v (Rolls Ser. 57, 1874), pp. 84–5. J. Sparke's edn of Whittlesey's chronicle, *Historiae Anglicanae Scriptores Varii* (1723), p. 128, has Colingham as the manor; this was the original reading of the MS, but it was amended, surely correctly, to show William of Hotot returning to live in state amongst his relations.

[47] *Rotuli Hundredorum*, ii. 332.

[48] BL Cotton MS Faust. A iv, fo 32r. A group of charters that was acquired in the 1230s contained two issued by W. le Eyr: *ibid.*, fos 117v, 118r.

[49] It was his manor which the Hotots were to hold; *VCH Bedfordshire*, iii. 112.

[50] **B 4 no 1**, in the translation of Bridges, ii. 368.

Dionisia's daughter was Emma, and she was given a second and more substantial portion of the Clapton estate on her marriage with William Dacus.[51] According to the estate book this comprised 120 acres of demesne land, the service of freeholders and villein tenants, along with a quarter of a knight's fee in Thurning. Richard Hotot was able to purchase this other Clapton estate, though not, inevitably, without a certain amount of incident along the way. William Dacus had two daughters, Isabella and Maud, and he divided his estate between them. Isabella married twice. Her first husband was Richard of Haselbergh, 'who was found in a wood barbarously murdered, with his head cut off'.[52] This perhaps cured her from any further affection for men of the west country, and her second husband was Hugh of Ringstone in Lincolnshire.[53] According to the family history the lands were conveyed to Ralph of Ringstone. Ralph then went to the Holy Land and sold the land to Hugh his brother for 100 marks.[54] Richard Hotot then bought the property for 170 marks (A 2; B 4 no 1). The final parcel was that of seven virgates of villeinage given by William Dacus to his daughter Maud on her marriage to Robert Grimbaud, and given by them in turn to their daughter Isabella on her marriage to Richard Pauncefot. This land was bought by Richard Hotot in 1248, for 160 marks (A 11), and with this transaction the twelfth century estate which Richard's great-uncle had alienated was in effect reconstituted in his hands. Richard occurs on 25 July 1250 (A 11), and must have died shortly thereafter.

Clapton was to remain the main base of the Hotots, but at Turvey also they had a substantial holding, the records of which play a prominent part in the estate book. It has been suggested that the family's interest here grew from land bought to Thomas Hotot by his second wife. It is beyond question that Richard Hotot was active in acquiring land here. 'First Richard of Hotot bought in Turvey from John de Lega the parson of Carlton the whole tenement which John had in the village, namely in demesnes and in rents owing to him, apart from the Boulogne fee' (A 7). The land cost 182 marks. That a younger son in orders had property of this value to alienate suggests he was a member of a family of some importance. And so he was. The de Legas held 10 fees of the barony of Wahull, and other land in chief of the crown; the ramifications of the family have been worked out by G. Herbert Fowler.[55] The land market in

[51] They were married by 1199, when they had to defend their right to this property against Rose of Polebrook, another of William of Clapton's nieces: *Curia Regis Rolls*, i. 117, 119-20, 295. William's base was in Somerset; for his assertion of this see *Curia Regis Rolls*, iii. 129-30 (cf J. C. Holt, *Magna Carta* (Cambridge, 1965), pp. 56-7), and for the evidence see his place in the public records, from 1194 (*Rotuli Curie Regis*, i. 85) to 1218-19 (*Pipe Roll 3 Henry III*, pp. 173, 181).

[52] B 4 no 1, in the translation of Bridges, ii. 368. William son of William held a small tenancy in chief in Haselbury Plucknett, Somerset in 1166: *Red Book of the Exchequer*, i. 229. Richard son of William of Haselbury occurs between 1202-3 (*Pipe Roll 5 John*, p. 159), and 1218-19 (*Pipe Roll 3 Henry III*, pp. 178, 181). Between Michaelmas 1219 and Trinity 1222 Isabella was claiming dower lands in Somerset as the widow of Richard: *Curia Regis Rolls*, viii. 69 and *passim* to x. 317; and the resultant fines, E. Green (ed.), *Pedes Finium ... for the County of Somerset, 1196-1307* (Somerset Rec. Soc. vi, 1892), pp. 38, 40-1.

[53] Whom she had married by Hilary 1224, *Curia Regis Rolls*, xi, no 1818, and to whom she was still married in 1258, *Somerset Fines*, p. 181. Ringstone is in Aveland wapentake, Lincs, where Hugh held by knight-service of the Bishopric of Lincoln and of the honour of Belvoir: C. W. Foster (ed.), *Registrum Antiquissimum*, i (LRS, 27, 1931), p. 173, and ii (LRS, 28, 1933), p. 85.

[54] See B 4 no 1 at note 179.

[55] *Red Book of the Exchequer*, i. 322; G. H. Fowler (ed.), 'Records of Harold Priory', *Beds. Hist. Rec. Soc.* xvii (1935), pp. 190-3, and map and pedigree (no 5) facing p. 224.

Turvey in the second quarter of the twelfth century was clearly very active. Richard Hotot also spent 20 marks on buying a virgate from Richard de Ardres, his name still recording the famous castle-town in Normandy from which his ancestors had come.[56] In addition to this there were 37 smaller acquisitions of land, all but two of them sales, representing the outlay of a further £33 6s 8d (A 7). He was not the only man active in the Turvey land market in the mid-century. St Neot's priory was building upon the twelfth century grants to it.[57] And in the later thirteenth century there is continuing evidence for an active land market here.[58] The reason for all this activity may be found in returning to *Domesday Book*. Turvey was a village of 12 hides. This land was divided between eight different lords. Only one of these estates, the four hides held by the bishop of Coutances, was described as being a manor. The *Victoria County History* has traced with great skill the numerous tenancies which resulted from the further fragmentation of this fragmented village.[59] The Hotot tenancy was 1½ hides, held of the barony of Belvoir. In 1278/9 only 20 acres of this estate remained in demesne;[60] by this time Thomas Hotot had been succeeded by his son William. From this small base, William Hotot was able to play as active a part in Bedfordshire politics as he did in those of Northamptonshire.[61]

The Hotot Estate Records

MS A is a volume which needs to be seen to be appreciated. It is written in a considerable variety of hands, with marginal additions, and several complex series of foot-notes. Four plates have been chosen to illustrate the variety of the material, and to help fill the place of a full description of it. The careful binding by the British Library confirms the accuracy of the foliation established by the Sotheby catalogue: 'gatherings of 8 + 4 + 4 + 2 (the second a stub) + 7 leaves'.[62] The size of the first 17 leaves is 280 × 175 mm, and of the last 7 leaves 220 × 115 mm. The earliest dated entry in the main text is from 1248–9 (A 6). Much of the material added refers to the years 1249 and 1250 (A 5, 10, 11, 15). It seems likely from this that the earliest text dates from the 1240s, the final decade of Richard Hotot's life, and the one which saw the majority of his acquisitions. The survey at the head of the final gathering is dated 1272–3 (A 41), and so the volume cannot have been bound in its present form until after that time.

A partial description of MS B can be given from Bridges' transcripts.[63] His transcripts from the two books which he saw are in three parts: (i) pp. 15–25, notes from the Northamptonshire sections of MS A, up to and including no 13; (ii) pp. 28–56, the inquisition of 1255–6 from MS B; (iii)

---

[56] A 7. Ernulf de Arde held one hide of the Boulogne fee in 1086: *Domesday Book*, i, fo 211a; see Round, *VCH Bedfordshire*, i. 201–2, and for the descent of the holding *ibid.*, iii. 111–12.

[57] BL Cotton MS Faust. A iv, fos 113r–136v, *passim*. Many of these charters are precisely dated.

[58] The Northamptonshire Record Office holds several thousand loose charters from Turvey in the Stopford Sackville collection, and two cartularies (Davis, *Medieval Cartularies*, nos 1202, 1291).

[59] *Domesday Book*, i, fos 209b, 210a, 211a, 213b, 214b, 215a–b, 218b; *VCH Bedfordshire*, iii. 109–17.

[60] *Rotuli Hundredorum*, ii. 332.

[61] Katherine S. Naughton, 'The Gentry of Bedfordshire in the Thirteenth and Fourteenth Centuries' (Univ. of Cambridge, M. Litt. thesis, 1973), pp. 226–32.

[62] Sotheby catalogue, as cited in note 8, p. 33.

[63] Bodleian Lib. MS top. Northants c. 19.

pp. 57–68, miscellaneous notes from both manuscripts. Parts (i) and (ii) of this list are either printed or calendared in this edition. The value of part (iii), though it represents only jottings, is that it gives page references to both manuscripts. The pagination was supplied by Bridges himself. References to MS B, taken along with Bridges' other proprietary annotations to MS A (see plates 1 and 3), allow an outline at least of the contents of the missing manuscripts to be established.

MS B started with the text of the inquisition of 1255–6, which occupied pages 2 to 14. Pages 15 and 16 may originally have been blank, for they contain headings of enquiry to the manor court (in French), and an agreement between lord and villagers on the one hand and the parson on the other regarding tithes of livestock and dated 1285. There follows material which also was in MS A and likely was copied from it (A 8, 9, 12 and possibly one other item), on pages 17 to 20. What was on the next four pages cannot be established. Pages 25 and 26 contained the record of a recovery of a villein dated to 1376.[64] There is the note that Robert Hotot supported his claim to this villein by references to two registers, the Black Book and the White Book. Here then is the name of the two registers in the late fourteenth century, shortly before the lordship passed from the Hotot family.

MS B continued with further material also to be found in MS A. It had William of Clapton's grant to Thomas Hotot (A 20), and the record of Richard Hotot's acquisition of the Pancefot estate in 1247. Then there was Magna Carta (A 21), though there is no record here of the related documents (A 22, 23, 24). There are thereafter only a few references in Bridges' notes to later documents in MS B. On page 47 there is a note that the Bishop of Lincoln confirmed some of the village children when he passed through in 1254.[65] A 26 is noted as being on page 71 of MS B. And finally a note on forinsec service (A 18, and there in Thomas Hotot's own hand) is stated to have been on page 87 of MS B. It is thus clear that MS B was a good deal longer than MS A. Of the bulk of its contents, however, from around page 30 to around page 70, there is no record, other than Bridges' description of the volume as containing 'a register of charters relating to the manors of Clapton, Turvey and other manors and lands of the Hotot family'. The two volumes are clearly closely related. It was only when the charters had been organised that it was possible to annotate rentals in the way A 7 and 16 are annotated.

It is more difficult to establish who was responsible for the composition of the two registers. The concern with tithes, and the complexities of title to them in a village with a vigorous land market, is a distinctive feature of the 1255–6 inquisition in MS B. It adds force to Bridges' supposition that Martin of St Ives, the parson of the church, was responsible for the register.[66] If, however, Bridges thought that only the priest would have been able to write a document of this kind, he would have been mistaken. The evidence of the latter part of MS A, which since it related to Bedfordshire Bridges did not study, shows that Thomas Hotot wrote some of that volume in his own hand. The first of the entries which demonstrates this are A 19, which refers to rents 'due to us' (debitos apud nos) in Turvey, and A 18 which refers to 'my house' (mansio mea) in the same village. And in

---

[64] Bridges, ii. 369.
[65] ibid., ii. 372.
[66] 'Cuius autor ut conjicitur fuit Martinus de Sancto Ivone', Bodleian Lib. MS top. Northants c. 19, p. 28; thence Bridges, ii. 372.

A 32, a list of meadowland in Turvey, there is reference to land 'which my father bought' (*quam pater meus emit*). Each of these entries was written by Thomas Hotot. He may have written more. It would seem quite possible that he wrote much of MS A from **A 18** onwards, and that **A 43** represents his writing in the later years of his life. It would seem possible also that the same hand wrote some of the glosses. They were not the work of Richard Hotot, nor probably made in his time. According to Bridges, MS A was the the estate book of Richard Hotot, but this is a limited view.[67] It was Thomas Hotot who was responsible for MS A in its final shape, and it would appear for the shape of MS B also. Richard Hotot was the builder. His son, Thomas Hotot, was the organiser.

The title-page of MS B, preserved by Bridges, gives a brief statement of why organisation was required.

> This is the Register of Thomas of Hotot, of all the charters and final concords and exchanges wherever they were made and the acquisitions, made by Thomas of Hotot the grandfather of the said Thomas and by Richard of Hotot his son and by Thomas son of the said Richard, to provide evidence without sight of the original charters for all lawsuits that arise or for all unjust demands for forinsec service or rent and for giving reliefs according to the provisions of the charters.

The description would serve just as well for MS A, as an examination of some of the contents of the two volumes will show.

The main grants of land gave Richard Hotot a demesne and the service of dependent tenants to work it. **B 6** is a complete terrier of the demesne of the Peterborough abbey fee, which amounted to about 470 acres. This was the only demesne of any size in the village, for all but 24 acres of the Lovetot fee was divided among tenants **(B 8)**. The demesne comprised a number of small closes, and parcels scattered through the four main fields:

next the village	97 acres
Tornhilfeld	124 acres
Hulkefeld	64 acres
Medwefeld	62 acres
Westfeld	122 acres
Total	469 acres

The entry in the terrier adds that Westfield was attached to (*sociatur ad*) Meadowfield. It may be that it was attached to it for the purposes of cropping, but far from certain, for it is known that at this time the unit of cropping was the furlong. It can be established from elsewhere in MS B, however, thanks to its concern about tithes, that in the 1250s the demesne was sown on a three-course rotation.[68] A passage distinguishes between 'land in the fields which lies almost sterile each third year and land in the messuages and crofts which bears fruit annually' **(B 8)**. The church was most concerned to get its tithes from the fertile peasant gardens.[69]

The Clapton demesne was cultivated, at least in part, by the services of dependent tenants. If the records of those services do not bulk large in the Hotots' archives, it is likely because those services were not extensive. By

---

[67] He thought that Richard died *c* 1268, BL Add. MS 54228, p. iv, and his error was followed by the Sotheby catalogue, as cited in note 8, p. 33.
[68] Entries elsewhere in the Hotot records might have seemed to hint at a two-course rotation. Thus the reference to land, 'ex utraque parte adiacentibus' in **A 2** (William Hay).
[69] On which see E. Britton, *The Community of the Vill* (Toronto, 1977), pp. 157–9.

the 1240s the standard holding of the villein tenants was a half-virgate (A 12). Each tenant owed rent of 4s 3d a year, and in addition eight labour services in the autumn, a spring and a winter ploughing service, and work carrying hay from the fields and reeds from the marshes. They might keep their sheep in their own sheep-folds, though the sheep of those with less than a half-virgate had to lie in the lord's fold. These are light obligations, and it may be that they were bought out, for in 1272–3 the thirty-four villein half-virgaters owed 11s a year rent (A 41). At the same time the le Moine tenants in Barnwell owed 6s 8d a year rent, but heavier services.[70] Only a few miles away from each of these manors, villeins with similar holdings on the manors of Peterborough and Ramsey abbeys owed heavy and regular week-work and continued to do so until well into the next century.[71] Such light services are a characteristic of the small lay estate, and must indicate that the demesne was cultivated almost exclusively by the permanent farm staff (the *famuli*) or by hired labour.[72]

In many ways the resident villein tenants seem to have been the least of the Hotots' worries. What did worry them can be seen from a reading of what they were concerned to write down. In MS A they can be seen first of all keeping a track of their rents, and of any other services owed to them. They owed services in their turn, rents to neighbours for land purchased, and in some cases homage if the land was held by military tenure. The Hotots needed to keep on top of their charters, and the careful annotation of the lists which forms so attractive a part of MS A was made for this utilitarian purpose. Most of the charters themselves do not survive; these were the routine bits of MS B, which Bridges did not transcribe. The inquisition made in the 1250s shows in more detail the Hotots' concerns. Chapters 13 to 21 of B deal with 'forinsec services', those owed to the royal government, 'unjust demands' of which the register was designed to prevent. Scutage was the first of these. Scutage was levied on the knight's fee. Divided lordship in Clapton made for problems, and it can be seen that to distinguish the fees was important both for the lord and the rector of the church. Entries regarding forinsec services in Turvey are in Thomas of Hotot's own hand. Thus when parcels of different fees were exchanged, different tithing arrangements might become confused (A 7). Other forinsec services were for sheriff's aid, for the repair of Northampton town walls, the *murdrum* fine and responsibilities to criminal justice. *Quot* and *quantum* are the words that recur in the inquisition; the Hotots needed to quantify. Some of the services though fell on the village community as a whole; there is more than one reference to the *villatus* (B 20) or the *communitas villae* (B 16, 17, 18), organised to meet its obligations.

Edward I's land legislation was concerned to protect lordship.[73] 'Because of the machinations of their tenants lords were losing customs and services that properly pertained to the defence of the realm.' There is not much in the Hotot book about the defence of the realm, only a few pence owed for castle-guard at Belvoir and at Rockingham (A 35; B 16).

---

[70] *Cart. Ramsey*, i. 49–50: an interesting survey, probably made *c* 1275, when the manor was acquired by Ramsey Abbey.
[71] At Elton, Hunts, a manor of Ramsey Abbey, holders of a full virgate *c* 1250 owed three days' work a week and a variety of customary services.
[72] E. A. Kosminsky, *Studies in the Agrarian History of England in the Thirteenth Century* (Oxford, 1956), pp. 275–6; R. H. Britnell, 'Minor Landlords in England and Medieval Agrarian Capitalism', *Past & Present*, no 89 (1980), p. 10.
[73] T. F. T. Plucknett, *Legislation of Edward I* (Oxford, 1949); the quotation which follows is from the preamble of the statute *Quia Emptores* (1290).

But there is a revealing passage under the heading, 'these men are owed homage in Northamptonshire' (A 27). It lists eight individuals and then continues: 'there are others to whom it is owed, but through the passage of time by purchase we have their homage and service freely from their chief lords, by which the said homage is no longer to be done, for the chief member of the homage does only the service owed'. It was the passage of time that was so insidious, and the fragmentation of holdings that went with it.[74] These small lords *were* lords. They maintained what trappings of lordship they could. They held courts in their halls, and hoped that their neighbours would attend. Thomas Hotot was distrained for services at the courts of Simon de Borhard at Clifton and Simon de Beauchamp at Dilwyk; and in each case established by a fine that the mesne tenant owed the service.[75] In 1268 though he did do homage to Isabella Pauncefot 'in her hall at Blisworth'. And in 1254 he had done homage to Hugh of Ringstone not in Lincolnshire or Northamptonshire but 'in London, in the house of the abbot of Peterborough at St Sepulchre' (A 43). This is a nice reminder that lordship retained its social function. The houses of their lords in London provided for the local gentry somewhere to hang their hat, or rest their feet after a hard day's shopping.

The London of 1254 was an active centre of political debate, and the abbot of Peterborough's house was a good place to keep in touch with it.[76] That men like the Hotots did keep in touch is a safe assumption. They had amongst their muniments copies of 'The Charters', i.e. of Magna Carta and the Charter of the Forest (A 21, 22). When these texts are seen in monastic cartularies they can easily be taken for granted. But when, seemingly copied out at a monastic house, they are found amongst the records of a minor knightly family, their central position in the political life of the thirteenth century comes over very clearly. What impression is to be gained from the inclusion here of the two letters by which King John made his peace with the papacy in 1213 is less clear (A 23, 24). For Matthew Paris, Richard Hotot's contemporary (and Richard's elder brother was abbot of a Benedictine house), this was a charter 'detested by the whole lay estate', which showed the humiliation of King John.[77] The Hotots may have asked for them as important historical records; alternatively they may have come in as a make-weight. The relaxation of the Interdict which followed in 1214 was a date no less memorable than that of Magna Carta (A 10). This was a family that liked its history. The stories about the Anglo-Saxons and the list of the kings of France are concluding jottings no less appropriate than the family history which starts off the work (A 44, 46).

[74] As an example of this from the Basset records: the Brampton fee was divided between five parceners. Two only of the five appeared to do homage; the parcels of the other three were taken in hand. BL Sloane MS 31 no 7 rot. 9r.
[75] *Bedfordshire Fines*, nos 564–5.
[76] John of Caux, the abbot at this date, served as an itinerant justice in the 1250s and became Treasurer in 1260. He was criticised by Matthew Paris as a bad monk, and characterised by Professor Tout as insignificant. But the activities which called for such comment will have made his house an excellent centre for the Hotots and their kind. For references see King, *Peterborough Abbey*, p. 95 and note 6; *The Roll of the Shropshire Eyre of 1256*, ed. A. Harding (Selden Soc. xcvi, 1981), pp. xii–xiii.
[77] *Chronica Majora*, ii (1874), pp. 135, 146; and see C. R. Cheney, *Pope Innocent III and England* (Päpste und Papstum, 9; Stuttgart, 1976), pp. 333–5. It may be noted that the reconciliation with the papacy came just after the mustering of John's army on Barham Down (A 1 at note 86). 'The well-informed and vivid author who wrote the "Coventry" chronicle gives an account of the state of tension and expectancy in England': Cheney, p. 331.

Note on editorial method

MS A was a working document. It was heavily annotated in the 1250s and 1260s, and John Bridges in his turn left his mark on it. The annotations are of different kinds. The first logically are the foot-notes, which were added as the family archive was put in order (and later copied into MS B). These notes, which can be foot-notes or head-notes or marginal notes, but in each case are intended as a commentary on the text, have been printed in italic. There follow changes to the text, particularly in lists of names and rents, which were intended to bring it up to date. Brackets have been used for this material, and distinguish between later additions to the text (shown in round brackets), and deletions in the text (shown in angle brackets, with the original matter shown within the brackets if it is still legible). Thus:

(   ) additions to the text
⟨   ⟩ deletions in the text

The further emendations to the text are editorial. Matter supplied by the editor is added in square brackets, as is normal practice. Square brackets have been used for Bridges' headings to MS A, supplied from MS B where the original heading had faded. Bridges' other annotations, though they have been used above to help establish the text of MS B, have not been printed. The one exception to this stern rule is the pagination, supplied by Bridges in a bold hand which so dwarfs the British Library's recent foliation of the volume that the editor has reluctantly retained it.

[   ] editorial matter

A consideration of John Bridges' treatment of MS A leads to a consideration of his transcription of MS B. What is printed below from MS B is his fair copy of the 1250s enquiry, and not the notes which he made from other parts of the manuscript. Bridges deserves great credit for seeing the importance and interest of the enquiry. But his text is not immaculate. A comparison of the text of MS A with his transcriptions reveals little fault in material such as lists of names and rents. But the enquiry is in parts a more literary text, and it is the more literary parts of the text that cause the difficulty. The stories about members of the Hotot family are material of this kind; they were reproduced in Bridges' history of the county, and some of them have been quoted in the introduction to this volume.[78] The statement that the passages are quoted 'in Bridges' translation' is made advisedly. A comparison of text and translation in these cases will show that the translation is free, and at times inaccurate. It is clear that Bridges did not always understand his text. There are passages in the text which make no clear sense. The editor has made some obvious emendations, and has indicated a few of the more difficult passages. But he has not harried John Bridges, if only because he is conscious that later historians will be no less aware of his own imperfections.

[78] See above at notes 22, 50 and 52.

A

British Library, Additional MS 54228

1 The history of lordship in Clapton, Northants. After the Norman Conquest Alfred de Grandcourt held a knightly tenancy of the Lovetot fee and of Peterborough Abbey. The property descended to Walter and then William de Grandcourt. William alienated parts of the estate to Thomas Hotot and William Dacus. Thomas Hotot granted his land in Clapton to his son Richard.

page 1 Toroldus abbas de Burgo Sancti Petri dedit Rogero de Luuetot baroni de Sudho feodum duorum militum in Cloptun Pokebroc. et in Catteworte ad tenendum de predicto abbate & suis successoribus.[79]

Rogerus idem de Luuetot dedit Alfredo de Gravntkovrt militi suo totum feodum quod habuit de dono dicti abbatis in Cloptune scilicet quatuor hidas pro pheodo vnius militis. & idem Rogerus dedit eidem Alfredo in eadem villa de Cloptune vnam hidam et vnam virgatam terre pro quarta parte pheodi militis et illa hida & illa virgata sunt de propria baronia dicti Rogeri de Sovdho de nullo pertinencia ad Burgum preter tantum quod sunt in libertate ipsius abbatis.[80]

Idem Rogerus dedit eidem Alfredo in Pokebroc pheodum dimidii militis & duodecimam partem vnius feodi de feodo de Burgo. & vnam hidam et vnam virgatam terre de propria baro/*page 2* nia ipsius Rogeri de nullo pertinencia ad Burgum sicut predictum est. [81] parte vnius feodi militis.[82]

Dictus Rogerus dedit dicto Alfredo vnam hidam et vnam virgatam terre in Thirnninge pro quarta parte vnius feodi de sua propria baronia de nullo pertinencia ad Burgum sicut predictum est.[83] dictus Alfredus totum predictum tenementum integre obtinuit omnibus diebus uite sue.[84]

Valterus filius et eres dicti Alfredi successit patri suo tenens integre predictum tenementum in Cloptune. Pokebroc. et in Thirnninge.

Post Valterum de Graunkort successit eidem filius & heres Villelmus nomine et allii tres filii milites. Robertus Valterus et Ricardus. et tres sorores scilicet. Alicia. Deonisia. et Rohesia.

De Alicia ita est. Robertus de Hotot de Cariltona duxit illam in uxorem et generauit Thomam de Hotot filium et eredem suum. Villelmus predictus a/*page 3* [Plate 1] wunculus eius dedit eidem Thome *pro 20 marcis quas*

[79] Turold, abbot of Peterborough 1070 × 1098. Roger of Lovetot succeeded after 1086 to the lands of Eustace the sheriff, and died *c* 1116: *Pytchley*, pp. 90–102; *VCH Northants*, i. 366; *Early Yorkshire Families*, ed. C. Clay (Yorks Arch. Soc. cxxxv, 1973), pp. 53–6.

[80] There were three holdings in Clapton in 1086: (1) Eustace held of the abbot of Peterborough 3 hides, 3 virgates and a third of half a hide; (2) Elmer held half a hide of the abbot; (3) Alfred held of Eustace the sheriff 1 hide and 1 virgate: *Domesday Book*, i, fos 316b, 350a.

[81] A space was initially left in the MS at this point. An entry was made later, and then erased.

[82] There were two holdings in Polebrook in 1086: (1) Eustace held of the abbot of Peterborough 4 hides less a virgate; (2) Eustace the sheriff held of the king in chief 1 hide and 1 virgate: *ibid*. i. fos 315b, 349b.

[83] In 1086 Thurning lay partly in Huntingdonshire and partly in Northamptonshire. In Northants Peterborough abbey held ½ hide in demesne: *ibid*. i. fo 314a. The two main holdings were in Hunts: (1) Eustace held 1⅓ hides of Crowland abbey; (2) Eustace held 5 hides in chief, which Alfred and Gozelin held of him: *ibid*, i, fo 342b, 350a.

[84] For Alfred and his successors as tenants of land in Clapton see the introduction.

aquietauit in iudeismo sexaginta acras de dominico suo et illam virgatam terre quam Albricus filius Quene solet tenere et illam virgatam quam Valterus le Archer solet tenere et abere.[85] Predictus Thomas generauit. Robertum. Thomam. Reginaldum. de Alicia de Olebi et de secunda scilicet de Alicia de Evri generauit. Villelmum. Ricardum. Valterum. Rogerum. et Fulconem. Thomas pater istorum octo fratrum dedit Ricardo filio suo totum tenementum quod abuit de dono awunculi sui in Cloptune. eodem anno quo rex Iohannes vnauit exercitum. super Berehamdune.[86]

Villelmus de Grantkurt dedit Villelmo le Daneis qui Emmam filiam Dionisie sororis sue duxit in vxorem sex viginti acras terre de dominico suo de Cloptune et servicium liberorum hominum et ⟨quatuor *erased*⟩ virgatas de vilenagio.[87] et quartam partem vnius feodi in Thirninge.

2 The consolidation of Richard Hotot's holding in Clapton. He acquired the holding which had descended from William Dacus, and made other purchases of land.

page 4 Succedente tempore Rohesia de Pokebroc filia Roberti de Cloptun frater et heres Villelmi de Cloptun existentis implacitauit Villelmum Dacun de illo tenemento *per auxilium episcopi Wintonie qui tunc tempore erat cancellarius regis et auunculus dicti Villelmi le Daneis* & facta est finalis concordia in curia regis pro sex solidis annuatim eidem Rohesie et heredibus suis dumtaxat soluendis.[88] Ille Villelmus Dacus dedit Isabelle filie sue quicquid habuit in Cloptun *videlicet per cartam de feffamento*. Hugo de Ringisdone duxit predictam Isabbellam in uxorem. Ille Hugo et eadem Isabella dederunt Radulfo de Ringisdone totum tenementum quod habuerunt in Cloptone per cirograffum factam in curia domini regis. Idem Radulfus vendidit Hugoni fratri suo quando iter aripuit in terram sanctam totum illud tenementum pro centum marcis. Predictus Hugo vendidit Ricardo de Hotot totum illud tenementum sine aliquo retenemento in perpetuum *pro 170 marcis*.[89] Idem Ricardus emit de Accellino de Cloptone *pro 113 marcis* quaterviginti acras terre in Cloptone et parumper amplius et toftum et croftum quod fuit Henrici Fabri et servicium servientis Roberti cum servicio Gilberti capellani et servicio Hugonis clerici et ad ultimum emit virgultum dicti Accellini pro 18 marcis.[90] Dictus Ricardus emit de Radulfo de Vigornia illam virgatam terre quam Torstanus le chapelein

[85] The grant is printed below as **A 20**. It does not mention any indebtedness to the Jews. See further introduction at note 43.

[86] In the spring of 1213 King John mustered a large army on Barham Down, between Canterbury and Dover: A. L. Poole, *From Domesday Book to Magna Carta*, 2nd edn (Oxford, 1955), p. 459.

[87] The grant to William Dacus does not survive. The information here is likely taken from the foot of fine of June 1199 (see the following note), which does not clearly distinguish villein from free holdings—hence possibly the gap left in the MS. According to **B 4 no 1**, when William Dacus transferred this land to his daughter it included 3½ virgates of villein land.

[88] See introduction at note 51. The case was heard in 1199 and 1200: for the pleading see *Curia Regis Rolls*, i. 117, 119-20; for the fine PRO CP 25(1) 171/5/40, which gives valuable detail, though the document is faded and in part eaten away. The bishop of Winchester at this time was Godfrey de Lucy. The chancellor was Hubert Walter, archbishop of Canterbury. Neither of these men can be connected with William Dacus. But it should be noted, even though the families cannot be connected, that in 1210 a Robert of Hotot was a tenant and an official of the bishop of Winchester: *VCH Hants*, iv. 219; *The Pipe Roll of the Bishopric of Winchester 1210-1211*, ed. N. R. Holt (Manchester, 1964), p. xxxix.

[89] Cf **B 4 no 1**, and see then the discussion below note 179.

[90] It is clear from this entry that Ascelin of Clapton held a small manor in Clapton. In addition to this he gave 10 acres of demesne and 44 acres of tenant land to William Hay, which later came to Thorney abbey: Cambridge Univ. Lib. Add. MS 3021 ('Red Book of

solet tenere *pro 20 marcis*.[91] Emit eciam de monialibus de Chikesand octodecim acras de dominico pro octodecim marcis *pro 18 marcis*.[92] Ille Ricardus dedit Hugoni filii Henrici dimidiam virgatam terre et sexdecim marcis argenti pro quieta clamacione matris sui de terra et tenemento Henrici filii Galfridi avi sui inperpetuum. Emit eciam de Ranulfo Grimbaut *pro 5 marcis* unum quarterum terre. Emit eciam de Willelmo Hay *pro 52s* totum ius et clamium quod habuit in solo vel comuna in Oldeforde grene et comunam in omni tempore quod habuit in quatuor acris preter unam rodam ex utraque parte adiacentibus pro quinquaginta solidis et pro quodam tofto quod Ranulfus de Tichemers solet/*page 5* tenere.[93]

3 A list of the parsons of Clapton. Reginald, a younger brother of William of Clapton, is recorded as the first parson, as having rebuilt the church in stone and as having been bald from his birth, which was eight weeks premature.

Reginaldus primus persona de Cloptone frater iunior Villelmi de Cloptone fundavit ecllesiam de Cloptone de lapide que prius fuit lingnea. Hic natus est de matre sua ante tempus maturum per spacium octo septimanarum ex quo sibi crines defecerunt a nativitate sua ab occipite usque ad frontem. Post illum successit persona de Cloptune Radulfum de Achirche. Et post illum successit persona de Cloptune magistro Johannes Caluus. Et post illum successit Hugo de Dauintre. Post illum vero Martinus de Sancto Iuone.[94]

4 A list of tenants in Clapton. According to the heading there were five hides, but only three and a half hides are listed here; for the balance see **no 17**.

[ANNO REGNI REGIS HENRICI FILII REGIS JOHANNIS ... ISTI VIRI TENEBANT QUINQUE HIDAS IN VILLA DE CLOPTONE DUMTAXAT][95] HIDA PRIMA. Villelmus Akari et Gilbertus de Blaisworte 1 virgatam. Margeria uxor Micaelis et Walterus filius Micaelis 1 wirgatam. Marsilia et Hugo filius Henrici 1 wirgatam. Johannes Lodeman et Henricus filius Radulfi 1 wirgatam. Walterus Monacus et Rogerus le Paumer 1 wirgatam. Ricardus de Hotot et Walterus filius Accellini 1 wirgatam. Dupla pars dimidie wirgate Roberti filii Galfridi respondeat cum ista hida. HIDA SECUNDA. Galfridus filius Henrici dimidiam uirgatam et 1 quar-

Thorney'; hereafter cited as TRB), fos 212r–213r. The second of these grants was for 12 marks to redeem his debts to the Jews, to whom 'omnes terre mee obligate fuerunt'. Ascelin was the son of Ralph of Clapton (*ibid.* fo 212v), who was the first tenant listed in the fine of 1199 (above note 88), and who was still alive in 1220 (*Rotuli Hugonis de Welles*, ed. F. N. Davis, ii (LRS, 6, 1913), p. 190). Ralph was the son of Geoffrey (*VCH Northants*, iii. 128), who is probably the Geoffrey *miles* who held of William of Clapton in **B 7** and **B 12**. And Geoffrey may be the son of the Ralph of Clapton who occurs in 1149 (*Early Charters*, p. 62).

[91] There is more information in **B 4 no 1**.

[92] See **B 4 no 7**. The grant by William of Clapton was among those confirmed by Henry II in a charter of 1163 × 1179: G. H. Fowler, 'Early Charters of the Priory of Chicksand', *BHRS*, i (1913), p. 123.

[93] This represents one of two exchanges of land made with William Hay and recorded in the Thorney cartulary: TRB fo 214v, which does not record the payment of any money. See further **B 12** and notes. For Ralph of Titchmarsh see further below note 120, and **B 4 no 6**, at note 189.

[94] The list of the first incumbents of Clapton printed in Bridges, ii. 371 is taken from here. Reginald and Ralph of Achurch are not otherwise recorded. *magister* John Calvus occurs in a fine of 1199 (PRO CP 25(1) 171/5/36), and in an undated charter in the Thorney cartulary (TRB fo 212r). His successor, Hugh of Daventry was instituted in 1219: *Hugh of Wells*, i (LRS, 3, 1912), pp. 160–1. Martin of St Ives was instituted in 1230: *ibid.* ii. 156, 239–40. His successor, Hugh of Colingham, was instituted in 1267: *Rotuli Ricardi Gravesend*, ed. F. N. Davis (LRS, 20, 1925), p. 109. See further **B 9** and the notes thereto.

[95] The heading is faded, and the precise date has been lost, but it is not likely to be far distant from that of **A 6**, of 1248–9. This heading has been supplied by Bridges from MS B.

terum. Hugo le Strange et Hugo Caperon 1 wirgatam. Willelmus le Frankelein 1 wirgatam. Wido filius Galfridi et Johannes Carpentarius 1 wirgatam. Ranulfus de Tichemers et Henricus de Nordfolk 1 wirgatam. Nicolaus filius Roberti et Willelmus filius Laurencii 1 wirgatam. Micael Faber et Gilbertus de Holdernesse 1 wirgatam. Galfridus filius Leuerici 1 dimidiam virgatam. Tercia pars dimidie virgate Roberti filii Galfridi debet respondere cum ista hida.

HIDA TERCIA. Valterus Grimbaut 2 virgatas. Gilbertus le Frankelein 1 wirgatam. Walterus de Blaisworte et Ranulfus de Blaisworte 1 wirgatam. Johannes Biscop et Robertus filius Reginaldi 1 wirgatam. Gilbertus le Franceis et Hugo le Bret 1 wirgatam. Galfridus Trip et Reginaldus de Biterne 1 wirgatam. Willelmus Trakilissone et Walterus filius Leuerici 1 wirgatam. Ranulfus de Tichemers et Micael filius Willelmi 1 wirgatam.

DIMIDIA HIDA. Almonerus de Burgo 1 wirgatam. Persona wnam wirgatam. Micael Faber et Gilbertus de Holdernesse cum Rogero le Scot 1 wirgatam. Henricus de Bernewelle et Alicia uxor Walteri Waket 1 dimidiam wirgatam. Hugo de Tichemers dimidiam wirgatam.

5 A note of the construction of a chapel in the cemetery of Clapton in the year 1249–50.

Memor est quod anno regni regis Henrici filii regis Johannis 34 et anno pontificatus Roberti Lincolniensi episcopi 15 constructa fuit capella in cimiterio de Clopton in honore Sancte Trinitatis.[96]

6 The tenants of a hide of land in Turvey, Beds, in 1248–9.

page 6 ITA ERAT SITU HIDA WYMUNDI IN TURVEYE ANNO REGNI REGIS HENRICI FILII REGIS JOHANNIS 33

HIDA WIMUNDI IN TORWEYE. Willelmus Martel dimidiam wirgatam. (Domina Agatha unam virgatam terre) Nicholaus de Gatisdene 3 quarteros et Robertus Bataille. Rogerus filius Simonis et Galfridus filius domini 1 quarterum (et media sedes Villelmi filii domini). Galfridus de Bosco 3 quarteros (dimidiam virgatam). Ricardus de Hotot cum residuo Roberti le Rowe wnam wirgatam et unum quarterum. Et in hac hida non est amplius.

7 Notes of the land acquired in Turvey by Richard Hotot. The sum paid to John de Lega, the parson of Carlton, Beds, indicates a substantial holding, but the majority of the other grants listed here are of small pieces of land.

[HEE SUNT EMPTIONES RICARDI DE HOTOT IN TURVEY][97] Ricardus de Hotot emit primo in Torveye de Johanne de Lega persona de Karilton totum tenementum quod idem Johannes habuit in eadem willa, scilicet in dominicis et redditibus omnibus sibi preter feodum de Bolonia pro 182 marcis.[98] Postea idem Ricardus emit in eadem villa de Waltero Russel tres acras de hida Wimundi pro 4 marcis. Deinceps idem Ricardus emit de Ricardo de Ardris unam virgatam de feodo de Trailli pro 20 marcis.[99] Deinceps idem Ricardus habuit ex dono eiusdem Ricardi de

---

[96] The 34th year of Henry III ran from 28 October 1249 to 27 October 1250. The 15th year of Robert Grosseteste ran from 17 June 1249 to 16 June 1250.

[97] The heading has been supplied by Bridges from MS B.

[98] For the de Lega family and John's position in it see the introduction at note 55. In a fine dated Michaelmas 1249 Nicholas son of Geoffrey of Gatisdene confirmed 40 acres of arable, 3 acres of meadow and 12s annual rent to John de Lega, who granted the land to Richard Hotot: PRO CP 25(1) 2/22/11. John de Lega was active in the land market in Turvey at least as early as 1236: Bedfordshire Fines, nos 364, 385, 451; cf Fowler, 'Early Records of Turvey', BHRS, xi (1927), pp. 62–4, 91.

[99] On Richard de Ardres ibid. pp. 81–2 and pedigree 4; and see further introduction at note 56.

Ardris duas acras in inlond *ex dono.* Idem R de Willelmo clerico unam acram *pro 1 marca.* Idem R de alio Willelmo clerico unum mesuagium quod Rogerus le Fotor tenuit *pro 4 marcis.* Idem R de Henrico filio Steffani per excambium totum Gatisdenecroft *6 marcas.* Predictus Ricardus emit de Henrico filio Steffani 16½d redditus et ab eodem homagium et totum servicium Ricardi le Thein *pro 15s.*[100]/*page 7* Emit eciam de Nicholao de Gatisdene 5d reditus *pro 5s.* Emit eciam de Willelmo clerico reditum 2½d *pro 2s.* Emit eciam de Simone simentario unam rodam prati *pro 10s.* Habuit eciam de Roberto le Rowe tres acras terre et dimidiam *propter concordiam.*[101] Emit eciam de Galfrido carpentario dimidiam acram terre *pro 3s.* Emit eciam de Roberto de Suelleston dimidiam acram terre *pro 5s 6d.* Emit eciam de Huberto Mauduit quinque rodas terre et reditum quatuor denariorum *pro 22s.*[102] Emit eciam de Stephano Ilger dimidiam acram *pro 5s.* Emit eciam de Galfrido filio domini croftum quod iacet iuxta curiam eiusdem Ricardi *pro 43s.* Emit eciam de Petro filio Willelmi unam acram terre *pro 1 marca.* Emit eciam de Nicholao de Gatisden 5 selliones et 2 buttas *pro 6s.* Emit eciam de Huberto Ledeyeman dimidiam acram *pro 5s.* Emit eciam de Simone Martel 3 rodas terre *pro 9s.* Emit eciam de Symone Eyron 1 acram et reditum 4d *pro 12s.* Emit eciam de Britelino 5½ acras *pro 4 marcis.* Emit eciam de Samsone le Mansel unam acram *pro 10s.* Emit eciam de Willelmo Bigge 2 acras *pro 17s.* Emit eciam de Ada Weyredole 1 rodam prati *pro 10s.* Emit eciam de Sibilla Martel sextam partem 3 rodarum prati *pro 3s.* Emit eciam de Milisent totum dominium quod habuit in Torweye *pro 6s.* Emit eciam de Nicholao de Gatisdene unam dimidiam acram prati et unam dimidiam acram terre *pro 18s.* Emit eciam terciam partem de crofto *pro 30s.* Emit eciam de Radulfo le Duc duas partes unius acre prati *pro 22s.* Emit eciam de Nicholao de Gatisdene 4 acras super Vitelond *pro 34s.* Emit eciam de Henrico filio Steffani 3 rodas terre cum redditu 3½d *pro 7s.* Emit eciam de Milisent 1 acram terre *pro 16s.* Emit eciam de Ada filio Roberti 1 rodam prati et 1 acram terre *pro 19s.* Emit eciam de Helewisa 1 acram terre *pro 11s 6d.* Emit eciam de Willelmo Sanar 1 acram terre *pro 11s.* Emit eciam de Henrico de Chisilhamtone 6 selliones et 1 goram pro quatraginta solidis *pro 40s.* Emit eciam de Nicholao de Gatisdene quietam clamacionem redditus 2d de pitil iuxta wiam et 1d del Halowe et ½d de Willelmo de Bordeleys pro 2 rodis terre Roberti Bataille *pro 3s.*

8 Services owed by Richard Hotot for land in Clapton.

page 8 HEC SUNT SERVICIA QUE RICARDUS DE HOTOT DEBET IN CLOPTONE

De[103] Roberto de Hotot pro quadam particula terre decimam partem feodi unius militis.[104]

---

[100] In the mid-1250s Richard le Thein transferred part of his land to his son-in-law Thomas de Evermodio, and the remainder to St Neot's priory in return for a corrody: NRO SS 2881; BL Cotton MS Faust. A iv, fo 139r.

[101] PRO CP 25(1) 2/22/11 also transferred to Richard Hotot a messuage, 6 acres of arable and a half acre of pasture which Robert son of Roger le Ruwe held.

[102] A Hubert Mauduit witnessed charters dated Easter 1247 and 3 May 1269: NRO SS 2856, 417.

[103] The author seems here to have been copying from a list of acquisitions. It took him a couple of entries to work out how to amend the list to answer the question which he had set himself.

[104] A **42** below shows this obligation as arising from the time of Thomas Hotot, from which it is clear that the Hotots of Clapton owed the Hotots of Carlton the service of a tenth of a fee, as in A **20**.

De Hugone de Ringisdune aliam particulam terre propter unum par calcarium deauratorum vel 6d ad Pascha & pro eadem terra Roberto le Flemmec 6s ad festum Sancti Michaelis.[105]
Accellino de Cloptune pro una particula terre unam libram piperis vel 7d ad Natale Domini.[106]
Wydoni Grimbalt pro una particula terre 6d scilicet 3 ad festum Sancti Michaelis et totidem ad Pascha.[107]
Johanni Papilon pro vna virgata 12d scilicet ad festum Sancti Michaelis.[108]
Domino de Uadenho pro tribus acris prati in Brantisheie 12d ad festum Sancti Michaelis.[109]
Valtero Monaco pro terra Ranulfi Grimbalt 2d ad Pascha.[110]
Heredibus Roberti filii Petri pro Nonnedole 3d ad festum Sancti Michaelis.
Heredibus Vydonis Roc 2d ad mediam Quadragesimam.
Monialibus de Chikisend pro octodecim acris terre unam libram piperis ad Pascha vel 12d.[111]
Radulfo de Vygornia pro vna virgata terre 2s ad Pascha sed idem Radulfus debet nobis 6d de eadem virgata.[112]
Ricardo Pancefot unum par calcarium deauratorum vel 6d ad Pentecosten pro omni servicio.[113]
Henrico de Folkesvorthe pro uno tofto et crofto 2d ad Pascha.[114]
Berengero Monacho 2 capones pro dimidia virgata que fuit Roberti de Melcheburn in Bernewell.[115]
Templariis pro tribus toftis in Hogereston 2s et 6d medietatem ad festum Sancti Michaelis et tantundem ad Pascha.[116]
Philippo de Vassensle pro octodecim acris in Vassensle 12d ad festum Sanctorum Petri & Pauli.[117]

[105] For Hugh of Ringstone see **B 4 no 1** at note 179. Robert the Fleming is the same man as Robert son of Rose of Polebrook: the suggestion made in *VCH Northants*, iii. 102 receives confirmation in the gloss to Cambridge Univ. Lib. Peterborough D & C MS 1 ('Swapham's Cartulary'; hereafter cited as Swa), fo 181v, which is a grant of his manor in Polebrook, Kingsthorpe and Clapton to Peterborough Abbey in 1252. The gloss refers to Swa fo 261v, in which he had previously remitted to the abbey his rights in Clapton church.
[106] See above note 90.
[107] **A 25** states that he paid 9 marks for this land. Guy Grimbald witnessed a charter of Ascelin of Clapton: TRB fos 212v–213r. The family of Grimbald who are freeholders in Clapton must be distinguished from, though it may be related to, that of Grimbald which held in Hardwick, Houghton and elsewhere, of the honour of Huntingdon: W. Farrer, *Honors and Knights' Fees*, ii (1924), pp. 304–5.
[108] See **B 4 no 6**, and the notes thereto.
[109] In 1242–3 Peter de Grendon held half a knight's fee in Wadenhoe: *Book of Fees*, p. 937; cf Bridges, ii. 388–91.
[110] **A 2** states that Richard Hotot purchased a quarter virgate from Ranulf Grimbald. On Walter Monachus see **B 4 no 1** at note 183.
[111] See **B 4 no 7**.
[112] See **B 4 no 1**.
[113] See **A 11** and notes.
[114] Henry of Folksworth, Hunts, held two knights' fees of the earldom of Oxford: *VCH Hunts*, iii. 173–4.
[115] This Berengar or his son of the same name held an estate in Barnwell, Hemington and Crowthorp, which he sold to Ramsey abbey in 1276: *VCH Northants*, iii. 71–3; *Cart. Ramsey*, ii. 339–40. The half-virgate which Robert of Melchbourne held in villeinage came to Reginald Hotot, who granted it to Ramsey around the time it acquired the main Barnwell estate: NRO Buccleuch Deeds H 19; printed *Cart. Ramsey*, ii. 343.
[116] According to **A 25** this land was bought from Adam the clerk. Oggerston in Morborne parish, Hunts, is now a deserted settlement, but in the 13th century it was on a major road and the headquarters of a *baillia* of the Templars: Lees, *Records of the Templars*, p. cxc and note 7; Sir Frank Stenton, *Preparatory to Anglo-Saxon England* (Oxford, 1970), p. 242 note 2.
[117] Washingley, Hunts, is now also largely deserted. This tenancy is recorded as part of a decayed serjeanty in *Book of Fees*, p. 1217, where the value of the messuage and 18 acres was given as 6s a year.

9 Rents owed to Richard Hotot for land in Clapton.

page 9 REDDITUS RICARDI DE HOTOT IN WILLA DE CLOP-
TONE[118]

Gilbertus le Frankelen tenet vnam virgatam pro 4s ad quatuor terminos partim solvendis.[119]

Andreas filius Hendrici tenet dimidiam virgatam et debet ad Natale Domini 2 capones & ad Pascha 6d.

De Radulfo de Tichemers pro dimidia virgata 6d ad festum Omnium Sanctorum.[120]

De Reginaldo de Beumis pro vna hida in Tirninge quartam partem feodi vnius militis.[121]

Johannes de Veston tenet unum quarterum terre et debet ad festum Sancti Michaelis 6d.

Robertus Serviens tenet unum quarterum et ad eundem terminum debet 6d.

Roheysia Grimbaut tenet quinque akras et debet ad Natale 1d.

Henricus Grimbaut tenet unum toftum cum tribus rodis terre pro 5d scilicet ad Pascha. Et preterea pro una roda et dimidia 1d ad festum Sancti Michaelis.

De Emma filia Rogeri de Blaisworte pro uno tofto et pro sex acris terre 4s quadripartitum ad quatuor tempora anni.

De Gilberto de Blaisworte sacerdote pro sex acris 1d ad Pascha et de eodem 16d ad quatuor tempora pro tofto cum crofto cum tribus rodis.

De Roberto de Tichemers pro sex acris et dimidia 1½d ad festum Sancti Michaelis.

Henricus de Norfolk tenet dimidiam virgatam pro 4s 3d ad quatuor tempora, scilicet ad quodlibet festum 12d et ad Natale 15d.

Hugo filius Henrici tenet dimidiam virgatam pro 4s ad quatuor tempora.

De Waltero Monaco pro 1 virgata et dimidia 1 libram piperis et 6d ad 2 terminos.

De Johanne de Armiston pro quatuor acris terre cum tofto 12d sex ad festum Sancti Michaelis et sex ad Pascha.

De Rohesia filia Ranulfi pro dimidia virgata terre 1d ad Natale.

Dictus R emit de eadem Rohesia *pro 10s* tres rodas terre et iacent super le Longehopewold de predicto tenemento cum servicio ½d quem magister Jordanus debet.

10 Memorable dates in English history. A note that the 33rd year of the reign of Henry III was 5448 years from the beginning of the world, 1249 years from the birth of Christ, 1216 from Christ's death, 544 from the building of Peterborough, 184 years from the Norman Conquest, 79 years from the martyrdom of Thomas Becket and 34 years from the relaxation of the Interdict.

Anno rengni regis Henrici filii regis Johannis tricesimo tercio adposa erant ab origine mundi 5448 anni. ab incarnacio Domini 1249. a passione Christi

---

[118] The heading is supplied by Bridges from MS B.

[119] The names here should be compared with those in **A 4**. Gilbert the franklin witnessed charters in TRB fo 213r.

[120] In Titchmarsh there was a small Waterville fee held of Peterborough Abbey (*Pytchley*, p. 42), and a larger fee held of Ferrers. In 1242-3 Ralph of Titchmarsh held ⅓ fee there of John de Plassiz who held of Ferrers: *Book of Fees*, p. 937. He witnessed several of the Clapton charters in the Thorney cartulary: TRB fos 212r-214v. See further **B 4 no 6** and note 189.

[121] In 1236 Reginald de Beaumis held in Thurning of Richard Hotot, who held in turn of Lovetot: *Book of Fees*, p. 923. The family were tenants also in Sawtry, Hunts, and held land in Barnwell of le Moine: *VCH Hunts*, iii. 108-9; *Cart. Ramsey*, i. 48.

1216. a constructione Burgi 644. ab adventu Normannorum in Angliam 184 anni. a passione Sancti Thome 79 anni a relaxatione interdicti 35.[122]

11 Two further notes of acquisitions of land by Richard Hotot in Clapton and in Winwick. Logically, as noted by Bridges with both texts in front of him, these entries should be added to **no 2**.

page 10 Predictus Ricardus emit de Ricardo de Doufre totum illud tenementum quod habuit in villa de Winewyc ex dono Johannis le Bere de Elintona sine aliquo retenemento die sancti Jacobi apostoli *anno regni regis Henrici filii regis Johannis 34* [25 July 1250] *pro quaterwiginti marcis argenti.*[123]

Predictus Willelmus le Daneis dedit Roberto Grimbaut in liberum maritagium cum Matilda filia sua septem virgatas terre de villenagio in villa de Cloptone. Idem Robertus et Matilda uxor eius dederunt Ricardo Pancefot in liberum maritagium cum Isabella filia sua illud totum predictum tenementum. Dictus Ricardus Pancefot et Isabella uxor eius dederunt Ricardo de Hotot totum illud tenementum predictum per cirograffum in curia domini regis confectum pro centum et sexaginta marcis.[124]

12 The services owed by customary tenants in Clapton. The main services listed are payment of 4s 3d a year rent, eight days' work at Harvest time, and specified ploughing and carrying services. Half-virgaters might retain their sheep in their own folds, but those of smallholders had to lie in the lord's fold.

HEE SUNT CONSUETUDINES OBSERVANDE IN VILLA DE CLOPTUNE[125]

Ad quatuor tempora anni ad quodlibet terminum de dimidia wirgata 12¾d. In autumno octo diebus operari. Quelibet wirgata ad festum Sancti Michaelis habeat unam karetam cum duobus equis una die ad kariandum turbam de marisco vel faciant equipollenciam kariagii ad dispositionem seruientis. Quelibet dimidia virgata debet kariare in autumno duas karecatas bladi. Dabunt ausilium ad festum Sancti Michaelis. Ad semen yemale dimidia virgata debet arare unam rodam. Et cratare una die integra. Ad Natale Domini quelibet virgata dabit unum panem de quantitate dimidii

[122] According to the figures given here the world was created in 4199 BC, Peterborough Abbey was founded in AD 605, the Norman Conquest was in AD 1065, the death of Becket in AD 1070, and the relaxation of the Interdict in AD 1214. The latter two dates are correct, and the error in the date of the Conquest may be accounted a slip of the pen. The earlier two dates cause more difficulty. According to Hugh Candidus Peterborough was founded 5,800 years after the beginning of the world, in AD 656; this would make the creation in 5144 BC (*Hugh Candidus*, p. 7 and notes). According to Walter of Whittlesey the monastery was founded in AD 655 (*ibid.*), which would square with the Hotot figure, reading dcxciiij for dcxliiij. According to Bede, the Jews dated the creation to 3952 BC, while Isadore of Seville had 5154 BC, and Eusebius of Caesarea and St Jerome 5198 BC (*Chronica Maiora* (MGH, Auct. Ant. xiii, 1898), pp. 281-2). The last of these might be thought the nearest approximation to the Hotot date.

[123] Richard of Dover held the Lutton fee of Peterborough abbey in the 1240s: *Pytchley*, pp. 46-9. For John le Bere of Ellington see *Cart. Ramsey*, i. 43, 95; ii. 305.

[124] It is presumed that this Robert Grimbald is the tenant of the honour of Huntingdon, on whom see above note 107. Richard Pancefot held a fee in Great Easton, Leics, of Peterborough abbey: *Pytchley*, p. 135. Bridges, ii. 368 says that the estate was transferred to Richard Hotot by a fine levied at Gloucester in 32 Henry III, 1247-8. The original of the fine has not been traced.

[125] The heading has been supplied by Bridges from MS B. After transcribing this entry Bridges added the following from MS B: 'Omnes tenentes singulis annis operabuntur in autumpno ad equipollenciam 16d, aut invenient 1 hominem aut mulierem per 10 dies ad metendum, allocantes homini 2d, mulieri 1½d. Debent eciam redimere sanguinem suum, si filios vel filias vel alios alio modo a tenemento domini recederent, ad voluntatem domini vel ballivi. Et si filie corporaliter deliquerint infra custodiam patris vel matris dabunt leyrwyte' (MS B, p. 65, which may have been added there as a gloss to the entry here printed).

busselli. In eodem tempore dimidia virgata dabit 3 gallinas et unum gallum. Ad semen quatragesimale dimidia virgata debet arare unam rodam et *page 11* cratare una die integra. Vertent fena et levabunt. Et quelibet dimidia virgata debet de consuetudine kariare vnam karecatam tantum. Oves dimidiarum virgatarum sunt in ovili suo proprio si habeant ovile vel si pares sint coniucgti (scilicet duo vel tres sed non ulterius) et compostaverint terram suam propriam.[126] Sin autem omnes sint in ovili domini. Omnes bidentes hominum minus habencium quam dimidias virgatas plenarie sint in ovili domini. Et omnes angni eorum et dimidiarum virgatarum non admodum ut supradiximus habencium ovilia pascant cum angnis domini in dominicis sine tributo usque in vigilia Pentecostes.

13 Note of a case pursued by Durand son of Henry of Brampton and Alice his wife against Thomas Hotot and Gunnora his mother, between 1252–53 and the summer of 1262. There is information on the pleading but none on the substance of the case.

page 10   Text: not printed.

14 Note of a grant of two virgates of land by William of Clapton to Richard his brother.

page 11 Predictus Willelmus de Cloptone dedit domino Ricardo fratri suo wirgatam terre quam Turstanus le chapelein solet tenere et dimidiam virgatam terre quam Galfridus filius Martini solet tenere et illam dimidiam wirgatam quam Waremannus et Quena uxor eius solent tenere.[127]

15 The rents and farms owed to Richard Hotot for land in Clapton in 1249–50. The total owed is £13 3s 0½d.[128]

Tricesimo quarto anno regni regis Henrici filii regis Johannis isti fuerunt redditus et firme Ricardi de Hotot apud Cloptone, scilicet totalis firma ad festum Sancti Michaelis 66s 3¾d, ad Natale Domini 65s 2¾d, ad Pasca 66s 7¼d, et ad festum Sancti Johannis Baptiste 64s 10¾d.
Summa totalis quatuor terminorum £13 3s 0½d.

16 The rents and farms owed to Richard Hotot for lands in Turvey. The acquisition of much of this land is recorded in **no 7**.[129]

page 12   REDDITUS ET FIRME DE TORVEYE
AD FESTUM SANCTI MICAELIS
De Willelmo Martel 3d *pro dimidia virgata.*

---

[126] The arrangement which allowed the customary tenants but not the smallholders to keep their sheep in their own folds was quite a common one. It is found, e.g., on the Peterborough abbey manor of Cottingham, Northants: BL Cotton MS Nero C vii, fos 94r–95v. It is unusual for it to be spelt out, as is done here, that what was at issue was the manure.

[127] Bridges has annotated this entry with the remark, 'this should come on page 4'. The entry there says that Richard Hotot bought from Ralph of Worcester the virgate of land which Thurstan the chaplain used to hold. **B 4 no 1**, below at note 182, states that Ralph had this virgate from William Dacus. Earlier in the same narrative, it is stated that Isabella daughter of William Dacus bought from Walter son of Richard her kinsman the half-virgate which Geoffrey son of Martin used to hold. This establishes the descent of part of this land from William of Clapton to Richard his brother; from Richard to Walter his son; from Walter to William Dacus; from William to Ralph of Worcester; and from Ralph to Richard Hotot.

[128] It may be that this represents the totals from a fuller rental, but if so it has not survived; cf the rental of 1272–3, below **A 41**.

[129] By contrast to **A 15** there is a full rental of the Hotot estate in Turvey, the chief interest of which lies in the elaborate series of foot-notes which identify the land for which the rent was paid. Page 14 of the MS A is reproduced here as plate 2; and page 12 was printed by M. T. Clanchy, in *From Memory to Written Record* (1979), plate XV.

De Radulfo clerico 8d *pro medietate feodi de Beuver que tenet.*
De Roberto Gerin 3d *pro duobus acris.*[130]
De Willelmo filio Ade 9d *pro mesuagio et crofto.*
De Rogero filio Simonis 6d *pro 2½ acris terre cum mesuagio.*
De Waltero le Packere 3d *pro quinque acris terre et dimidia de terra Michaelis.*
De Ricardo de la Leye 3d *pro sex acris terre.*
⟨De Henrico filio Steffani⟩ 1d *pro sex acris terre.*
De Radulfo de Nordho 3½d[131] *pro eo que sequntur.*[132]
⟨De Agnete le Chalf⟩ 4d
⟨De Alano Scip⟩ 5d
⟨De Hugo le Corteis⟩ (de Waltero Mauvallet) 6d *pro una acra.*
De Galfrido de Bosco 3d *pro uno quarterio terre.*[133]
De Willelmo le Macon 4d *pro tribus acris.*
De Amicia Camerarie 1d.
De abbate de Sancto Iacobo 1d *pro inferiori sedetrium.*[134]
De Willelmo filio Radulfi 1d.
De Waltero le Packere 1d *pro mesuagio iuxta Robertum Bataille.*
De Nicolao de Gatesdene 3½d *pro tribus acris.*
De Roberto Mauvallet 3d.
⟨De Willelmo Linel⟩ 1d *pro una acra de feodo Huberti Mauduit.*
De Ada Prest 9d *pro eo que subsequntur.*
De Ada filio Hugonis 9d *pro eo que subsequntur.*
De Henrico veteri de Gatisdene 3d.
⟨De Radulfo Peiteral⟩ 7d.
De Gilberto Baywel 3½d *pro duobus acris terre et de Henrico filio Steffani fuit emtum.*
De Milisent 4d.
De Accelot Martel 2d.
De Willelmo de Tichemers 1d.
De Waltero de Pikishille ½d *de Roberto le Velu fuit emtum pro 5d pro una acra in Sortestcroft.*
De Thomasin unum clavum gariofili *pro eo que subsequntur.*
De Willelmo le Huliere 2d.
De Radulfo de Nordho 12d.
De Willelmo Gerin unam acram.
De Waltero le Pakkere ½d *pro dimidia acra in tribus selionibus de terra libbe.*
De Galfrido le Karpenter de Stachedene ¼d.
De Roberto filio Lece ¼d.
AD FESTUM SANCTI MARTINI
De Willelmo filio Lece 5d.

---

[130] Robert Gerin witnessed NRO SS 2856 (dated Easter 1247), 2857.
[131] Ralph of Nordho witnessed 'Turvey Records', pp. 99–100.
[132] The first of a number of foot-note references which refer the reader to information in the foot-notes on a subsequent page. It is clear from this, and from the fact that the order of the foot-notes does not always follow the order of the text, that this section was annotated piecemeal, as the relevant charters came to hand.
[133] Geoffrey de Boys or de Bosco witnessed NRO SS 2857 and 'Turvey Records', nos 14, 15, 18. In the 1290s and 1300s *magister* Warin de Boys acquired a considerable estate in Turvey. NRO SS 4186 is a roll of around 200 of his charters (= Davis, *Medieval Cartularies*, no 1202), and many of the originals survive loose in the same collection.
[134] The abbey of St James, Northampton had land in Turvey from the de Lega family: 'Turvey Records', pp. 62–3; cf *VCH Beds*, iii. 114.

De Henrico de Hardmad' 8d.
De heredibus Oswaldi 1½d pro forinseco.
AD FESTUM OMNIUM SANCTORUM
De Willelmo filio domini unam libram cimini *pro una acra supra boscum Johannis de Bovele.*
De Steffano Lauerke ½d *pro tribus sellionibus super Brouningiscoll.*
De Willelmo Kiggil 1d *de Henrico filio Steffani fuit emtum.*
De Waltero Mauwallet unam libram cimini.
De Rogero serviente 1d.

page 13
AD FESTUM SANCTI ANDREE
De Waltero de Pikishille 3d *pro decem acris ad Natale Domini.*
AD NATALE DOMINI
De Waltero le Packere 1½d *pro acra et dimidia de terra Russell.*
De Roberto Bataille 1d *pro mesuagio cum crofto.*
De uxore Johannis le Broyn 1d *pro una roda in uno mesuagio.*
De Willelmo filio domini 2d *pro uno mesuagio et crofto.*
De Radulfo de Nordho 1d *pro una acra terre et alia prati.*
De Micaele le Macon ½d *pro uno mesuagio.*
De Johanne le Huliere 1d *pro dimidio mesuagio et pro dimidia acra terre.*
⟨De Rogero le Fotor⟩ 12d *pro una mansione.*
⟨De Alano Scip⟩ 5d.
De Willelmo le Macon ½d *pro mesuagio et tribus acris.*
De Rogero le Bidil 1d.
De Willelmo Sanar 1d *de Nicholao de Gatisdene patri fuit emtum et est pro una acra terre, scilicet super Frilond 1 dimidia acra et versus Edvinismade 1 roda et ad Coppiddemor tres butte.*
De Willelmo filio Radulfi 1½d.
⟨De Roberto . . .⟩ 2d *pro tribus acris.*
De Nicolao Fabro ½d *pro terra de Simone Eyron, pro una acra terre in tribus sellionibus super Ferifurlong quam Petrus tenet.*
⟨De Roberto Serviente⟩ (Ada Prest) 9d *pro mesuagio et tofto.*
⟨De . . . . . .⟩ 9d *pro mesuagio et tofto.*
De Helewisa ½d *pro una acra et una roda, scilicet una acra super Banlond et una roda sub Nordbroc, de Nicholao de Gatisdene fuit emtum.*
De Waltero Pakkere 1d *pro una acra de Galfrido de Gatisdene.*
⟨De Accelot Martel⟩ 2d.
⟨. . . . . .⟩
De Radulfo de Nordho 1 libram cimini.
De Willelmo filio Filippi ¼d.
De Willelmo filio Lece ½d.
AD FESTUM SANCTE MARIE IN MARCIO
De Amicia 1d *pro mesuagio et acra et dimidia terre.*
De Galfrido filio domini 1d *pro mesuagio et crofto trium acrarum.*
De Radulfo clerico 6d.
De Roberto Gerin 3d *pro duabus acris.*
De Willelmo filio Ade 9d.
⟨De Accelot Martel⟩ 1½d.
De Rogero filio Simonis 6d *pro terra prescripta.*
De Waltero le Packere 1½d *pro terra prescripti Micaelis.*
De Ricardo de la Leye 1½d *pro septem acris.*
De Rogero le Budil ¼d *pro una acra terre.*
⟨De Hugone le Corteis⟩ (Waltero Mauvalet) 6d *pro terra prenotata cum mesuagio.*

De Galfrido de Bosco 3d *pro terra prenotata.*
⟨De Henrico filio Steffani⟩ 1d *pro sex acris terre.*
De Willelmo le Macon 4d.
⟨De Nicholao de Gatisdene⟩ 1½d *pro tribus acris terre.*
De abbate de Sancto Iacobi 1½d *pro uno mesuagio.*
De Willelmo filio Radulfi 1d.
page 14 [Plate 2]   De Waltero le Packere 1½d *pro octo sellionibus terre et una particula prati in Smalidol'. de Simone Eiron fuit emtum pro acra et dimidia terre et una roda prati in Dalmade.*
⟨De Roberto Mauvallet⟩ 3d.
⟨De Willelmo Linel⟩ 1d *de Huberto Maudut fuit emtum et est pro eo quod ad festum Sancti Michaelis.*
De Elya le Champion 1½d *de Huberto Maudut fuit emtum et est pro duabus rodis terre sub Wolloniswic.*
De Willelmo de Bosco 1d pro 5 rodis terre iuxta Robertum de Bosco *de eodem* [*Simone Eiron*] *fuit emtum.*
⟨De Willelmo Sanar ½d.⟩
⟨De Simone le Macon⟩ ½d *iuxta foraria monacorum in Wytelond pro duabus rodis.*
⟨De Willelmo filio Henrici ½d.⟩
⟨De Ricardo de Sarnebroc ½d⟩ *de Henrico de Gatisdene fuit emtum et est pro duabus rodis terre in Witelond iuxta foraria monacorum.*
De Hamone Molendinario ½d *de eodem* [*Simone Eiron*] *fuit emtum. pro dimidia acra terre ad Horspitbroc iuxta W le Wolmonere.*
De Henrico veteri de Gatisdene 3d.
De Radulfo Peiterel 7½d.
De Thoma molendinario ½d *de Henrico filio Steffani fuit emtum et est pro una acra terre inter cheminum ducendo de ponte ad ... et cheminum que dicitur Arneborneweye, et cum hoc redditu condonatur ½d que Villelmus filius sacerdotis debuit Henrico filio Steffani per eandem cartam nobis ab illo factam.*
⟨De Accelot Martel 2d.⟩
De Waltero Mauwallet ½d pro 2 selliones terre in Hokedecroft *de eodem* [*Simone Eiron*] *fuit emtum pro duabus sellionibus terre ad Hokidecroft.*
De Roberto de Bosco ½d *de Henrico filio Steffani fuit emtum pro Hokidecroft.*
De dono Galfridi filii Galfridi. [*the four following entries bracketed together*] Willelmo de Thichemers ½d. De Symone filio Galfridi ¼d. De Hugone filio Galfridi ¼d. De Ricardo de Wermintona ¼d.
De Ada Prest 9d.
De Ada filio Hugonis 9d.
AD PASCA
⟨De Rogero le Fotor 12d⟩ *pro eo et de eo quod ad festum Sancti Johannis.*
⟨De Alano Scip 5d.⟩
De Henrico de Gatisdene ½d *de persona de Kariltona fuit emtum et est pro uno forario super Blakemanniscroft.*
De Roberto Bataille 1d *de persona de Kariltona fuit emtum et est pro uno mesuagio cum crofto.*
De Willelmo Sanar 1d *de persona de Kariltona fuit emtum et est de mesuagio uno cum dimidia acra.*
De Iohanne tectore ½d *pro eo quod ad Natale Domini.*
⟨De Alicia le Chalf⟩ 4d.
De Waltero de Dunstable 1d *de Simone Eyron fuit emtum pro duabus sellionibus in le Wetelond.*

De Radulfo de Nordho 1d *de Nicholao de Gatisdene fuit emtum et est pro una acra abuttante super Ridwellmade.*
De Henrico de Gatisdene ½d *pro duabus rodis terre in fine crofti quas habemus in excambio de Henrico veteri.*
De Willelmo Sanar ½d *de Willelmo clerico de Pikishill fuit emtum et est pro duabus acris terre.*
De Willelmo Sanar ½d *de Simone Eyron fuit emtum et est pro duabus rodis terre supra Portweye.*
⟨De Roberto Serviente⟩ (Ada Prest) 9d.
De Willelmo le Wistlere 9d.
De Henrico de Hardmad' 12d.
De Willelmo de Bordeleys ½d.
De Waltero Lanator ½d *de Helewisa ... fuit emtum pro una roda prati in Brocholis iuxta Valterum de Nordho.*
De Willelmo le Huliere ½d *de eodem.*
De Ricardo de Wermintona ½d et 1 salutationem.
De Gilberto Molendinario 10s.
De Hugone filio Filippi 1d, de Ada de bosco ad Pasca ½d, de Matheo le Blund ½d, de Waltero Mauwalet ½d *de Henrico filio Steffani fuit emtum.*
De Radulfo de Nordho 4d *de Henrico filio Steffani fuit emtum pro Haspelond harisdinis.*[135]
De Henrico filio Johannis ½d.
page 15
AD FESTUM SANCTI JOHANNIS
De Rogero le Fotor 12d *de Willelmo filio Ricardi de Pikishill fuit emtum et est pro uno mesuagio iuxta Adam filium Roberti cum tofto.*
De ⟨...⟩ 5d. De ⟨...⟩ 9d. De ⟨...⟩ 9d.
De Gilberto Baywel forinseco *de persona de Kariltona fuit emtum et non dat nisi forinsecum pro uno quarterio.*
De Henrico de Hardmad' 12d.
⟨De Accelot Martel 2d.⟩
De Petro filio Willelmo unam rosam.
De Ada filio Hugonis 10d.
De Ada Prest 10d.
De Ada coopertore 3d *de Symone Martel fuit emtum pro dimidio mesuagio et crofto.*
AD FESTUM GULE AUGUSTI
De Willelmo Martel 4d *de persona de Kariltona fuit emtum et est pro eo quod ad festum Sancti Micaelis.*
De Waltero Pakkere ½d *pro dimidia acra in tribus sellionibus de terra libbe.*

17 A list of tenants in Clapton; a continuation of and a gloss upon **no 4**.
RESIDUUM HIDARUM IN CLOPTONE
Omnes prescripte virgate terre et dimidie sunt de antiquo dominico Willelmi de Grantkort et debent respondere ad dominicum in omnibus forinsecis et scutagiis et geldis. Et quod deest de dimidia hida dominico tenetur conplere omnino.
HIDA QUARTA. Persona Willelmi de Cloptone tenet unam virgatam (Ricardus de Hotot), Willelmus Bodi et Willelmus de Tirningge unam virgatam, Ranulfus Bricwold et Torstanus filius Galfridi unam virgatam, Henricus filius Widonis et Rogerus filius Andree unam virgatam.

---

[135] NRO SS 2858 contains a reference to 'illa forera que vocatur Haspelondes Havedens'.

18 A note of the forinsec services owed from Turvey, concerned to establish the responsibility of Thomas Hotot and that of other tenants. The reference to 'mansio mea' suggests that this entry is in Thomas Hotot's own hand.

page 16 Bis in anno dantur forinseca servicia domino regi, scilicet ad festum Sancti Johannis Baptiste et ad festum Sancti Martini. Et respondet dominus cum domina ad quinque hidas, scilicet ad hidam Wymundi, et ad hidam Durandi, et ad hidam Warneri, et ad hidam de Muttlepit, et ad hidam Hugonis de Auno, videlicet pro tales quantitates subscriptas. Scilicet requirendum est ad feodum Wymundi de tribus partibus unius virgate, et ad eundem feodum Rad' clerico de uno quarterio. Et ad feodum Durandi requirendum est de uno quarterio quod est mansio mea; de alio quarterio pro domino Galfridi de Burdeleys et hoc iniuste; et pro dimidio quarterio contra Walterum de Pikishill. Et ad feodum Warneri pro dimidio quarterio, et pro crofto Peyteral. Et ad feodum de Muttlepit pro dimidio quarterio. Et ad feodum Hugonis de Auno pro una virgata et dimidia.

Et sciendum est quod ad festum Martini datur auxilium vicecomitis et secta, et ad festum Sancti Johannis auxsilium vicecomitis tantum, sub tali forma. Scilicet ad festum Sancti Martini virgata de hida Wymundi 13d ex quo pars nostra scilicet tres partes illius 9¾d. Et ad eandem hidam Radulfo clerico pro uno quarterio 3¼d. Et preterea ad eandem hidam pro dimidia virgata que fuit Henrici de Bosco 6½d. Et ad eundem terminum ultimo pretactum ad hidam Durandi pro quarterio mansionis mee ego absque domina 1½d, pro quarterio Galfridi de Bordeleys ego absque domina 1½d sed hoc iniuste, et pro dimidio quarterio contra Walterum de Pikishille 3¾d cum domina. Et ad eundem terminum ad hidam Warneri ego cum domina pro dimidio quarterio in Estcroft ½d et domina Agatha ½d ... ipsa ¾d et nos ad festum Sancti Johannis 3d scilicet pro nobis et ipsa, preterea nos pro crofto Peyteral ½d. Et ad hidam de Muttlepit ad terminum pretactum pro dimidio quarterio ¾d cum domina, quia croftum damsele cum Hokidecroft tenetur ad aliam medietatem quarterii. Et ad eundem terminum ad hidam Hugonis de Auno pro una virgata si debeat dari sicut solet 9d sed si secta debeat aumoneri 3d cum domina sicut prius. Preterea pro dimidia virgata Iacobi de Ardres 3¼d. Summa totalis de hida Durandi in festo Sancti Martini pro auxsilio vicecomitis et secta 2s.

In rei veritate sciendum est de hida Durandi quod isti in perpetuum respondendum sunt ad forinsecum bis in anno danda scilicet ad festum Sancti Martini et ad festum Sancti Johannis Baptiste. Atque responsurum ad omnes geldas amerciamenta et tallagiis scilicet ad festum Sancti Martini pro forinseco scilicet auxilium vicecomitis et secta dimidia virgata 3d ad festum Sancti Johannis dimidia virgata 1½d scilicet ad auxsilium vicecomitis tantum.

page 17 Sciendum est quod ad festum Sancti Johannis datur auxsilium vicecomitis tantum et quam collectores sumus omni forinsecorum de hida Durandi pro terra quondam Henrici que vocatur Clipsweni. Ideo atorn' discernendum est quantum quisque tenencium de hida Durandi solvendus est ad forinsecum in festo Sancti Johannis scilicet dimidia virgata de hida Durandi 1½d quarterio ¾d. Summa totalis ad auxilium vicecomitis 12d.

Respondendum est ad hidam Wymundi ad istum terminum pro tribus partibus unius virgate contra Johannem Lefre scilicet 2¼d et ad eandem hidam pro dimidia virgata Henrici de Bosco 1½d. Item ad eandem hidam Agathe de Bosco pro una quarterio ¾d.

Respondendum est ad hidam Warneri nos simul cum domina Agatha pro uno quarterio in Estcroft ¾d. Ita tamen quam conventum est inter nos quod ipsa solvat ad festum Sancti Martini ¾d ad auxilium vicecomitis pro nobis et ipsa scilicet ad istum terminum ¾d pro omnibus. Preterea respondendum est ad hidam Warneri pro crofto Peyteral. Respondendum est ad hidam de Muttlepit pro dimidio quarterio et de mansione Demisele Maud et Hokidcroft pro alio dimidio quarterio scilicet in toto integro ¾d.

Respondendum est ad hidam Hugonis de Auno pro una virgata de Sancto Georgeo ¾d. Preterea ad eandem hidam pro dimidia virgata Iacobi de Ardres.

19 Rents owed to Thomas Hotot in Turvey. Portions of these rents, most commonly a third, were to be paid to 'the lady', who is presumably Thomas's mother Gunnora. From the reference to the rents being owed 'to us' this section also may be identified as being written by Thomas Hotot.

page 16 SCIENDUM QUOD ISTI SUNT REDDITUS DEBITOS APUD NOS IN VILLA DE TURVEYE SECUNDUM QUOD ...[136]
AD FESTUM SANCTI MICHAELIS
Ricardo de Borhard 1 marcam domina terciam partem.[137] Johanni Velu ½d domina medietatem. Symoni de Holewell 1½d domina terciam partem.[138] Ricardo de Hardres ½d domina medietatem. Ade filio Roberti ½d domina totum. Item eidem Ade ½d pro una acra terre. Willelmo le Mordant 2d domina terciam partem.[139] Radulfo de Northo 1d domina terciam partem. Nicolao le Champeun 1d. Symoni de Gatisdene unum clavum ferreum. Albredo de Pikishill 1d domina totum. [*three further entries illegible*]
AD FESTUM NATALE
Huberto Maudut ½d domina terciam partem. Willelmo cum barba 1d domina terciam partem. Stephano Ylger ¼d domina totum. Brechelino 1d domina terciam partem. Huberto Maudut ¼d domina totum. Roberto Piscator ¼d. Johanni de Pikishill ½d domina terciam. Huberto Maudut ½d domina totum. Johanni de Pikishill ½d domina medietatem. Heredibus Willelmi de Mitlepit ½d. Symoni de Holewell 1 libram cimini. Sibilla filia Rogeri unum clavum ferreum. [*one entry illegible*]
AD FESTUM SANCTE MARIE IN MARCIO
Waltero Mauvalet ½d domina totum. Ricardo de Hardres unam libram piperis domina terciam partem. Symoni de Holewell 1½d domina terciam partem. Ricardo Borhard 1 marcam. Willelmo de Bosco 1d domina totum.
AD PENTECOSTEN
Henrico filio Steffani unum clavum ferreum.
AD PASCA
Johanni de Pikishill ½d domina terciam partem. Agatha de Bosco ½d. Johanni de Pikishill ½d domina terciam partem. Willelmo le Mordant 1d domina terciam partem. Radulpho de Northo ½d domina totum. Johanni de Pikishill 1d domina totum. Henrico Wygem 1d domina terciam partem. Heredibus Willelmi de Mitlepit 1d domina terciam partem. Ricardo de Hardres unam libram piperis domina terciam partem. Rogero servienti 1d.

---

[136] Under the heading, the last word of which has not been deciphered, the list of rents is written in a cramped hand in five columns.

[137] On the family of Borhard see the full notes of G. H. Fowler in 'Turvey Records', pp. 73-5 and pedigree 3. Simon de Borhard still occurs in 1257: Richard de Borhard occurs by 1264.

[138] Simon of Holewell is a frequent witness to charters of the 1240s and 1250s: NRO SS 2856-7, 2880-1; 'Turvey Records', p. 62.

[139] In 1254 William le Mordant and Richard de Ardres held of Simon de Borhard the land of the Belvoir fee in Turvey: 'Turvey Records', p. 79. William had succeeded Eustace le Mordant by 1247, and died before 1279: *ibid.*; NRO SS 2856. For the later importance of the family see *VCH Beds*, iii. 110-11.

Radulfo le Duc ½d. Hugoni filio Filippi ½d pro una roda prati. [*one entry illegible*]
AD FESTUM SANCTI JOHANNIS BAPTISTE
[*blank*]
AD FESTUM OMNIUM SANCTORUM
Heredibus Willelmi le Mordant unam libram cymini.[140]
AD FESTUM SANCTE MARIE MAGDALENE
Ricardo de Ardres 1d pro terra Iacobi fratris sui.

20 Charter of William of Clapton granting land in Clapton to Thomas Hotot. The grant comprised three peasant families with two virgates of land, and demesne land with the furlongs identified and amounting to 113 acres. Thomas paid William 20 marks for this grant and was to hold by the service of a tenth part of a knight's fee.[141]   [c 1190]

page 17 Sciant presentes et futuri quod ego Willelmus de Clopton dedi et concessi et hac presenti carta mea confirmavi Thome de Hotot in feodum et hereditagium in willa Cloptonie toftum et croftum quod Acarius filius Quene tenuit plenarie et toftum quod fuit Hubertici Tillarii et Albrici filii Willelmi cum tofto et crofto et wirgata sua terre et omnibus pertinenciis que ad predictam terram pertinent et Quene matrem eius et omnes infantes eius et virgatam terre quam Walterus le Archer tenuit cum tofto et crofto et cum omnibus pertinenciis que ad predictam terram pertinent. Et preterea de dominico meo pratum quod iacet pro septem acris in Pitfurlong et culturam que iacet pro 10 akris iuxta domum Roberti de Norfolc et le Ofrecolecroft quod iacet pro septem acris et terram que iacet inter wias pro tribus acris et terram de Witisdale quod iacet pro tribus acris et terram de Longelond que iacet propius ville pro septem acris et terram de Mikelebewic que iacet pro 5 acris et terram que iacet versus Madeslade pro una acra et terram infra fossum prati que iacet pro 6½ acris. Et terram in Stocfolde que iacet pro tribus acris et terram de Coppidemere que iacet pro duobus acris et terram in Tornhilslade que iacet pro septem acris et terram inter moras que iacet pro duobus acris et terram versus divisam de Torp *page 18* que iacet pro duobus akris et terram de Brocfurlong que iacet pro quatuor akris et terram super Enol que iacet pro una acra et dimidia et terram in Middilfurlong que iacet pro quatuor akris et terram in Olvismerefurlong que iacet pro tribus acris et terram de Klaihil que iacet pro quatuor acris et terram in Hungerhilslade que iacet pro duobus acris et terram ad Bagwest que iacet pro una acra et terram de Nelond in Sarpislade que iacet pro una acra et terram in Sortebanlond que iacet pro duobus acris et terram ad Thornihil que iacet pro quatuordecim acris et terram de Brocfurlong que iacet pro decem acris et quatuor selliones ad Brocfurlong que iacent pro una acra. Hanc predictam terram dedi predicto Thome de Hotot et heredibus suis in feodum et hereditatem tenendam de me et heredibus meis pro homagio suo et servicio suo et viginti marcis quas mihi dedit libere et quiete in pratis et pasturis in exitibus et in omnibus libertatibus que ad predictam willam Cloptonie pertinent pro omni servicio que ad me pertinet scilicet servicium decime partis feodi unius militis faciendo. Hanc predictam terram debeo ego et heredes mei warantizare Thome de Hotot et heredibus eius et si eam warantizare non possimus commutaci-

---

[140] The rents due at the final two terms were added later, by which time William le Mordant had died.

[141] The prominence afforded this charter suggests that it may have been seen as in some way the 'foundation charter' of the Hotot estate. When the parcels of demesne here are set alongside those in the 1250s terrier (**B 6**), it will be seen that the furlongs were scattered over three of the village's four fields.

onem ei faciemus ad walitudinem de nostro feodo. Hiis testibus. Willelmo
Lancelin. Radulpho filio Willelmi. Galfrido filio Ade. Henrico filio Galfridi. Rogero filio Galfridi. Widone filio Willelmi. et multis aliis.

21 Magna Carta 1225. A full text of the final revision of Magna Carta, issued by
King Henry III when he came of age.[142]
pages 19-22 [No Heading]
Text: Statutes of the Realm, i. 22-5; and see further Holt, *Magna Carta*,
pp. 313-37.

22 Charter of the Forest 1217. **Nos 21** and **22** together make up 'the Charters'
which were frequently reissued in the course of the thirteenth century.
pages 22-4 INCIPIT CARTA REGIS HENRICI FILII REGIS
JOHANNIS DE LIBERTATE FORESTE QUAM FECIT IN
PRINCIPIO CORONACIONIS SUE
Text: Statutes of the Realm, i. 20-1; and see further Holt, *Magna Carta*,
pp. 350-8.

23 Letter patent by which King John made his peace with Pope Innocent III. He
agreed to accept Stephen Langton as Archbishop of Canterbury, and to pay
the church compensation for the losses it had suffered. 13 May 1213.
pages 24-5 ISTA EST CARTA QUAM REX ANGLIE JOHANNES
FECIT ECCLESIE ROMANE ET PAPE INNOCENCIO QUANDO
EXCOMMUNICATUS FUIT
Text: Foedera, I. i, p. 111; and see further Cheney, *Innocent III and
England*, p. 331 note 26.

24 Letter patent by which King John resigned England and Ireland in fee to Pope
Innocent III, undertook to pay an annual tribute of 1000 marks and to do liege
homage to the pope. 15 May 1213.
pages 25-6 HEC EST CARTA J REGIS DE TRIBUTO ...
FACIENDO[143]
Text: Foedera, I. i, pp. 111-12; see further Cheney, *Innocent III and
England*, p. 332 note 29.

25 A list of Richard Hotot's main purchases of land: 'these are the purchases of
Richard of Hotot in lands and tenements in Clapton, besides the great costs of
building'. The total sum given for purchases in Clapton and elsewhere is £534
5s 4d.[144]
page 26 ISTE FUERUNT PERQUISICIONES RICARDI DE
HOTTOT de terris et tenementis tamen in villa de Cloptona preter mang-
nos sumptus edificii.
Hugoni de Rincgesdone ducentum marcas et triginta marcas.
Ricardo Pancefot et Ysabella uxore sue novies viginti marcas et tres
marcas.
Accelino de Cloptona centum marcas et tresdecim marcas.
Radulfo de Wygornia viginti marcas.
Alexandro capellano viginti marcas.

---

[142] A **21**, **22**, **23** and **24** need to be taken together. They cover eight sides, and they look
just like four leaves from a monastic cartulary. The texts of **nos 21** and **22** would have been
easily accessible. The texts of **nos 23** and **24** were more out of the way; they have not been
found in any of the surviving Peterborough abbey cartularies.
[143] One of the words of the heading is illegible.
[144] The majority of the tenants listed here are identified in the notes to **A 2, 8** and **11**; and
to **B 4**.

Monialibus de Chicsonde decem et octo marcas.
Willelmo de Musca quindecim marcas.[145]
Priore de Stanle sex marcas.[146]
Hugoni de Hotot quinque marcas.
Hugoni filio Henrici quindecim marcas.
Willelmo Hay quinquaginta et duos solidos.
Thoma le Blond duas marcas.
Ade filio Henrici tres marcas.
Wydoni Grimbaut novem marcas.
Henrico filio Galfridi septem marcas.
Ranulfo Grimbaut quinque marcas.
Hugoni clerico quatuor marcas et dimidia.
    Summa istarum parcellorum 658 marcis 8s 8d.
Preterea apud Wynewic Ricardo de Dovere quaterviginti marcas.
Preterea apud Bernewell Accelino, Johanne fratri eius, Roberto de
Melcheborne, Rohesie et Elene de le Haycroft triginta marcas et vinginti
solidos.
Ade clerico de Ogereston decem et octo marcas.
Henrico de Folkesworthe viginti solidos.
Willelmo fratri suo duas marcas.
Ade de Asseby in eadem tres marcas.
Radulfo de Beaumes in eadem sex marcas domino.

26 Meadowland in Northants, much of it recorded as being of the marriage-
portion of 'the lady', who is probably Thomas Hotot's mother; cf **A 19** and **35**.
page 27 [Plate 3] In Littleholm de maritagio domine in superiori loco
iuxta pratum Radulfi de Dive[147] scilicet superius quatuor perticas et
quinque pedes et iuxta aquam tres perticas et quatuor pedes.
In eodem prato de maritagio domine scilicet superius tres perticas et decem
pedes et iuxta aquam tres perticas et 9 pedes iuxta pratum Turkilbuon de
Broc.
In Brantisseye de maritagio domine scilicet superius tres perticas et iuxta
aquam decem et nouem perticas in latitudine.
In prato de Torp et Archirche sub aula comitis de Wadinho[148] widelicet
iuxta aquam 11 perticas et octo pedes et iuxta terram novem perticas et
talis est latitudo ibidem.
In eodem prato scilicet in Mikilholm equaliter scilicet sursum et deorsum
quatuor perticas et 2 pedes et dimidium. et ita sunt quatuor acre prati
quarum longitudo sub Wadino est 40 perticarum et in Mikilholm 55
perticarum quas dominus Reginaldus de Waterwill dedit Ricardo de Hotot
pro servicio suo.[149]

---

[145] William de Musca witnessed three charters in the Thorney cartulary (TRB fos 212r-v,
214r-v), but there is no other evidence of Richard of Hotot's dealings with him. A William de
Musca gave land in Aldwincle to the Templars before 1185: Lees, *Records of Templars*, p. 116.
[146] Presumably Stanley priory, Glos, though no information that would make sense of
this connection has been found.
[147] The Dive family were sub-tenants of the family of Waterville of Marholm: *Pytchley*,
pp. 44-5.
[148] Thorpe Achurch and Wadenhoe lay on either side of the river Nene. In 1254 Edmund
earl of Lincoln granted Wadenhoe to Roger de Quency, earl of Winchester, for life. Roger
died in 1264, and the manor reverted to the Lacys: *VCH Northants*, iii. 150.
[149] The Waterville family held Marholm in the Soke of Peterborough, and land in Thorpe
Achurch, Titchmarsh and Clapton itself: *Pytchley*, pp. 41-5. An assise of novel disseisin was
taken at Clapton on 4 November 1240, which shows Reginald of Waterville succeeding his
father and establishing his lordship in Marholm; he died in 1287: *Curia Regis Rolls*, xvi,
no 2465; *Pytchley*, p. 45 note.

27 A note of those to whom homage was owed in respect of lands in Northamptonshire. In other cases the homage had been bought out.[150]   [1263 × 1272]
ISTIS TENETUR HOMAGIUM IN NORHAMTONESCHIRE
Roberto de Hotot pro decima parte feodi militis.
Radulfo de Ringesdone pro una carucata terre dominice et quatuor virgatis in vilenagio et cum servicio liberorum hominum.
Domine Ysabelle Pancefot pro septem virgatis de vilenagio et sex acris de dominico.
Priori de Chikesaunde pro decem et octo acris de dominico.
Domino Berengario pro virgata et dimidia in Bernewelle.
Cecilie de Ferariis pro dimidia virgata.
Domino Reginaldo de Wateruile pro 4 acris prati in Torpmade.
Johanni de Douere pro terra de Wynewic.
Reliqui sunt quibus debebatur set per successionem temporis per emcionem habemus eorum homagia et servicia plena de suis capitalibus dominis ex quo illud homagium de cetero non est faciendum quia capud membro de eodem homagio non faciet set tantum servicium.

28 A note of those to whom homage was owed in respect of lands in Bedfordshire.[151]
ISTIS TENETUR HOMAGIUM IN COMITATU DE BEDEFORDIE
Heredibus vel assingnatis Johannis de Lega.
Ricardo de Ardres pro virgata terre et dimidia et pro duabus acris terre in inlond.
Symoni de Holewelle pro uno quartero terre et pro alio quartero damisele Maud.
Agathe de Bosco pro uno quarterio quadraginta et octo acrarum.
Henrico Wygem pro suo feodo.
Willelmo le Welbe et Matilde uxori eius et heredibus ipsius Matildis.
Heredibus Willelmi le Mordant pro terra de Roberto le Mordant.

29 A list of rents owed in respect of lands in Turvey; the majority of the tenants are named in **no 19**.
page 28
Text: not printed.

30 A list of the tenants of a hide of land in Turvey.
page 29   ISTA EST HIDA DURANDI[152]
Prior de Santo Neoto tenet unam dimidiam virgatam terre que fuit Willelmi de Antioche. Radulfus clericus dimidiam virgatam. Ricardus le Theyn dimidiam virgatam. Ricardus de Hotot dimidiam virgatam. Stefanus Iocewine dimidiam virgatam. Walterus Mauvalet et Simon Ilger dimidiam virgatam. Gilbertus Paynel unum quarterum. Galfridus le Bordeleis unum quarterum. Simon de Norwico dimidiam virgatam.

---

[150] This list may be compared with **A 8**, which dates from before 1248 (see **A 11**). Ralph of Ringstone stands in the place of Hugh, who died some time between June 1258 and Nov 1265 (*Somerset Fines*, p. 180; *Final Concords of the County of Lincoln*, ed. C. W. Foster (LRS, 17, 1920), p. 224); Isabella Pancefot has been widowed, and her husband was still alive at Easter 1263 (PRO CP 25(1) 92/12/246); and John of Dover has succeeded Richard. Cecily de Ferrers was the daughter of Sir Hugh de Ferrers of Bugbrooke, Northants, who was dead by 1257; Cecily died 28 July 1290: *Complete Peerage*, v, pedigree between pages 320 and 321.
[151] This would appear to be written at the same time as **A 27**. It must be a little later than **A 19**, for William le Mordant has died. William was still alive in 1257, and his heirs held in 1278-9: NRO SS 2880 and note 139 above.
[152] Though written in the time of Thomas Hotot, the entry refers to Richard Hotot's time.

31 The rents owed by tenants of the fee of William of Polebrook in Turvey, and the rents 'which we owe' for the same tenement.
Text: not printed.

32 A list of meadowland in Turvey. Marginal notes indicate those from whom some parcels of this land had been purchased. One of these refers to land 'which my father bought'; and so this section and **no 31** would seem to be in the hand of Thomas of Hotot.[153]

In Alfeldecroft dupla pars unius acre iuxta Robertum Gerin *de Radulfo le Duc fuit emptum.*

In Nordmade dimidia roda iuxta Adam le Wite *de Iacobo fuit emtum.*

In Nordmade dimidia acra iuxta pratum Radulfi clerici *de Willelmo filio Radulfi.*

In Riderwellmade 3 acre et amplius de Roberto le Rowe *de persona de Kariltona.*

In Nordmade dimidia acra inter Willelmum Stronge et W de Hill et 4 pedes superius *de wirgata de Sancto Georgio.*

In Nordmade dimidia acra inter Willelmum Martel et Radulfum clericum et 4 pedes superius *de wirgata de Sancto Georgio.*

In Nordmade 1 roda inter Radulfum Pitele et Radulfum clericum et 2 pedes superius.

In Dalemedwe wna acra de feodo Wimundi iuste latitudinis et optime longitudinis inter pratum domini Henrici de Lega et pratum Roberti le Rowe *de persona de Kariltona.*

Item una roda prati in Alfeldecroft equalem longitudinem inter pratum Henrici de Lega et pratum Ade filii Roberti *de wirgata de Sancto Georgio.*

Item una particula prati in Smalidole videlicet iuxta aquam mensura rode et iuxta terram dimidia roda inter pratum Henrici de Lega et pratum Roberti le Mordant *de virgata de Sancto Georgio.*

Item una roda prati in Dalemedwe inter pratum Walteri le Prude et pratum Roberti le Champion scilicet ad Blakewell equali longitudo et amplius *de terra Russell quod pater meus emit cum crofto Russell.*

Item una roda prati in Dalemedwe inter pratum Hugonis Tabar et pratum Henrici de Montibus *de persona de Karletona cum quartero terre Walteri de Norhamtona scilicet damiselle Maud fuit emtum, quod quidem pratum supra tactum Hugonis Taabard Thomas de Hotot emit de Iacobo de Ardris scilicet rodam et dimidiam iuxta Adam le Wite ex quo sunt ibi nunc simul due rode et dimidia.*

Item dimidia roda in Dalemedwe inter pratum Willelmi Aswi et pratum Henrici de Montibus *quod quidem participemus cum Iohanne le Huliere scilicet unam rodam quam rodam Stephanus de Gatesdene et Radulphus de Gatesdene emerunt de Gilberto Chiroc de feodo de Mutleput ex quo medietatem habemus per personam de Carlitona qui emit de Galfrido de Gatisdene.*

Item una particula prati in Brocholis inter pratum Roberti le Mordant et pratum Roberti Gerin scilicet Suadt *de virgata de Sancto Georgio.*

Item apud Dolepat 12 pedes superius et preterea sextam partem trium rodarum in Dalemade et in Nordmade *de Sibilla Martel.* [*a second footnote illegible*]

Item in Alfeldecroft 1 roda prati inter pratum Ricardi de Hotot et pratum Willelmi Duretest *de Ada filio Roberti.*

Item in Nordmade 1 roda prati inter pratum Radulfi clerici et pratum quod fuit Johannis de Nordho *de Ada filio Roberti.*

[153] The last of the carefully annotated entries which show the concern of Thomas Hotot to keep control over his property in Turvey.

33 A list of lands in Turvey, giving amounts and location. The first entry reads: sub Monkisgate una dimidia acra.
page 30
Text: not printed.

34 In the margin to **no 33** there is what appears to be a list of Thomas Hotot's own purchases of land in Turvey, while foot-notes to these marginal notes give the prices paid.
Thomas de Hotot emit de Milisent 2 seliones in crofto suo pro 10s 2 bussellis frumenti.
Emit eciam de Heylot unam acram terre pro 7s *2 bussellis frumenti.*
Emit eciam de Simone Martel dimidiam acram terre et unam rodam et dimidiam cum prato in Dalmade *pro 10s 2 bussellis frumenti.*
Emit eciam tres selliones in Brouningiscoll' de Stefano Laverke *pro 5s 4d.*
Emit eciam de Rogero de Beydene 4 selliones sub Ordilho *pro 4s.*
Dedit eciam uxori Rogeri de Goldintoun pro quieta clamio dotis de Goldintounvike et pro grava ibidem et pro 22½d redditus dimidiam marcam ad comitatum de Bedeford anno regni regis Henrici 38 die lune proxima ante festum Sancti Nicolai [1 December 1253].
De Willelmo Bigge 2 selliones *pro 4s 10d.*
Preterea de Henrico Fabro una roda *pro 3s.*
De Ricardo Vauclin una acra *pro 8s.*
De Simone Martel dimidia roda prati et tres denarios redditus *pro 5s 3d.*
De Simone Eyron 1¾d redditus *pro 13½d.*
De Heylot 1d redditus *pro 10d.*
Pro terra Iacobi de Ardris *13 marcas 4s 8d.*
Pro terra Floris de Beydene *pro dimidia marca.*
Item pro terra Simone Martel ad Riderswellemade *pro 4s.*

35 Further notes of meadowland in Turvey, noting the person from whom the parcels had been bought, and their location in terms of the neighbouring tenant or tenants.[154]
page 31
[1] In Alfeldecroft dupla pars unius acre, de Radulfo le Duc fuit emptum, inter Petrum filium Willelmi et Robertum Gerin.
Item in Alfeldecroft dimidia acra (domina totum),[155] una roda de virgata, alia de Ada filio Roberti, inter Willelmum Durtest' et Radulfo Pirot.
In Dolepat iuxta aquam una roda iuxta terram 12 pedes, de Simone Martel et libbe fuit emtum, iuxta Walterum le Packere.
In Smaledole iuxta aquam una roda iuxta terram dimidia roda, de virgata de Sancto Georgio, inter Radulfum Pirot et Robertum le Mordant.
In Dalemad una acra scilicet Wimundi (domina terciam partem), de persona de Carletona, inter Radulfum Pyrot et Rogerum seruientem.
Item in Dalemad una roda, de terra Russel, inter Radulfum le Duc et Radulfum clericum.
Item in Dalemad dimidia roda (domina totum), de persona de Carletona fuit emtum, iuxta Rogerum seruientem.
Item in Dalemad due rode et dimidia, de persona de Carletona 1 roda, de Iacobo de Ardres roda et dimidia, inter Adam le Wite et Henricum de Montibus.

[154] Sections 1 and 2 of this list would seem to cover the same ground as **A 32**. The changes in the names of neighbouring tenants between the two lists suggests an active market in small parcels of meadowland.
[155] Notes of the land owing rent to Thomas Hotot's widowed mother are written above the line in a minute hand; cf **A 19**.

In Brocholis dimidia roda (domina totum), de virgata de Sancto Georgio, inter Radulfum Pyrot et Robertum Gerin.

[2] In Nordmad una acra et dimidia et 12 pedes supra, una Willelmi Porthors, alia Nicholai de Gatesdene et tercia Simonis Martel et libbe, inter pratum de Stiuetona et Radulfum clericum.
Item in Nordmad dimidia acra, de virgata de Sancto Georgio, iuxta Simonem de Holewell.
Item in Nordmad dimidia roda, de Iacobo de Ardres fuit emtum, iuxta Adam le Wite.
Item in Nordmad una roda et 2 pedes supra dimidiam pedem subtus, de virgata de Sancto Georgio, inter Ricardum ... et Radulfum clericum.
Item in Nordmad una roda 2 pedes supra dimidiam pedem subtus (domina totum), de Ada filio Roberti, iuxta pratum Walteri de Northo.
Item in Nordmad dimidia acra (domina totum), de virgata de Sancto Georgio, inter Reginaldum le Strange et Robertum Mordant.

[3] In Riperswellemad tres acre (domina terciam partem), de persona de Carletona fuit emptum, sub Beydene et preterea ibid de Symone de Hole-well et Hugone serviente due particule prati per finalia excambia.
In le Halew (domina terciam partem), de Willelmo Porthors fuit emptum.
In Crowlebroc (domina terciam partem), de Willelmo Porthors fuit emptum.
In Estlirreuesbroc (domina terciam partem), de Willelmo Porthors fuit emptum.
In crofto extra murum, de Henrico filio Stephani fuit emptum.

36 A list of payments owed in commutation of the duty to perform castle-guard at Belvoir Castle.
ISTI SUNT DEBITORES DE WARDA DE BEWVER
Thomasin 2½d pro inlond quod fuit Ricardi le Theyn.[156]
Henricus filius Stephani 2½d pro terra in nouo Stocking.
Hugo filius Phillippi seruientis ¾d in Blakemannescroft.[157]
Item Hugo filius Phillippi seruientis et Simon de Holewelle ¾d pro terra in Mittlepit inlond.
Prior de Sancto Neoto 1¼d pro quinque acris sub Liuerunhey.
Sibilla filia Henrici de Gatesdene veteris ¾d pro tribus acris in suo Estcroft.
Walterus le Packere ¾d pro tribus acris in crofto suo.
Robertus le Rue 1½d pro crofto Cibbe et pro tribus acris ad Liuerunehey-gate.
Galfridus de Ringstede ½d pro crofto Bigge.
Johannes Hareng de Carletona 2d pro octo acris iuxta Middelhotherd pro Henrico filio Stephani.
Thomas de Hotot 1d pro tribus acris ...
Item ¾d pro tribus acris iuxta Middelhotherd.
Item 2¼d pro novem acris super Wllowswic.
Willelmus Thurgod ¾d pro tribus acris super viam del Pirie.
Agatha uxor Radulfi clerici 5d pro quindecim acris in Crowlestocking et pro quinque super ... [*MS torn*]

---

[156] The 2½d here mentioned was specifically reserved when Richard le Thein granted land in Turvey to Thomas de Evermodio: NRO SS 2881, and see note 100 above.
[157] The father occurs as Philip serviens or Philip serviens hundredi, and witnessed charters at Christmas 1251: BL Cotton MS Faust. A iv, fos 133v–134v, and 'Turvey Records', pp. 63, 99. The son occurs as Hugo filius Philippi servientis domini regis de ballivo de Wylie, in a charter which is unlikely to date from earlier than the 1270s: NRO SS 2867.

Willelmus de Tichemers 1d ... [*MS faded*]
page 32 blank

37 Charter of Robert le Seriant of Clapton by which he granted to Thomas Hotot his lord 2s annual rent from his tenement in Clopton, in return for the payment of 'a certain sum of money'. Witnessed by Gilbert le Moine and others (not named). 28 May 1268.
page 33
Text: not printed.

38 Charter of Gilbert of Holderness by which he granted to Thomas Hotot his messuage and the land with appurtenances which came to him from Emma of Holderness his wife, with the service of his free tenants. Thomas Hotot and his heirs undertook to pay 7s a year rent to the nuns of Stamford, and to give Gilbert 'sustenance' for the rest of his life in the terms of the charter issued to confirm this. Witnessed by Gilbert le Frankeleyn and others (not named).
Text: not printed.

39 Charter of Robert le Sergant of Clapton by which he granted to Thomas Hotot his lord a rood of land lying next to the messuage of Gilbert son of Guy, in return for the payment of 'a certain sum of money'. Witnessed by Richard le Frankeleyn and others (not named).
Text: not printed.

40 Charter of John of Holderness son and heir of Emma of Holderness by which he granted to Thomas Hotot the service of Hugh le Waleys and the service of Hugh le Ginnur, which latter tenement lay between the house and the croft formerly of Walter le Ginnur and to the east next the house and croft formerly of Walter of Weston. Witnessed by Gilbert le Frankeleyn, Richard his son, Hugh son of Henry, Roger son of Andrew.
Text: not printed.

page 34 blank

41 The rents and farms owed to Thomas Hotot in Clapton, 1272–3.
page 35   ISTI SUNT REDDITUS ET FIRME THOME DE HOTOT ANNO PRIMO EDWARDI IN VILLA DE CLOPTON AD FESTUM SANCTI MICHAELIS
De Gilberto le Moyne 3d. De Ricardo le Fraunkelein 12d. De Hugone filio Henrici 12d. De Hugone filio Galfridi 2s 6d. De Henrico de Nortf' 12d. De Radulfo le Waleys 2d. De Henrico de Fagenham 12d. De Willelmo sacerdote 5d. De Hugone le Ginnur 6d. De Waltero Grimbaut 2s. De Roberto le Sergaunt 19d et dimidiam libram cimini vel 1d. De Hugone de Weston 6d. De Henrico Grimbaut 1d. De Alicia de Cotingham 1½d et unum diem in messe. [*three later additions faded*]
De triginta et quatuor dimidiis virgatis villanorum de quolibet 2s 9d.
De Roberto Lyoun 4d. De Roesia 4d. De Waltero preposito 2s et de eodem 1¾d. De Roberto Allekario 12d. De Willelmo de Makesey 4d. De Willelmo filio Michaelis 16d. De Galfrido de Torveye 2½d. De Ada filio Agnete 8d. De Ranulfo Cirot' 12d. De Matilda Michaelis 12d. De uxore Hugonis de Tichemers 9d. De Willelmo mercatore 9d. De priore de Huntedon 2s. De Hugone le Ginnur 12d. De Waltero de Hyrst 9d. De uxore le Batour 6d. De Willelmo sutore 1d. De uxore fabri 16d. De Hugone Widerward 5d. De Henrico Grimbaut 20d. De Willelmo bercario 18d. De Waltero Biscop 6d. De Waltero Cirot' 12d. De Gilberto le Moine 12d. De Willelmo Cut 9d.
De molendinis 20s.

page 36 [Plate 4]   FESTUM NATIVITATE CHRISTI
De Waltero Grimbaut 2s. De Henrico de Fakenham 12d. De Hugone filio
Henrici 12d. De Willelmo le Heir ½d. De Henrico de Nortf' 15d. De
Hugone filio Galfridi 2s 6d. De Alicia de Cotingham 1½d. De Roesia le
Grimi 1d et forinsecum dimidii quarterii. De Rogero filio Andree 2 altilia.
De Ricardo le Frankelein 12d. De Willelmo sacerdote 4d. De Matilda filia
Widonis 2d. De Albrico 1d.
De triginta et quatuor virgatis dimidiis de quolibet 2s 9d.
De Roberto Lyun 4d. De Waltero preposito 2s et de eodem 1¾d. De
Waltero le Kareter 1d. De Rogerio Allekario 2d. De Willelmo de Makesey
3d. De Willelmo filio Michaelis 16d. De Galfrido de Torveye 2¼d. De Ada
filio Agnete 8d. De Ranulfo Cirot' 12d. De Matilda filia Widonis 4d. De
Matilda Michaelis 12d. De uxore Hugonis de Tichemers 9d. De Hugone le
Ginnur 12d. De Waltero de Hyrst 9d. De uxore le Batur 6d. De Willelmo
Sutore 5d. De uxore fabri 16d. De Hugone Widerward 5d. De Henrico
Grimbaut 20d. De Willelmo mercatore 9d. [*one later entry faded*] De
Willelmo bercario 18d. De Waltero Biscop 6d. De Waltero Cirot' 12d. De
Gilberto le Moyne 12d. De Willelmo Cut 9d.
De molendinis 20s.
   Summa totalis £7 3s 3¾d.
page 37 [Plate 4]   FESTUM PASCHE
De Roberto le Sergaunt 12d. De Hugone le Waleys ¼d. De Henrico Grim-
baut 5d. De Gilberto le Moyne 3d et unam libram piperis. De Henrico de
Fakenham 12d. De Hugone filio Henrici 12d. De Henrico de Nortf' 12d.
De Hugone filio Galfridi 2s 6d. De Radulfo le Waleys 2s. De Waltero
Grimbaut 2s. De Alicia de Cotingham 1½d. De Rogero filio Andree 6d. De
Ricardo le Francelein 11½d. De Willelmo sacerdote 4d. De Albrico 1d. De
Hugone le Ginnur 6d.
De triginta et quatuor dimidiis virgatis villanorum de quolibet 2s 9d.
De Roberto Lyun 4d. De Waltero preposito 2s et de eodem 1¾d. De
Waltero le Kareter 1d. De Roberto Allekario 7d. De Willelmo de Makesey
3d. De Willelmo filio Michaelis 16d. De Galfrido de Torvey 2¼d. De Ada
filio Agnete 8d. De Ranulfo Cirot' 12d. De Matilda Michaelis 12d. De
uxore Hugonis de Tichemers 9d. De Hugone le Ginnur 12d. De Waltero
de Hirst 9d. De uxore le Batur 6d. De Willelmo sutore 5d. De uxore fabri
16d. De Hugone Widerward 5d. De Henrico Grimbaut 20d. De Willelmo
bercario 18d. De Waltero Biscop 6d. De Waltero Cirot' 12d. De Gilberto
le Moyne 12d. De Willelmo Cut 9d. [*one entry illegible*]
De molendinis 20s.
   Summa £7 4s 5¼d.
page 38   FESTUM SANCTI JOHANNIS
De Waltero Grimbaut 2s. De Henrico de Fakenham 12d. De Hugone filio
Henrici 12d. De Henrico de Nortf' 12d. De Hugone filio Galfridi 5s 6d. De
Alicia de Cotingham 1½d. De Ricardo le Frankelein 12d. De Willelmo
sacerdote 4d. De Albrico 1d.
De triginta et quatuor dimidiis virgatis villanorum de quolibet 2s 9d.
De Roberto Lyun 4d. De Waltero preposito 2s et de eodem 1¾d. De
Waltero le Kareter 1d. De Roberto Allecario 7d. De Willelmo de Makeseye
3¾d. De Willelmo filio Michaelis 16d. De Galfrido de Torvey 2¼d. De Ada
filio Agnete 7d. De Ranulfo Cirot' 12d. De Matilda Michaelis 12d. De
uxore Hugonis de Tichemers 9d. De Hugone le Ginnur 12d. De Waltero
de Hirst 9d. De uxore le Batur 6d. De Willelmo Sutore 5d. De uxore fabri
16d. De Hugone Widerward 5d. De Henrico Grimbaut 20d. De Willelmo
Bercario 18d. De Waltero Biscop 6d. De Waltero Cirot' 12d. De Gilberto

le Moyne 12d. De Willelmo Cut 9d. De Willelmo mercatore 9d.
De molendinis 20s.
  Summa istius terminum £7 1s 7¾d.
page 39   Ad Gulam Augusti de Henrico Grimbaut 3d.[158]
Ad festum Sancti Martini de Waltero Grimbaut 1 libram cimini.
Ricardus de Hotot die Sancte Trinitatis 1d.
Galfridus de Ringsted eodem die 1d.
Ricardus frater meus ad festum Sancti Petri 1 rosam.
Gilbertus le Moyne ad Pasca 1 libram piperis.
Rogerus de Beumis quartam partem feodi militis.[159]
Prior de Finnishevid decimam partem militis ad scutagium.[160]
Walterus de Hotot unam libram cimini.
Henricus Grimbaut forinsecum bis in anno pro uno quartero terre.
Ricardus de Hotot 17d per annum ad sustentationem unius lampade
perpetui coram altarem beate Marie Magdalene.
De Reginaldo de Hotot unam libram cimini scilicet ad Natale pro Berne-
welle.[161]
Item de eodem 1d pro mesuagio iuxta Willelmum sacerdotem ad festum
Sancti Leonardi.

page 40 blank

42 Services owed for lands and tenements purchased by Thomas Hotot and
  Richard Hotot in Clapton.[162]
page 41   HEC SUNT SERVICIA QUE DEBEMUS PRO TERRIS ET
TENEMENTIS DE PERQUISICIONE THOME DE HOTOT PRIMI
IN WILLA DE CLOPTON
Roberto de Hotot de Kariltona decimam partem feodi unius militis.[163]
Heredibus Widonis le Frankelein ½d.
Heredibus Widonis Roc 2d sed Thomas de Hotot secundus illos redemit.
HEC SUNT SERVICIA QUE DEBEMUS PRO TERRIS ET TENE-
MENTIS QUE RICARDUS DE HOTOT PERQUISIVIT IN WILLA
DE CLOPTON
Heredibus Widonis Grimbaut 6d sed Thomas secundus illos redemit.
Heredibus Henrici filii Galfridi 5d sed idem Ricardus illos redemit in
posterum.
Heredibus Roberti filii Petri 3d.
Heredibus Accellini 7d.
Heredibus Hugonis de Ringesdene 6d vel unum par calcarium deaurato-
rum.

[158] The rental is completed by a note of the obligations of various neighbours and relatives.
The reference to 'Ricardus frater meus' establishes that the text was written by Thomas Hotot
in the last years of his life.
[159] Roger de Beumis occurs as witness to a charter dated 13 Oct 1264, and on 8 Sept
1272 granted land in Barnwell to Armston hospital, 'for the souls of Reginald de Beaumis my
father and Isabel my mother': NRO Buccleuch Deeds A 40, H 33; and see above note 121.
[160] See the Fineshade priory cartulary, Lambeth Palace Library Ff 291, fos 20v–21r, which
contains the grant by Richard of Folksworth son of the late Richard Hotot of 32s rent from
'Berndon', saving the service of a tenth part of a knight's fee, 'si quod fuit faciendo'. The
cartulary is late, and its compiler seems to have conflated in the one section grants in
Barrowden in Rutland and Barnwell in Northants.
[161] A kinsman had been given the acquisitions made in Barnwell by Richard Hotot
(A 25). Shortly after this the lands were purchased by Ramsey abbey; see note 115 above.
[162] Most likely contemporary with A 41, of 1272–3; at most a year or two later. There is
a clear echo of A 8 (Richard Hotot's obligations) and A 27, 28 (Thomas Hotot's obligations
in his earlier years). The coherence of this final gathering with the earlier material with which
it was bound, might suggest that the binding took place in Thomas Hotot's lifetime.
[163] See note 104 above.

Heredibus Isabelle Pancefot 6d vel unum par calcarium deauratorum.
Thome de Lollintona 12d.
Willelmo de Wircestre 18d.
Abbati de Burgo 6s.
Gilberto le Moine 2d.
page 42 Priori de Chikesaund 12d vel unam libram piperis.
Heredibus Hugonis de Ferrariis 3s pro terra in Bernewell.
Domino Belengario 2 altilia pro dimidia virgata terre in Bernewell.
Heredibus Ricardi de Dofre 1d pro quaterwiginti acris terre in Wynewic et pro homagio et servicio heredum Willelmi de Badbornham.
Roberto de Tichemers 2s scilicet pro prato de Brantisseye 12d et pro virgata terre Gilberti Gray 12d.

43 Notes of homages performed: (1) Thomas Hotot to Hugh of Ringstone, 16 June 1254; (2) Thomas Hotot to Isabella Pancefot, 24 September 1268; (3) William of Worcester to Thomas Hotot, 30 April 1273.[164]
page 43 Anno regni regis Henrici filii regis Johannis 38 die martis proxima ante festum Sancti Botulfi apud Lundoniam in domo abbatis de Burgo ad Sanctum Sepulcrum Thomas de Hotot secundus fecit homagium Hugoni de Ringisdone qui eadem hora solvit illi duo paria calcarium deauratorum coram domino Radulfo fratre suo cui dedit unum par illorum.[165]

Anno regni regis Henrici filii regis Johannis quinquagesimo secundo die Lune proxima ante festum Sancti Michaelis Thomas de Hotot secundus fecit homagium domine Isabelle Pauncefot in aula sua apud Blaysworte et que ipsum implacitaverat ante de eodem tenemento de quo tunc cepit homagium pro finali concordia anterius facta.[166]

Anno primo Edwardi die dominica proxima ante Invencionem Sancte Crucis Thomas de Hotot secundus cepit homagium Willelmi de Wircestre in aula sua apud Clopton pro duobus virgatis terre in Clopton et idem Thomas fecit illi homagium pro medietate illius terre propter tenorem carte de feofamento.[167]

two pages 43* blank

44 Notes on the careers of the later Anglo-Saxon kings of England.[168]
page 44 Ethelredus rex Anglie filius Edgari nobilissimi regis et frater Edwardi coram ducibus Anglorum sacratus est in regem apud Kingiston. Homine sinistro sicut de eo cum parvulus esset Sanctus Dunstanus profetabat mingxit ramorum cum baptizaretur in sacro fonte unde vir domini exterminium terre Anglorum in tempore eius futurum dixit. Cum rengnasset triginta et septem annis post multos labores et angxietates uite sue

---

[164] According to the heading to MS B, homage had to be performed 'according to the terms of the charters'; and this was done in the three entries which follow.
[165] The service owed at Easter by the terms of the grant to Richard Hotot; see below **B 4 no 1** at note 179.
[166] The service owed at Pentecost by the terms of the grant to Richard Hotot; see below **B 4 no 1** at note 180. Blaysworte is presumably Blisworth, but it is not clear how she came to have lordship there.
[167] See below **B 4 no 1** at note 181.
[168] This material has been extracted from the chronicle of Henry of Huntingdon: *Henrici Archidiaconi Huntendunensis Historia Anglorum,* ed. T. Arnold (Rolls Ser. 74, 1879), pp. 167–8, 182, 185–6. Compare T. Wright (ed), *Feudal Manuals of English History* (1872), pp. 15–17. The texts there printed are from rolls, one of which is illustrated in Clanchy, *From Memory to Written Record,* plate XIII. Wright commented, a little quaintly but none the less accurately, that these records 'give us the amount of knowledge relating to the history of his country which it was considered that an English baron or gentleman of the feudal period ought to possess, as well as its special colour and character' (p. x).

decessit in Lundonia ante quam navigium ostile advenisset. Post quem
Edmundus filius eius electus est in regem qui vocatur eciam irinside videlicet ferreum latus quia maximi vigoris et mirabilis patiencie bellicis erat in
negociis. Edmundus rex post paucos dies ex hinc proditione Edrici ducis
infidissimi occisus est apud Oxenforde. Sic periit Edmundus cum rengnasset uno anno et sepultus est iuxta Edgar avum suum in Glastingbiri.

45 Charter of William Hotot by which he granted to Reginald his brother and
Alice daughter of William of Nottingham his wife the tenancies which Richard
le Bere and W. frater Haildrici formerly held in villeinage of Thomas his father
in Barnwell, with their villein tenancies and their families (sequela). He also
granted them the homage and service of the prior of Armston, magister Anger
of Barnwell, Nicholas his brother, Robert of Sutton and William brother of
magister Jordan of Barnwell, with all the tenancies which they formerly held of
Thomas in that village. Date: *c* 1280.

Text: not printed.

46 A list of the Christian kings of France, from Clovis to Louis VI.

page 45   Nomina regum Francie omnium qui Cristiani sunt. Clodoveus.
Clotarius. Chilpericus. Clotarius. Dagobertus. Cladoveus. Teodoricus.
Childebertus. Dagobertus. Teodoricus. Clotarius. Et post transmigrationem huius generacionis Pipinus. Karolus Magnus imperator. Lodowicus pius imperator. Karolus calvus. Ludovicus. Karolus simplex. Odo
Robertus et Radulfus isti tres fuerunt invasores rengni. Lodovicus. Lotar-
ius. Lodowicus ... rex ultimus. Et post transmigrationem huius generacionis Hugo filius Hugonis mangni ducis. Robertus. ... Henricus. Filippus.
Lodovicus.

B

Bodleian Library, MS top. Northants c. 19

HOC EST REGISTRUM THOME DE HOTOT DE OMNIBUS CARTIS ET FINALIBUS CONCORDIIS ET EXCAMBIIS UBIQUE FACTIS ET PERQUISITIS PER THOMAM DE HOTOT AVUM PREDICTI THOME ET PER RICARDUM DE HOTOT FILIUM EIUS ET PER THOMAM FILIUM PREFATI RICARDI AD EVIDENCIAM HABENDAM SINE VISIONE CARTARUM ORIGINALIUM PRO OMNIBUS CONTINGENTIBUS LITIBUS VEL QUESTIONIBUS FORINSECORUM INIUSTORUM VEL REDDITUUM ET PRO RELEVIIS DANDIS SECUNDUM TENOREM CARTARUM

All those both laymen and clerks who in the future should require clear evidence of the customs of the village of Clapton as it has descended from the time of Alfred de Grandcourt can read and find evidence on each point in what follows.[169] We have most carefully and earnestly established this and tested it from the ancient fathers who are left in the village, the old men with their venerable grey hairs.

Omnes qui in posterum indigeant tam laici quam clerici de consuetudinibus villatus de Clopton a tempore Alfredi de Grauntkort descendendo manifeste racionari et de unaquaque parte habere evidenciam indigentes subscripta perspiciant et intelligant. Quoniam prout diligenter et affectuose didici et expertus sum a senioribus patribus de villa de Clopton, quos residuos inveni senes crinibus veneranda canitie dealbantibus.

1 Concerning the village of Clapton and the fields adjacent to the village, how much remains there of the different baronies?

capitulum De villa de Clopton et campis eidem ville adjacentis, videlicet quot ibi restant diversitates baroniarum.

solutio Due sunt siquidem scilicet baronia de Luvetot et baronia de Burgo.

2 Which fees are there in each barony, or how many fees?

capitulum Et de qualibet baronia quot sunt ibi feodis vel quantum de feodis.

solutio[170] De baronia Burgi feodum militis fere unius, excepta quantitate 2d de Catteworthe. (Scilicet tertia decima parte militis, sed supersunt 2d ad completionem de Pokebroc et Catteworthe, quam quando scutagium est ad 40s Clopton dat 37s 2d, Pokebroc 24s 6d, Catteworthe 18s 4d[171] et ita 2d de Clopton, 6d de Pokebroc et 4d de Catteworthe complent octogesimam partem sex marcarum pro duobus feodis de tribus villis pretactis quando scutagium fuerit per 40s videlicet ad baroniam de Burgo.) Et baronia de Luvetot revera quarta pars feodi unius militis.

---

[169] In the text the articles of enquiry are first given in full, and then the answers are given. For this edition the two have been amagamated; each question (*capitulum*) is given, with a translation, and is followed by its answer (*solutio*).

[170] Material in brackets is inserted from MS B, p. 55; a note on p. 32 indicates that it should have been transcribed at this point.

[171] 24s in MS, but the correct figure, which makes up the total of 80s, is found below in **B 13**.

3 From the time of William the bastard king of the English until the 40th year of the reign of king Henry the son of King John, 1255-56, how many and which were the lords who succeeded by inheritance, the son following the father

capitulum   Et a tempore Willelmi Bastardi regis Anglie usque ad quadragesimum annum regni regis Henrici filii regis Johannis quot et qui ibi fuerunt domini hereditarii succedentes, scilicet filius post patrem descendendo.

solutio   Abbas Thoroldus de Burgo cognatus regis Willelmi conquestoris dedit Rogero de Luvetot qui primus erat dominus baronie de Soudtho totum tenementum quod suum erat et in dominicis et in feodo preter unam virgatam, quare illa vocatur virgata Honeware.[172] Quam quidem successores illius Rogeri habentes hereditarium dominium de Clopton tenuerunt de abbate et successoribus eius in paragio,[173] testante Johanne abbate in libro suo apud Burgum, illo dico abbate qui proximus erat antecedens abbatem Martinum Britonem,[174] usque in ultimis diebus Willelmi de Grauntkort qui vocabatur Willelmus de Clopton ab inferioribus, quoniam facilius erat lingue eorum cognomen Anglicum quam Normannum. Idem Rogerus dedit Alfredo de Grauntkort socio suo et militi nobili quantumcumque habuit in Clopton cum de sua baronia propria tum de tenemento quod tenuit per vavassoriam de Burgo. Walterus de Grauntkort filius et heres dicti Alfredi successit eidem tenens integre dominium tocius ville tum in dominico cum in servitio, scilicet 5 hidas nichil excepto, sicut testatur venerabilis abbas Johannes predictus in registro quod fecit de feodis suis apud Burgum. Willelmus de Grauntkort filius et heres dicti Walteri successit eidem hereditarie primo recipiens et tenens integre, qui postea dispersit dedit et vendidit. Et tot erant heredes de Clopton, ut ita dicam filius post patrem.

4 How many men were enfeoffed thereafter, and by whom? Who were they? In what way did they gain entry?

capitulum   Et quot postmodum feofati fuerunt et qui et a quibus et quo genere ingressus.[175]

solutio   [1 William Dacus.][176] Dictus Willelmus de Grauntkort dedit et vendidit Willelmo Daco totum tenementum quod habuit in Clopton preter terras quas emit de Waltero filio Ricardi militis, qui fuit frater eiusdem

[172] The account here may be compared with that given in **A 1**.

[173] In the Peterborough Abbey survey of knights' holdings made *c* 1105 there is the entry: 'Walterus filius Aluredi v hidas de feodo Rogeri de Luvetot, et de abbate 1 virgam cxl acras in paragio in Hamtonascira' (E. King, 'The Peterborough *Descriptio Militum* (Henry I)', *EHR*, lxxxiv (1969), p. 100 no 37.

[174] If the phrase might seem to suggest a little uncertainty as to the identity of the abbot before Martin Brito (1226 × 1233), it was called for, for his predecessor was not John but Alexander (1222 × 1226). The statement that this abbot made a feodary, from which the Hotots gained their information about the early history of their estate, is an interesting one. The feodary should be added to the list of lost manuscripts in Janet Martin, *The Cartularies and Registers of Peterborough Abbey* (NRS, xxviii, 1978), pp. 46-7. This early feodary was superseded by that made by Henry of Pytchley *c* 1400, which preserves no record of it; but cf the beginning of the Lovetot entry in *Pytchley*, p. 90 with that found here.

[175] The simplicity of the descent to William of Clapton is deliberately contrasted with his treatment of the estate, 'qui postea dispersit, dedit et vendidit'. The *solutio* here, which deals with William's alienations, represents a considerable feat of organisation, only possible after the family's charters had been put in order (an order which may have been followed in the cartulary itself). The long narrative or count has been broken up by supplying headings, and some paragraphs, neither of which are found in the original transcript.

[176] For the material in this section see the introduction at notes 50 to 54, and **A** at notes 87 to 89. It may be presumed that the first sentence here summarises the charters in the Hotot archive which named William Dacus as a beneficiary. It seems possible, however, that the text here and elsewhere identifies as an original grant what was in fact a confirmation.

Willelmi et ab eo feofatus, et preter terras quas disrationavit ad bancum super Galfridum de Normanvill et Symonem fratrem eius, et preter terras quas quondam habuit per exscambium de priore et conventu Sancti Neoti. Idem Willelmus Dacus duxerat in uxorem Emmam filiam et heredem Roberti de Hofford et Dionisie uxoris sue,[177] que soror dicti Willelmi in tempore regis Stephani dum adhuc puella esset quadam die induta tunica armatoria et galero cervici imposito munita tantum scuta concavo militem quendam de Warmistura de givildeni[178] ictu haste prope Warmislowe prostravit et dextrarium domi reduxit.

Qui Willelmus Dacus succedente tempore dedit Isabelle filie sue unam carucatam terre in dominico et tres virgatas et dimidiam tenentium per villenagium et tria cotaria et servitia omnium liberorum hominum suorum. Que Isabella emit de Waltero filio Ricardi predicti consanguineo suo illam dimidiam virgatam quam Galfridus filius Martini solet tenere, et de Waltero Monacho partem mesuagii quod Britwoldus filius Ricardi solet tenere. Ipsa Isabella in posterum desponsata fuit a domino Ricardo de Hasilbewe et non peperit cum ipso. Denique capite ipsius in nemore persciso per quandam fraudelentem ambitionem relicta facta est. Postea desponsata de Hugone de Ringkesdone, qui annuente uxore terram suam quantumcumque habuerunt in Cloptone sine ullo retenemento, qui postea summoniti per breve warancie carte coram justiciariis apud Leychestre dederunt scilicet Radulpho de Ringkesdone warancia celeriter facta incontinenti sit inter ipsos finalis concordia.[179] Movente comite Ricardo Cornubie in terram Ierosolomitanam crucis signatus est dictus Radulphus personaliter adhiendum, sed scensu improvisus adivit fratri suo Hugoni petens ab eo quoquo modo posset centum marcas. Et igitur[180] Hugoni fratri suo et heredibus suis vel assignatis dictam terram de Clopton daret et redderet. Quo facto Hugo de Ringkesdone sumpsit de Aaron de Everwic centum marcas per cartam suam solvendo infra annum centum libras. Et hoc facto et soluto transeunte biennio prefatus Hugo vendidit Ricardo de Hotot totam illam terram de Clopton pro octies viginti marcis et decem in perpetuum reddendo per annum unum par calcarium deauratorum vel 6d per annum scilicet ad Pascha, et faciendo pro ipso Hugone et heredibus suis ipse Ricardus et heredibus suis capitalibus dominis feodi illius servitia que ad illud pertinet.

Idem Willelmus Dacus dedit Roberto Grimbaud cum Matilda filia sua septem virgatas terre de villenagio suo in Clopton et sex acras de dominico

---

[177] Ufford in the Soke of Peterborough. A Robert of Ufford occurs in 1202 (*Assise Rolls 1202 and 1203*, p. 1), and held 24 acres of land in Clapton in 1199 (PRO CP 25(1) 171/5/40).

[178] sic MS; possibly a garbled version of the name of the lord in whose household the unfortunate knight lived.

[179] PRO CP 25(1) 173/31/443, dated January 1240, is the grant of a carucate of land in Clapton by Hugh of Ringstone and Isabella his wife to Ralph of Ringstone, to hold of them by the rent of a pair of gilt spurs annually. According to the text which follows this land was granted by Hugh to Richard of Hotot two years later, i.e. in 1242. That grant does not survive, but the date is supported by the record of consequential litigation in the *curia regis* in 1242 and 1243. Ralph of Ringstone sued his brother Hugh for the return of four charters, and then (possibly having obtained them) sought to recover the Clapton estate from Richard of Hotot. Richard called Hugh of Ringstone to warrant him, which finally he did. *Curia Regis Rolls*, xvii, nos 69, 114, 162, 218, 289, 397, 1125, 1254, 1712. It is possible to reconcile the text printed here (which amplifies the version of the same story given in A 2) with what survives in the public records. Richard of Cornwall did indeed go on crusade in 1240, and Aaron of York was most active around this time: N. Denholm-Young, *Richard of Cornwall* (Oxford, 1947), pp. 38–44; M. Adler, *Jews of Medieval England* (1939), pp. 127–73. Equally it is possible that what can be seen here is the making of legend; that the date of the fine suggested the crusade; and that the story was built up in layers.

[180] A possible extension of the abbreviations transcribed in the MS.

suo quas Galfridus filius Badewini solet tenere.[181] Idem Robertus Grimbaud et uxor eius Matilda dererunt Ricardo Pauncefot cum Isabella filia
sua et herede de dicta Matilda progenita in liberum maritagum predictas
septem virgatas et sex acras de dominico suo. Dicti vero Ricardus et
Isabella vendiderunt Ricardo de Hotot totam illam predictam terram
quam habuerunt in Clopton; et postea summoniti fuerunt per breve warancie carte coram justiciariis itinerantibus apud Gloverniam, qui compa-
ruerunt et warantizaverunt factis chirographis in curia domini regis reddendo per annum unum par calcarium deauratorum vel 6d scilicet ad
Pentecosten.

Idem Willelmus Dacus dedit Radulpho de Wigornia nepoti suo duas
virgatas in villa de Clopton de villenagio,[182] scilicet illam virgatam quam
Turstanus le Chapeleyn tenuit et aliam virgatam quam Walterus Goldring
solet tenere. Contigit eciam quod idem Radulphus de Wigornia implaci-
tatus fuit de una dimidia virgata per Henricum filium Galfridi qui Radulphus fecit atornatum de Andrea Goldring et Henrico filio suo, et assignato
die litis coram justiciariis apud Neuport-Paynel tenens amisit per defaltam.
Et aliam dimidiam virgatam vendidit idem Radulphus dicto Andree reddendo 12d per annum. Et aliam virgatam vendidit Ricardo de Hotot
domino suo ratione huius quod perquisivit in feodum et hereditatem totum
tenementum et dominium quod fuit Willelmi Daci, et sic erat Radulphus
eidem Ricardo servivium faciens ut domino suo.

Sepedictus Willelmus Dacus dedit Albrico Monacho cognato uxoris sue
unam dimidiam virgatam cum tofto et crofto quam Willelmus de Waleys
solet tenere reddendo unam libram piperis per annum.[183]

[2 Thomas of Hotot.][184] Dictus Willelmus de Grauntkort dedit Thome
de Hotot filio Alicie sororis sue sexaginta acras et dimidiam de dominico
suo et duas virgatas de villenagio, scilicet illam virgatam quam Willelmus
filius Hugonis et post eum Albricus filius eius solet tenere, et illam virgatam
quam Walterus le Archer solet tenere, et illam dimidiam virgatam cum
pleno tofto tocius virgate quam Willelmus filius Walteri filii Godwini
tenuit, cum corporibus catallis et sequelis dictorum virorum et quatuor
acras de dominico retro orream persone et unam acram in Langethuong et
dimidiam acram in Wlfeldakur et viginti quatuor acras de illa terra quam
Galfridus filius Baldewini tenuit, faciendo decimam partem feodi unius
militis.

[3 Stamford Priory.][185] Prefatus Willelmus de Grauntkort dedit monialibus de Stanford duas virgatas unam de villenagio et aliam de dominico
et preterea le Nunnedole pro tribus acris in elemosinam cum Emma filia

---

[181] See A 11 and note 124.

[182] Two virgates were granted to Ralph of Worcester. Their descent may be established as
follows. (1) The virgate which Thurstan le Chapeleyn held came to Richard Hotot by a route
charted in note 127. (2) The virgate which Walter Goldring held was divided. A half-virgate
was lost in the plea noted here, of which no other details have been found. The other half-
virgate was sold to Andrew Goldring. Andrew sold it to William Hay; and William granted
it to Thorney Abbey: TRB fos 213r–v, 214v–215r.

[183] Albricus Monachus was also granted land by William of Clapton: see B 4 no 5 below.
He granted to Peterborough Abbey his rights in three acres of land in Clapton: Swa fo 261r–v.
Isabella Dacus bought from Walter Monachus part of the messuage which Britwold son of
Richard used to hold. This material is not well controlled, but Walter (who witnessed a
charter in TRB fo 213r) may be the son of Aubrey, and part at least of this land came to
Richard Hotot.

[184] The original grant to the Hotots of land in Clapton. Compare A 20.

[185] Benedictine priory for nuns. Founded c 1155 by William de Waterville abbot of
Peterborough, and subject to the abbey. For Ivetta de Muskham see introduction at notes 22
to 25.

sua et herede si secularis duraret quam genuit de prima[186] uxore sua, scilicet de Ivetta de Muscham que fuit soror episcopi Cestrie quondam Galfridi de Muscham qui nascebatur prope Neuwerk. Nam cum idem Willelmus de Grauntkort duceret ipsam uxorem suam de predicta patria versus domum suam et apropinquantibus illis itur regale extra Witeringe prospiciunt flammam ignis ingentissimam apud Clopton aulam suam et cameras universas atque omnia que ad convivium fuerunt preparata devastantem et comburentem. Nec mirum siquidem de ultione divina, nam edificium fecerat de nobilissimo circuitu fraxinum sacri cimiterii de Clopton, et quod deterius est tempore regis Stephani cum ingenti multitudine fodiantium cimiterium predictum cum ossamentis infinitis patrum predecessorum crudelissime procidit et in usus seculares plusquam terciam partem cimiterii predicti reduxit. Nam circuitus antiquus secundum quod primo dedicatus fuit et benedictus visui apparet manifeste, et filia cuiusdam ditorum fodiantium mihi hoc manifeste declaravit et dictum circuitum secundum quod prius fuerat manu mihi patefecit.

[4 The Templars.][187] Idem Willelmus de Grauntkort dedit Templariis dimidiam virgatam in elemosinam.

[5 Albricus Monachus.] Idem Willelmus de Grauntkort dedit Albrico Monacho unam virgatam liberam que prius fuerat de villenagio et acram et dimidiam de dominico.

[6 Matthew Papiliun.][188] Idem Willelmus de Grauntkort dedit Matheo Papiliun unam virgatam de villenagio et unam acram de dominico. Nam idem Matheus et heredes sui de feodo sunt collectores scutagii tocius baronie Burgi in comitatu Norhamtone excepto Nasso. Idem Matheus vendidit illam virgatam et illam acram Radulpho avo domini Thome de Tichemers.[189] Et de Radulpho successit Robertus ut filius et heres, qui illam dedit Gunnore filie sue in liberum maritagium.

[7 Chicksand Priory.][190] Idem Willemus de Grauntkort dedit monialibus de Chikesonde viginti quatuor acras de dominico, sed sex ablate fuerunt per abbatem Benedictum et residuum vendiderunt in posterum Ricardo de Hotot.

[8 Guy Rok.][191] Idem Willelmus de Grauntkort dedit Widone Rok

---

[186] Priore MS.

[187] Lees, *Records of Templars*, p. 116 and note 10, where the gift is recorded as a full virgate.

[188] Papley in Warmington parish, Northants. According to *PN Soc Northants* (Cambridge, 1933), p. 216, the name means 'Pap(p)a's clearing'. But it may be noted that just two miles east of here there was a serjeanty in Washingley, Hunts, 'ad custodiendum parvum papilionem cum arcubus et sagittis': *Book of Fees*, p. 1217. In Swa fo 265r Ralph of Ashton and John Papilun accounted for ward of Rockingham Castle and were described as *ballivi feodati*. It might be that the office gave the name to the man, and the man gave his name to the village. The village is now deserted, its tents folded away: *RCHM Northants*, i (1975), pp. 108-11. For the Papley fee see *Pytchley*, pp. 117-19. The tenant in the late 12th century was Martin, who transferred a substantial holding to Robert of Braybrooke: BL Sloane MS 986 fos 15r-16v. Matthew might be another member of the same family, or the name might have been transcribed in error for Martin—but if so the error goes back to the fine of June 1199 (PRO CP 25(1) 171/5/40), where Math' Papillun was recorded as a tenant in Clapton, and initially as refusing service to William Dacus (*ibid.*; *Curia Regis Rolls*, i. 295).

[189] In TRB fos 212v-213r there are two charters witnessed by Ralph of Titchmarsh (on whom see note 120 above) and by Thomas son of Robert of Titchmarsh. The latter is established by this entry to have been, and the former may also have been, a grandson of the Ralph who held in the 1190s, to whom part of the tenancy which came to William Dacus had earlier been leased: *Curia Regis Rolls*, i. 119-20. [190] See **A** note 92.

[191] Dingley, Northants was a property of the Knights Hospitallers. According to Dugdale, William of Clapton gave the Hospitallers a substantial estate in Clapton, including 169 acres of land: W. Dugdale, *Monasticon Anglicanum* (1661 edn), ii. 546; thence in Bridges, ii. 305. The grant cannot have taken effect.

quinque acras et plus aliquantulum per elemosinam francam et respondendo ospitale de Dingele.

[9 Walter of Hotot.]¹⁹² Idem Willelmus de Grauntkort dedit Waltero fratri Thome de Hotot nepoti suo unam virgatam de villenagio et quinque acras de dominico, quam terram Hugo de Hotot filius et heres eiusdem Walteri dedit Ricardo de Hotot cognato suo et heredibus suis tenendam de ipso Hugone et suis heredibus.

[10 Roger Grimbaut.] Rogerus Grimbaut accepit in Medwefeld de dominico quandam particulam¹⁹³ pro exscambio quam fecit et concessit Willelmo domino pro parte crofti sui inclusi in Ympecroft.

[11 Peterborough Abbey.]¹⁹⁴ Idem Willelmus de Grauntkort dedit et concessit domui de Burgo virgatam Huneware de dominico et preterea triginta et tres acras de dominico cum capitali mesuagio suo, et factus est ibi monachus et ibi mortuus est.

5 How many hides are there of the barony of Peterborough, and how many of the barony formerly of Nigel of Lovetot baron of Southoe?

capitulum Et quot hide de baronia Burgi, et quantum de baronia quondam Nigelli de Luvetot baronis de Soudtho.

solutio Sunt autem de feodo Burgi quatuor hide terre atque illa virgata que dicitur virgata Houneware et non amplius. De baronia siquidem de Luvetot una hida atque una magna virgata.

6 There should appear more clearly what before this was dark and difficult to discern, namely about the tithes of produce, both of the old demesnes of the two baronies and of the villein holdings which separately pertain to each barony.

capitulum Et ut manifestius appareat quod antea obscurum et tediosum ad discernendum erat, videlicet de decimis frugum tum de antiquis dominicis baroniarum duarum predictarum tum de villenagiis dictis baroniis separatim pertinentibus.

solutio Vetus dominicum de feodo Burgi quantum ad descimas dandas tripartitum est. Nam ab antiquo tercia garba penes Burgum remansit. Dictus Rogerus de Luvetot baro de Soudtho de eodem dominico de feodo Burgi aliam garbam ecclesie sue Sancte Marie de Hontedone quam fundaverat potenter canonicis in aumentum donavit. Nam omnes barones Normanni in primo conquestionis de victis Anglicis ad libitum quoque placeret statuerunt de decimis dominicorum propter anime salutem et peccatorum suorum diminutionem. Tercia garba de dominico eiusdem feodi relicta est rectori ecclesie de Clopton.¹⁹⁵

Sunt autem culture de dominico Burgi cuius descima sic debet tripartire sic iacentes et his locis et in tali quantitate acrarum,¹⁹⁶ videlicet in innome

---

¹⁹² A 21 establishes that he paid five marks for this land.

¹⁹³ particinam MS.

¹⁹⁴ What are noted here are the grants of demesne not of tenant land, which suggests that the source being used was not charters but the terrier of the demesne (**B 6**). The charters in the Clapton archive in Swapham's cartulary present considerable problems of interpretation. An indication of the problems, but not a solution to them, will be found in King, *Peterborough Abbey*, p. 91 note 5.

¹⁹⁵ The pleadings relating to Clapton church in 1219 established a three-fold division of tithes 'de antiquo dominico Willelmi de Cloptone': (1) St Mary, Huntingdon; (2) Sacrist of Peterborough Abbey; (3) Rector of Clapton. A pension of 25s 8d, of which there is no mention in this text, was owing to St Neot's, presumably from (3). *Hugh of Wells*, i. 160-1; ii. 190; and see *VCH Northants*, iii. 128.

¹⁹⁶ What follows is a very early and very detailed terrier. The Inhams were behind the peasant crofts to the north of the village, and this and the reference to Lillefordeslade confirm that what is printed here as the first paragraph deals with land immediately surrounding the

inter domum Henrici de Norfolk et domum Willelmi pastoris decem acre. Ad vetus molendinum tres acre, residuum vero impartibile ex utraque parte aumentatur ex villenagio. Ad Horsedole quatuor acre. Ad finem de Rissebalke tres acre. Versus Lillefordeslade tres acre. Ad Thornbalke una acra. Item versus Lillefordeslade tres acre diversis hominibus partite. Item versus Lillefordeslade tres rode et dimidia. Item ad finem de Stocfolddole una acra. In mansione et crofto quondam Walteri de Hotot due acre. In mansionibus et croftis Rogeri le Scot et Juliane de Holderness acra et dimidia. In mansione et crofto Gilberti Albi una acra. In innome versus Molecroftgrene uno loco una roda. In eadem quarentena tres rode et ambe particule de terra Templorum. In duobus Colecroftis undecim acre. Le Chalkedole quatuor acre, sed adhibetur preter hoc una roda que impartibilis est. In Wyttisdale tres acre. Item supra una acra. Item due acre ex opposito Baggewelle, et adhibetur una acra preter has impartibilis. Et due acre frisce[197] super Greneberwe. Et quatuor acre abbuttantes subter, sed adhibentur illis alie quatuor impartibiles. Super Greneberwe novem acre simul. Item in Greneberweslade due acre. Contra aldam sex acre. Ibidem non longe quinque acre. Ad Bidewelleslow due acre. Sub Greneberwe quinque acre de terra ecclesie. Foraria de Mardihe una acra.

Tornhilfelde. In Nunnedole tres acre, et adhibetur dimidia acra impartibilis. Ad Coppedemere de terra Almoneri quatuor acre. Item ad Coppedemere tres acre. Et in sorte Banelond due acre. In alto Banelond due acre et dimidia de terra Almoneri. Adhuc de terra ipsius tres acre non longe ab eadem. Versus Thornhilslade tres acre. Item versus Thornhilslade una acra in eadem quarentena de terra Almoneri. Item in eadem quarentena due acre de terra Almoneri. In eadem quarentena due acre, scilicet de Havedendole. Item due acre super abbuttantes super le Havedendole, scilicet Thungedole, sed adhibetur dimidia acra impartibilis. Preterea sex butte Hugonis Albi versus Scarpslade. Preterea quatuor dimidie rode Hugonis de Tichemers versus Wulfeldakergrene. Ad Wulfeldakergrene due acre, sed adhibetur una acra impartibilis. Super Worlochyl quatuor acre, sed preter hoc adhibetur una acra impartibilis. In eadem quarentena due acre. Et subter alie due. Et inferius sex acre. Nethermilneweye et Brimbelheg sex acre. Sub Thornhil versus Thorpmere tres acre. Super Thornhil cum Thornhilcroft quatuordecim acre. In Longethong uno loco sex acre, et adhibentur tres dimidie impartibiles. In eadem quarentena due acre. Sub Thornhil sex rode de terra Gilberti West. Super Mirihil septem acre versus Thornhilslade. Contra Thornhil due acre et dimidia. Super Redelond sex acre divise. Item super Redelond tres acre de terra Almoneri. Ad Wodeweygrene tres acre et dimidia, scilicet contra Banlond, et adhibetur una acra impartibilis. Versus Banlond una acra frisca. In Wodeweygrene una acra Thome filii Leverici. In eadem quarentena due acre. Item in eadem quarentena una acra. Ad Foxwelp tres acre. In eadem quarentena decem acre. Iuxta domum novi molendini de terra Templorum due acre.

Nunc de Hulkefeld. In longitudine Huntedoneweye tres acre. In eadem quarentena due acre frisce. Item in eadem quarentena una acra. Et preterea in eadem quarentena tres acre. In Sinewold duodecim acre. Supra versus Huntedoneweye una acra. Et in eadem quarentena acra et dimidia. Item in

---

village itself. Long Thong Farm and Wood Way, in Thornhilfield, are in the north-west corner of the parish. Mr David Hall, who has been kind enough to advise on the field-names, has in preparation a full field-survey of the parish. For a preliminary survey of the earthworks, see *RCHM Northants*, i (1975), pp. 27-9.
[197] Trustani MS (and *passim* in the text which follows).

eadem quarentena due acre. Preterea in eadem quarentena due acre. Ad
finem crofti Gilberti le Franceis septem acre. In Langelond versus le Hulk
acra et dimidia. In eadem quarentena tres acre. Item in eadem quarentena
due acre. Ad Casterisweye tres acre. In Westunedale tres acre Rogeri Scot
et participum. In capite de Westundale una acra Gilberti Monachi. In
Theuweye sex acre de terra Rogeri Scot et participum. In eadem quarentena due acre de terra Templorum. De eadem una acra in eadem quarentena. Item in eadem quarentena due acre, et adhibetur una acra impartibilis. Le Daneyscroft sex acre.

 Nunc de Medwefeld. Ad Roscelin due acre. Ad finem tres acre. In eadem
quarentena tres acre. Item in eadem quarentena tres acre de terra Almoneri. Item in eadem quarentena contra Sinewold due acre. In eadem quarentena una acra propinquior. In magno Bewic quinque acre. Contra
Winewicsrubbes due acre. In Pitfurlong sex acre. In goris sex acre, de
quibus Martinus rector ecclesie disracionavit omnem descimam. Adhibetur
predictis una acra impartibilis sicut et ipse sex facte fuerunt. In eadem
quarentena sex acre. In Dedakir sex acre. In Maddichfurlong propius
Madeslade una acra. In eadem una acra. In eadem tres acre consimiles-
duorum tenencium. Ad Withimere tres acre. Ad capud de Maddich
tres acre Hugonis de Tichemers. In Mathesonfurlong due acre de terra
Templorum. In eadem quarentena tres acre de terra monialium de Stanford.

 Nunc de Westfelde versus Tichemers que sociatur ad Medweyfelde ita est.
Ad Bagwellesladisoverend una acra de terra Walteri de Hotot. In eadem
quarentena due acre. In eadem quarentena tres acre de terra Almoneri. In
eadem quarentena exterius due acre. Foraria ad finem una acra. In Hun-
gerhilslade tres acre de terra Almoneri. Foraria subter due acre. Super
Hungerhil superior cultura due acre, et adhibentur due rode impartibiles.
In eadem quarentena due acre. In eadem quarentena una acra, scilicet
Hugonis de Tichemers. Sub Hungerhil tres acre. Le Hafdindole super
Bagewellehil quatuor acre. In eadem quarentena quatuor acre de terra
Almoneri. Ad Bagewelle una acra. Ad Depfurroes tres acre de terra Al-
moneri. Subter ad finem de terra persone quatuor acre. Le Hafdindole ad
Bagwellisladisnetherend due acre. Super Olvismerefurlong propius tres
acre, et adhibetur dimidia acra impartibilis. In eadem quarentena remotius
due acre, et adhibetur dimidia acra impartibilis. Versus le More contra
Ulvismerefurlong una acra, scilicet Roberti Raysun et Thome filii Leverici.
In eadem quarentena super Sortecnol eorundem una acra. In eadem
quarentena de terra Templorum due acre. In eadem quarentena le
Hafdendole due acre. Versus le Brohe sub Ulvismere quinque acre de terra
Almoneri ibidem divisim iuxta sex acre, et adhibetur una acra impartibilis.
In eadem quarentena quatuor rode de aumento Gilberti West. In eadem
quarentena una acra que Hugo de Tichemers solet tenere. In eadem quarentena quatuor rode quas Willelmus filius Willelmi et Hugo le Bret tenent.
Ad Grafthornthuertpadt tres acre. In eadem quarentena ad Halinessethorn
due acre, et adhibetur una acra impartibilis. Inter moras due acre Almoneri. Super Longdenol sex acre. Ad Thorpmere le Hafdindole due acre, et
adhibetur una roda impartibilis. Subter Nethermilneweie sex acre de terra
Almoneri. In eadem quarentena sex acre, et adhibetur dimidia acra impartibilis. In eadem quarentena due acre de terra Almoneri. In eadem quarentena una acra de terra Walteri de Hotot. In eadem quarentena dimidia
acra de terra Templorum. Wlfeldakerdole et Cleihil simul resorbentes et
ambe Almoneri undecim acre. In Cleihil sex acre et dimidia, et adhibetur
in medio septem dimidie acre et duo foraria super que faciunt novem et
sunt impartibiles.

7 From which lands, of what extent and where situated, is the parson of the church to receive the tithes in their entirety? From which lands, of what extent and where situated, is he to receive one sheaf, the sacrist of Peterborough another sheaf, and the prior of St Mary of Huntingdon the third sheaf? By what right was it so established, and by whose gift?

capitulum [1] Scilicet de qua terra et quanta et ubi persona de Clopton recepturus est decimas sine aliquo participe. [2] Et de qua terra et quanta et ubi recepturus est unam garbam, sacrista de Burgo aliam garbam, prior Sancte Marie de Huntedon terciam garbam. Et quo iure ita fuit dispositum et ex cuius dono.[198]

solutio Manifeste declaratio sit omnibus successoribus in perpetuum quod de omnibus libere tenentibus sicut de francillanis et de omnibus villanis qui tenent de feodo de Burgo sicut de villenagio quondam Willelmi de Clopton et preterea de toto dominico et de toto villenagio quondam Galfridi militis de Clopton danda est in perpetuum decima integra et sine aliquo participe rectori ecclesie de Clopton. Sed perspiciendum est caute quid vel quantum dictis villanis vel liberis in exscambium vel causa novi complementi vel in feodum liberis detur vel tradetur vel villanis ad firmam vel ipsis in exscambium post tempus Willelmi de Clopton de suo veteri dominico tradetur. Et quicunque liber vel servus de predicto dominico aliquam partem teneat decima frugum illius terre iuste triparciatur. Et rursum si qui liberi vel servi vel eciam capitales domini tenentes de feodo Burgi excambia fecerint in campis vel in villa ad edificia nova construenda cum tenentibus dominici veteris quondam Hugonis de Castillun vel cum tenentibus veteris dominici quondam Walteri le Stiward quorum dominica predicta de duabus garbis prioratui de Hontendon et de tercia persone de Clopton semper est respondenda. Videant ut de tali excambio locis antiquitus debitis et consuetis decimas iuste conservent et reddant. Et eciam e converso si qui servorum vel liberorum vel duorum[199] tenentium de veteri dominico quondam Willelmi de Clopton vel tenencium predictorum veterum dominicorum Walteri le Stiward vel Hugonis de Castillun excambia fecerunt cum dominis vel liberis vel servis qui tenent de villenagio quod est de feodo de Burgo de excambio sibi accepto quantum de decimis persone de Clopton plenarie et sine participe respondeant. Et pari forma fiat de excambiatis cum libere tenentibus de feodo Burgi quum ab initio tam liberorum quam rusticorum preter quam dominorum predictorum trium dominica [decime] omnis terre impartibiles rectori ecclesie semper remanserunt. Per specificationem autem que fiet continuo in posterum, scilicet de quantitate ipsius feodi de Luvetot atque ipsorum tenentium visibiliter aparebit quodquod residuum est baronie Burgi subjaceat et ad omnia consueto more respondeant.

8 From which lands, of what extent and where situated, is the prior of Huntingdon to receive two sheaves of the produce and the parson of Clapton the third sheaf? By what right, and when, and by whose gift were the tithes of the village so arranged?

capitulum Et de qua terra et quanta et ubi dictus prior de Huntedon recepturus est duas garbas frugum et persona de Clopton terciam garbam,

---

[198] The heading to section 7 asks two questions, the second of which has already been answered in section 6, which deals with the demesne land of the Peterborough fee. Section 7 answers the first question concerning the land from which the parson took the whole tithe. This is identified as the peasant land, and the lands of the former demesne of Geoffrey of Clapton (on whom see A note 90).

[199] MS, possibly for dominorum.

et quo iure et quando et ex cuius dono ita fuerunt decime ville prenominate statute.[200]

solutio Quum Rogerus de Luvetot baro domini regis cuius baronia dependet ad Soudtho in prima conquestione Normannorum ad diminutionem et veniam delictorum suorum et omnium successorum suorum prioratum Sancte Marie de Huntendone construxit, et ibidem canonicos regulares decenter disposuit, duas garbas omnium dominicorum suorum de sua tantum baronia in quocunque comitatu essent ad sustentationem dicti prioratus et canonicorum ibidem deo servientibus in puram elemosinam constituit.[201] Et terciam garbam de eodem dominico atque totam decimam integram tocius villenagii eiusdem feodi de Luvetot rectoribus ecclesiarum suarum sua sponte reliquit.[202] Videndum est in villa de Clopton qui quondam vetus dominicum de eodem feodo et quantum quisque per se tenuerunt et eciam qui villenagium de ipso feodo tenuerunt. Hugo de Castilun et successores sui tenent dimidiam hidam scilicet quatuor viginti acras in dominico de veteri dominico et in villenagio duas virgatas et dimidiam:[203] scilicet unam virgatam quam Albricus Swift tenuit, et unam dimidiam virgatam quam Rogerus Ioie solet tenere, et unam dimidiam virgatam quam Galfridus le Bret solet tenere, et unam dimidiam virgatam quam Hervicus filius Ailmeri solet tenere quam domina Emma de Castilun in proprios cultos reduxit et eundem Hervicum Mendicum dimisit, et predicte quatuor viginti acre respondent pro dimidia virgata. Walterus le Stiward et successor eius Galfridus de Normanvile et post ipsum Simon de Normanvile tenuerunt dimidiam hidam totam de antiquo dominico eiusdem feodi de Luvetot scilicet tres virgatas.[204] Sunt autem tenentes predictarum trium virgatarum isti uno tempore nominati: Rogerus le Franceis tenuit dimidiam virgatam, Reginaldus de Hitherne dimidiam virgatam, Willelmus filius Torkildi dimidiam virgatam, Robertus filius Reginaldi dimidiam virgatam, Henricus filius Galfridi le Neuman dimidiam virgatam, Hugo filius Galfridi le Bret dimidiam virgatam. Et isti tres virgate faciunt dimidiam hidam de feodo de Luvetot. Sed rector ecclesie de Clopton caute sibi provideat et inquirat si que terre in campis vel in croftis que annuatim fere seminantur de omnibus terris que sunt de feodo de Burgo preterquam de veteri dominico Willelmi de Clopton predictis tenentibus liberentur per excambia vel per aliquam aliam alienationem. Nam de feodo Willelmi de Grauntkort quod quidem pertinet ad Burgum preter quam de dominico predicto decimas integras sine participe est recepturus. Neque autem est equalis proportio terre campestris que collibet anno tercio quasi sterili ordinatur et terre mesuagiorum et croftorum que annualiter respondet fructifera. Aliud autem provideat idem rector quod sepius contigit. Contingit et continget de excambiis factis

---

[200] Section 8 deals with the demesnes of the Lovetot fee, from which land the parson received one-third and the prior of Huntingdon two-thirds.

[201] The Priory of St Mary, Huntingdon was founded by Eustace the sheriff before 1091. It adopted the Augustinian rule in the time of his successor, Roger of Lovetot: D. Knowles and R. N. Hadcock, *Medieval Religious Houses. England and Wales*, 2nd edn (1971), p. 160. For its possessions by the mid-12th century see the Bull of Pope Eugenius III printed in *Monasticon*, vi. 80.

[202] reliquid, MS.

[203] Hugh le Castilun was one of two sub-tenants who had earlier held the Lovetot fee in Clapton. A Hugh le Castillun granted Peterborough Abbey land in Stanwick, 1226 × 1233: Swa fo 237v.

[204] Walter le Stiward was the second of the two sub-tenants of the Lovetot fee. The Geoffrey de Normanville who is mentioned as his successor may have been the man of this name who was a younger son of Ralph de Normanville of Empingham, Rutland, in the 1210s: *VCH Rutland*, ii. 243.

scilicet quod illi qui sibi decimas integras debuerunt excambia fecerunt inequalia cum illis qui sibi tantum terciam garbam sunt solvendi sicut ipsis qui tenent baroniam de Luvetot et cum illis qui tenent vetus dominicum Willelmi de Grauntkort, dederunt enim dimidiam acram pro roda et dimidia et quidam pro roda et eciam acram pro tribus rodis que forte equaliter non respondent in decimis. Et pari forma provideat e converso predictus Prior de Huntendon et Sacrista de Burgo.

9 It should be established to which barony the advowson of the church of Clapton pertained. Which men in the past (no longer ago than just before the time of Robert of Lindsey abbot of Peterborough) had the advowson, and gave it to a number of priests and parsons in farm for the term of their lives? In what way, by what sort of plea and by whom were there ejected from the advowson those who from the time of the conquest of the Normans in England until the time of King Henry the son of King John had held it by the gift of lawful patrons, in peace.

capitulum Videndum est autem de advocatione ecclesie de Clopton cui baronia pertinebat et qui viri antiquitus (certe eciam non remotius quam semper ante tempus Roberti de Lindisheye abbatis de Burgo) habere consueverunt et ad firmam tradiderunt presbiteris pluribus et personis firmariis ad terminos vite. Et qualiter et quo genere placiti et a quibus eiecta est advocatio illorum qui verissime a tempore conquestionis Normannorum in Angliam usque ad tempus regis Henrici filii regis Johannis ex dono iusti patroni pacifice optinuerunt.

solutio Prefatus Rogerus de Luvetot patronus ecclesie de Clopton dedit prioratui de Sancto Neoto atque monachis ibidem deo servientibus dictam ecclesiam qui integre et pacifice illam tenuerunt et ad firmam sacerdotibus atque personis firmariis ad vita terminum tradiderunt usque ad obitum magistri Johannis Calvi.[205] Regente ergo tunc tempore abbasciam Burgi abbate Roberto de Lindisheye et Ricardo de Salfledebi predicte domus senescallo presentaverunt Hugonem de Daventre senescallum Eustacii de Faukumberge tunc tempore cancellarii domini regis ad ecclesiam de Clopton propter auxilium regie potestatis.[206] Et insuper ad cautelam consulentibus in unum ipso abbate et eius predicto senescallo miserunt pro brevi recti super priorem de Sancto Neoto de advocatione ecclesie de Hemmington et ipsos implacitaverunt. Fatigante priore de placito apud Ketene coram iusticiariis itinerantibus remisit advocationem ecclesie de Clopton dicto abbati et conventui in perpetuum, quatinus idem abbas de lite ecclesie de Hemmington quam in proprios usus tenebant omnino desisterent et facta est finalis concordia.[207] Sed Ranulfus de Clopton imposuit suum clamium quod inscribitur in fine facta. Et ita presentavit dictus abbas ipsum Hugonem et retinuit. Hoc autem in rei veritate predictus Ricardus senescallus Burgo anno Willelmi de Hotot abbatis secundo ad Pascha in

---

205 The succession of parsons is established in **A 3**, where references are given to their institution. What follows is the story behind the institution of Hugh of Daventry in 1219, after the death of John Calvus.

206 Robert of Lindsey, abbot of Peterborough 1214 × 1222. On Richard of Saltfleetby see King, *Peterborough Abbey*, p. 130. Richard was still steward in 1240 (Swa fo 207v), and may have held office until the death of abbot Walter in 1245. Eustace of Fauconberg was Treasurer (not Chancellor) 1217 × 1228, and Bishop of London 1221 × 1228. For Hugh of Daventry in his service, though not identified as steward, see *Curia Regis Rolls*, xi, no 2607; *Early Charters of St Paul's Cathedral*, ed. Marion Gibbs (Camden Soc. 3rd ser. lviii, 1939), p. 264. Two charters in the Braybrooke cartulary are dated from the consecration of Eustace as bishop: Richardson, *English Jewry*, p. 277.

207 The foot of the fine is PRO CP 25(1) 172/16/58. Another original, probably that from St Neot's, survives as NRO Buccleuch Deeds B 11.

aula Burgi narravit de consilio iniuste perquisitionis (*sic*) vehementer penitendo.[208]

10 There is also to be recorded how many hides of land there are in the village of Clapton.

capitulum   Reducendum est eciam ad memoriam quot hide terre sunt in prenominata villa de Clopton.

solutio   Ratum sit omnibus successoribus quod in villa de Clopton sunt quinque hide terre et due magne virgate, una scilicet quod est de feodo Burgi que dicitur virgata Huneware quam abbas Benedictus de Burgo disrationavit super plures in Clopton, et alia magna virgata de feodo de Luvetot quam Hugo de Castillun quondam tenuit in dominico.

11 How many hides of land are there in the one barony, and how many in the other?

capitulum   Et quot hide de una baronia et quot de alia.

solutio   Neque autem sit alicui ambiguum sed manifeste pateat in perpetuum quod in eadem villa de Clopton sunt quatuor hide terre et una virgata magna illa scilicet que vocatur virgata Huneware et ille sunt de baronia Burgi. Et de baronia de Luvetot una hida et una magna virgata.

12 Who were the predecessors of the tenants of this land, and who hold which parcels of land in modern times (we call modern the tenants of this land in the 39th year of King Henry, 1254–55)?

capitulum   Et qui tenentes predecessores fuerunt, et qui tempore moderno illas particulariter tenent; modernos quidem vocavi tenentes illarum terrarum anno tricesimo nono regni regis Henrici prescripti.

solutio   Fuerunt autem pridem tenentes feodi Burgi Willelmus de Grauntkort et omnes sui tenentes tam Galfridus miles quam omnes alii liberi tenentes sui et eciam omnes rustici preter hos duos subscriptos, scilicet preter feodum Walteri le Stiward et preter feodum Hugonis de Castilun que sunt de baronia de Luvetot, et ipsa predicta magna virgata eiusdem feodi est vetus dominicum quod fuit ipsius Hugonis predicti de Castilun. Moderni vero tenentes de feodo de Luvetot scilicet de feodo dimidie hide prefati Hugonis et prefati Walteri alterius dimidie hide. Est abbas de Torneie successor Hugonis tenens ipsius feodum et preter illud alias particulas de exscambiis et emcionibus Willelmi Hay de feodo Burgi et impartibiles.[209] Est autem successor Walteri le Stiward tempore moderno (prout prius modernum appellavi) Thomas de Hotot secundus respondentibus sibi de eadem terra sex villanis prescriptis de Clopton.[210]

---

[208] The transfer of the advowson from one religious house to another might not of itself seem a matter of great moment for the Hotots. But when members of the Clapton family sought to retrieve William of Clapton's alienations, John Calvus was confirmed in his possession of a half-virgate of land: PRO CP 25(1) 171/5/36. The name Calvus suggests John was a relative, possibly the son, of Reginald the priest, whose baldness is explained in A 3. It might be that the crime of which the old steward stood accused was the breaking of the family hold on the parish church.

[209] The grant to Thorney Abbey, and the archive lying behind it, are TRB fos 212r–214r, which establishes the date as 1238 × 1254, and states that William Hay had been steward of Thorney. The date is narrowed to 1240 × 1254 by PRO CP 25(1) 173/31/445. See also *Pytchley*, p. 43, and Sandra Raban, *The Estates of Thorney and Crowland* (Cambridge: Dept of Land Economy, 1977), p. 68. In 1242–43 William Hay held ⅛ part of a knight's fee in Clapton of Reginald de Waterville (Swa fo 283r; *Pytchley*, p. 41), and in Thrapston, Denford and Ringstead ¼ fee of the honour of Clare (Swa fo 284r).

[210] B 8 says that the land of Walter le Stiward came to Geoffrey de Normanville and then to Simon de Normanville. B 4 no 1 says that William Dacus obtained this land from Geoffrey and Simon. This establishes the stages of the transfer to Richard Hotot, even though they cannot be followed elsewhere.

13 All forinsec services are to be looked into. Concerning scutage, how much is owed by the village when scutage is granted by the magnates of the land both clerical and lay of their own free will at a rate of 20 shillings? How much is owed by the village when the scutage is at 40 shillings?

capitulum Et perspiciendum est de omnibus forinsecis servitiis, scilicet de scutagiis quantum ad eandem villam pertinet quando scutagium per magnates terre tam clericorum quam laicorum sua sponte conceditur ad viginti solidos.[211] Et quantum pertinet eidem ville quando scutagium est ad quadraginta solidos.

solutio Eternaliter autem manifeste appareat omnibus successoribus in Clopton de scutagiis concessis domino regi quod quando scutagium est ad viginti solidos tota villata de Clopton de iure dabit 18s 7d, Pokebroc 12s 3d, Catteworthe 9s 2d, et sic completur defectus integri militis in Clopton per duas villas predictas complecionem reddentes. Et cum sit ad quadraginta solidos duplare predictam asignationem cuiusque ville per se quum revera respondebunt pro duobus feodis ad baroniam Burgi.

14 When scutage is at 20 shillings how much does each hide pay? And how much when it is at 40 shillings?

capitulum Et cum sit ad viginti solidos quid pertinet unicuique hide solvendum. Et cum sit ad quadraginta solidos quantum unicuique hide pertinet.

solutio deest.[212]

15 How many virgates of land rightfully make up each hide? What is the size of each knight's fee if it is less than a full fee? Who ought and are accustomed to make up the deficit in what is lacking from a full fee? This concerns the fee of the barony of Peterborough and the tenants of the fee. Next the barony of Lovetot, what is the size of the knight's fee and who now holds it, both tenants of the ancient demesne and of the villeinage which pertains to the honour? In what way was that barony divided in three between sisters on the death of baron Nigel, and to which of the parceners was this land alloted?

capitulum Et quot sint virgate terre de iure in omni hida. Et de quantitate feodi militis quantum minus quam feodum integrum. Et qui defectum illum integritatis semper complere debent et consueverunt, quid scilicet feodum est de baronia Burgi, et tenentes illius feodi. Tunc de baronia de Luvetot quantum feodi militis. Et qui tenentes de illo feodo esse solebant, et qui nunc tenent tam antiquos dominicos quam tenentes villenagii quod ad honorem illum pertinet. Et quomodo baronia illa per obitum Nigelli baronis in sorores tripartita est et cui participi sortitum sit discernendum est.[213]

solutio Sunt autem de iure in omni hida de feodo Burgi septem virgate. Est autem in hida de feodo de Luvetot tota integritas sex virgatarum et sexta que dicitur magna virgata de Luvetot continet in se tres virgatas in quantitate secundum dico quod virgate statuuntur per villam. Post obitum

---

[211] Clause 12 of Magna Carta 1215 had asserted that the levying of scutage required consent. Subsequent reissues dropped this provision, but the idea lived on, as the *capitulum* makes clear. cf J. C. Holt, *Magna Carta* (Cambridge, 1965), pp. 286–7; and see also H. M. Chew, *The English Ecclesiastical Tenants-in-Chief and Knight-Service* (Oxford, 1932), pp. 103–12.

[212] A space is left in the manuscript, p. 51, with the note that the information under this heading is missing.

[213] Nigel died in 1219, and the inheritance was divided between his three sisters: I. J. Sanders, *English Baronies* (Oxford, 1960), pp. 80–1. A generation has been missed out by the Hotots: Margery de Vernon was the daughter of Alice, the third sister; and Nigel de Amundeville was the son of Ralph de Amundeville, who married the second sister, Amice.

siquidem Nigelli de Luvetot sortite fuerunt ista quarta pars militis in Clopton et totidem in Pokebroc et totidum in [Catteworthe][214] in partem Margerie de Vernon et heredum suorum, et duo feodi quod baro de Soudho tenuit in feodo in dictis tribus villis de baronia Burgi per vavassoriam sortite fuerunt in partem Nigelli de Amundevile qui fuit secundus particeps hereditatis.

16 How much must the village as a whole pay the men of Peterborough for what is called sheriff's aid? Why this much and not more? How much for the forinsec service which is called ward of Rockingham?

capitulum Quantum autem eidem ville communiter pertinet ad solvendum ipsis de Burgo pro hoc quod dicitur auxilium vicecomitis. Quare tantum et non amplius. Et quantum ad illud forinsecum quod dicitur warda de Rokingham.[215]

solutio Videndum est autem de hoc quod dicitur auxilium vicecomitis et de alio quod dicitur warda de Rokingham scilicet ad festum Sancti Michaelis ad magnum hundredum pro auxilio vicecomitis, 3s 11½d et non amplius quia alocatum semper fuit super terram Almoneri quantitas solutionis unius virgate scilicet 1½d et super terram persone 3d et super feodum Willelmi Hay 6d, quia idem Willelmus tempore Roberti abbatis de Burgo huiusmodi geldas et semper antea solvit cum communa ville et tunc tempore finem fecit per se pro feodo suo solvendo annualiter 12d quare 6d allocantur super illum ad illud debitum.[216] Et ad wardam de Rokingham die Sancte Michaelis 21½d et non amplius quia residuum semper computatur et alocatur super defectum militis integri et super quasdam terras Almoneri et persone quos nunquam vide solvere et attamen porcio quedam super ipsos semper alocata est. Et ad magnum hundredum post Pascha totidem ad auxilium vicecomitis quantum ad festum Sancti Michaelis et eisdem alocationibus quia integralis summa cum alocatis est 4s 10d bis in anno. Et die Pascha totidem denarios pro warda quot et die Sancti Michaelis et eisdem alocationibus quia ad integrum feodum de baronia Burgi ad wardam de Rokingham ubique solvendi sunt 2s.

17 How much then must each hide give for these two forinsec services last-named? How much has each half-virgate to pay?

capitulum Quantum vero quelibet hida dabit ad illa duo ultima forinseca nominata. Minutius autem propter evidenciam pauperum (*sic*) monstrandum est scilicet quid unicuique dimidie virgate contingit solvendum.

solutio Persolvet autem de iure quelibet hida ad istas duas predictas geldas 17½d scilicet dimidia virgata 1¼d. Sed de unaquaque hida ½d est retraendus de superfluo et ad voluntatem communionis ville disponendus.

18 How much is owed for the suit which once was known as ward-silver, and why not more? How is it to be collected from the village?

capitulum Pro secta siquidem que antea appellata erat argentum vigilie quantum reddendum est et quare non amplius. Et modus colligendi illam de villatu.

---

[214] Gap in MS.

[215] On sheriff's aid see H. M. Cam, *The Hundred and the Hundred Rolls* (1930), pp. 90–1; N. Neilson, 'Customary Rents', in P. Vinogradoff (ed.), *Oxford Studies in Social and Legal History*, ii (1910), pp. 124–9. The Abbot of Peterborough claimed the right to collect all scutages and aids due from his fee *per ministros suos*: Chew, p. 108. For the *ministri* collecting for ward of Rockingham Castle see Swa fo 265r. It was levied at the rate of 4s per fee, at which level it had been commuted in the reign of Henry I: King, *Peterborough Abbey*, p. 26 and note 2; Chew, pp. 101–3.

[216] Robert of Lindsey, abbot 1214 × 1222.

solutio In rei veritate pro vigilia quam Robertus de Braybroc statuit nomine secte sunt 17½d ad festum Sancti Martini annuatim reddendi quam coram predicto Roberto custode ex parte domini regis de baronia Burgi post obitum abbatis Benedicti de 2s postulatis per annum pro eadem vigilia relaxanda.[217] Thomas de Hotot primus obstitit[218] pro se et suis tenentibus in Clopton et respondit quod mallet vigiliam ad pontem de Lilleford cum necesse foret loricatus sustinere quam se et suos in perpetuum ad tributum tale inducere. Quapropter quantinus idem Thomas a contradictione desisteret nec alios p[ossunt] contradicere commodum abbatis consuleret quietus concessus est in perpetuum et sui de tali gelda et alocati sunt super feodum ipsius 3d. Et preterea super feodum Willelmi Hay 6d quia postquam semper responderat cum communa ville in posterum tempore abbatis Roberti finem fecit pro se et suis respondendi per se pro forinsecis annualiter 12d et ideo sit predicta alocatio super ipsius feodum.

19 At the view of frank-pledge how much is to be rendered in total, and how much by each of the four chief tithing-men, and by what right is it not more? It should be made clear at what times of the year this is owed.

capitulum Ad visum frankiplegii et quantum solvendum in toto et quantum quisque quatuor capitalium decennariorum pro se huic solvendus est et quo iure non amplius. Quibus autem temporibus anni hec sunt solvenda manifestabitur.

solutio Amplius autem videndum est scilicet de visu frankiplegii et sunt solvendi annualiter videlicet ad festum Sancti Johannis Baptiste 14d et non amplius quia 4d alocantur super antiquum feodum Thome de Hotot per causam prenotatam. Et pro licencia conducendi quadrigas abbatis de Burgo apud Cotingham cum feno annuatim per pratum Thome de Hotot in Karilton quod est de feodo de Belvero[219] et super feodum Willelmi Hay 6d quia ut predictum est separavit se a communa ville ut pretactum est.

20 How many perches of wall do we have to repair of the enclosure of Northampton (by us I mean the community of Clapton)? Where and between whom is our place? When part of the wall falls down and stands in need of repair, how is the collection made to repair what has broken down and to support the walls.

capitulum De parco vero de Norhamptone quot pertice muri nobis antiquitus ad reparandum nobis vero non dico id est communioni de Clopton (*sic*) et ubi et inter quos situs sit locus et cum pars muri ceciderit et emendationem indigerit quomodo imponenda sit collecta ad muros[220] sustentandos et ad quid diruptum est integre reparandum.[221]

[217] If Robert of Braybrooke was custodian after the death of abbot Benedict in 1193, the vacancy can only have been a short one, and has left no trace in the public records. On Robert's career see Richardson, *English Jewry*, pp. 100-2. Robert was custodian after the death of abbot Akarius in March 1210 until his own death in the summer of 1211, when his son succeeded him: *ibid.*, p. 271; *Pipe Roll 12 John*, pp. 215-16; *Pipe Roll 13 John*, pp. xxvi, 271-2. The term 'wardsilver' would seem here to be being used for the duty of guarding a local bridge: for such a use see Neilson, 'Customary Rents', pp. 133-4.

[218] obstilit MS. Some parts of the text which follows look unreliable.

[219] On frank-pledge, *ibid.*, pp. 157-62. The Peterborough Abbey manor of Cottingham lay adjacent to East Carlton, the ancestral manor of the Hotot family; and Carlton church was originally a chapel subject to Cottingham: *English Episcopal Acta I. Lincoln 1067-1185*, ed. D. M. Smith (1980), p. 7. But where a discussion of carrying-services in Cottingham fits into a discussion of frank-pledge is not clear. The final chapters of the enquiry, not based on charters, are not always well controlled.

[220] nuntios MS.

[221] The Hotots seem to have felt themselves under an ancient obligation to repair the walls of the county town. In their time, however, grants of murage were made in the form of a toll on goods brought to Northampton market: *Records of the Borough of Northampton*, ed. C. A. Markham and J. C. Cox (Northampton, 1898), i. 36-7, 41-3, 58-61; ii. 427-8. But see also Neilson, 'Customary Rents', pp. 141-2.

solutio   De parco autem de Norhamton sciendum est quod quatuor pertice et dimidia muri per villatum de Clopton sunt reparande et cum necessaria fuit reparatio exspense procuratorum et cimentariorum coliguntur per hidas.

21 It is to be established why the murdum fine is collected in two ways.
capitulum   De murdo autem discernendum est pro quo duplex sit collecta.[222]
solutio   Nam cum contingenter advenerit de viris vel mulieribus vel infantibus demersis vel arsis vel occisis quatuor villarum testes ad primum comitatum comparebit reddendi rationem de infortunio et ista sustentatio procuratorum ville debet colligi de omnibus domibus igne vescentibus. Alia vero collecta pro murdro quod ponitur per justiciaros itinerantes super hundredum solvenda est et colligenda per capitales decennarios sed non equaliter de omni.

Cetera hujus codicis B transcribuntur e codice A usque ad pag. 20; sequitur Magna Carta et registrum cartarum ad villas de Clopton, Turvy aliorumque maneriorum et terrarum ad familiam de Hotot etc spectantium, usque ad finem.

[222] On the *murdrum* fine at this date see C. A. F. Meekings (ed.), *Crown Pleas of the Wiltshire Eyre 1249* (Wilts Rec. Soc. xvi, 1961), pp. 61–5.

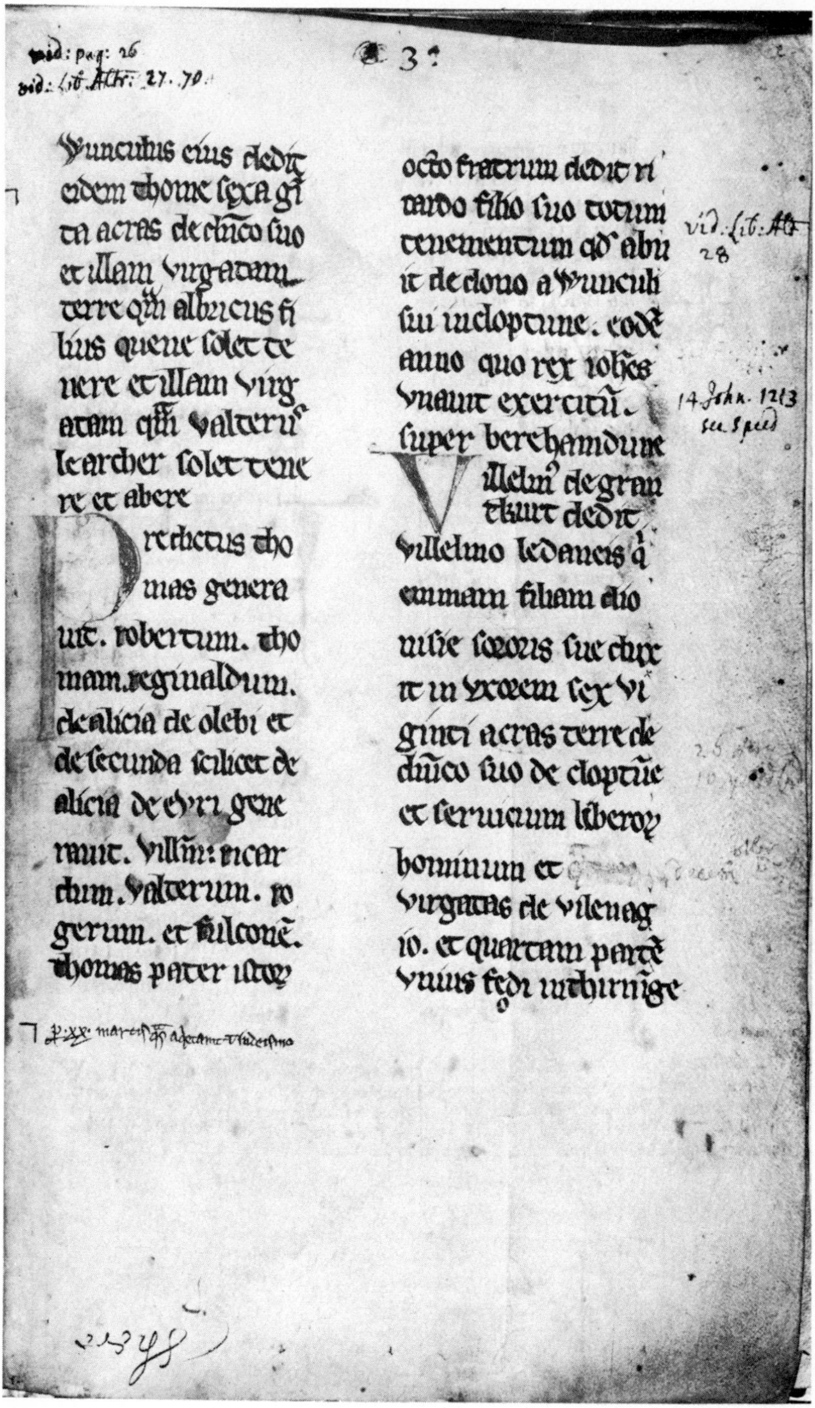

Avunculus eius dedit
eidem thome sexagin
ta acras de dnico suo
et illam virgatam
terre qm albricus fi
lius queue solet te
nere et illam virg
atam qm walterus
learcher solet tene
re et habere
Predictus tho
mas genera
uit. robertum. tho
mam. reginaldum.
de alicia de olebi et
de secunda scilicet de
alicia de evri gene
rauit. willm. ricar
dum. walterum. ro
gerum. et fulconem.
thomas pater istorum
octo fratrum dedit ri
cardo filio suo totum
tenementum qd habu
it de dono avunculi
sui in cloptune. eodem
anno quo rex iohannes
duxit exercitum
super berchamdune
Willelmus de gran
tkurt dedit
willelmo le daneis qui
emmam filiam avo
nisie sororis sue duxit
in uxorem sex vi
ginti acras terre de
dnico suo de cloptune
et servicium liberorum
hominum et
virgatas de vilenag
io. et quartam partem
unius feodi in thiringe

1 Hotot Estate Book, BL Add. MS 54228, page 3

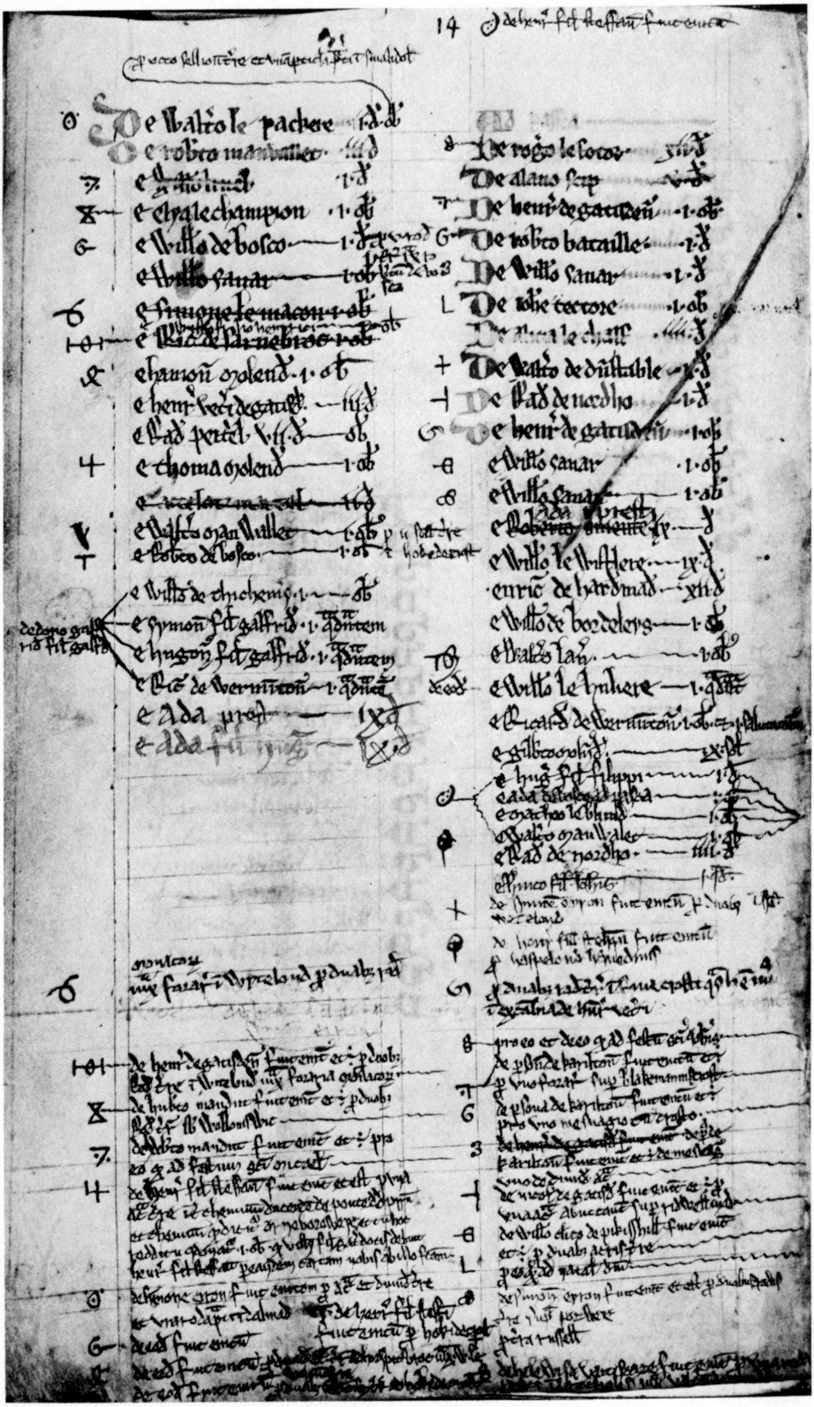

2 Hotot Estate Book, page 14

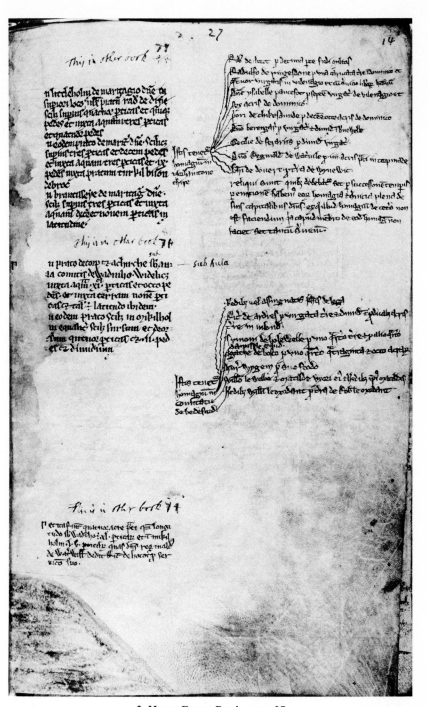

3 Hotot Estate Book, page 27

4 Hotot Estate Book, pages 36–37

Mr Affleck, Successor to Mr Taylor, has made no observation upon what Mr Allett & Mr Taylor have written in the following pages. So that we cannot know what forms & expences he was obliged to submit to on his appointment to this Curacy.

Alexander Akehurst held this Curacy from the 21st of Novr 1784 to the 5th of January 1789. He had no licence from the Bishop, nor was he required to take one out, tho he attended an Episcopal visitation at Towcester.
R.A.

+ The usual fee for exhibiting Letters of Orders at the visitation was paid by R.A.

On the subject of Licence. See Grey's System of English Ecclesiastical Law – Pages 287-312 – 2d Edit. Ao. 1732.

A true Copy of a writing left by ye Revd Mr Charles Allestree sometime Minister of ye Parish of Daventry.

The Preface giving an Account of ye following Treatise.

The trouble & duty of exercising ye Ministerial function at Daventry is very great & discouraging: & every Man living will find it so upon trial. I shall not therefore offer to describe it; experience will teach every future Minister as sensibly & as much to his vexation as it has instructed me.

But it will be reasonable & I sh set down (for ye benefit & information of my Successor) ye alteration of expences & ye casual income of ye Place yt he may depend upon for his invitation to undertake ye Charge & follow his employment here.

1. In ye first place he will find at his admission to ye Cure, yt as there is no need of Institution & Induction so no fees are demandable either by ye Bp, or his Officers (no, not so much, as at a visitation either by himself or his Archdeacon) but only for a licence to preach. wch nevertheless I avoided because I had a licence ad praedicandum per totam Angliam from ye University of Oxford.

2. The Minister of ye place is exempted from ye payment of Taxes to ye King. & his small Tythes never came under any valuation so as to be charged wth any debt to ye Crown.

3. Whatever House he rents for his accommodation is by ye favour of ye Parishioners freed from Parish duties, or Taxes to ye Poor.

4. Tho I have struggled hard & met wth great opposition yet I gaind ye point at last, that no abatement shd be made in times of publick Taxing, of ye twenty six pounds wch Mr Farmer is bound to pay to ye Minister here: This matter is settled beyond dispute, & is inserted in his lease.

5. Every time ye H Sacrament is administered ye Minister is allowd a Bottle of Tent wine for his refreshment after ye Service is over; & at every Visitation ye Ch Wardens pay ye Ministers Charges

5 Daventry Tithing Book, pages 4–5

The View of Daventre Church and of one side of the Priory.

CHURCH, AND REMAINS OF THE PRIORY, AT DAVENTRY.

6 *Above*. Daventry Old Church and Abbey Building by Peter Tillemans, about 1720.

Below. Daventry New Church, built 1752–58, and the Abbey Building; from *The Gentleman's Magazine*, 1826, shortly before the Abbey Building was demolished.

7 Part of the Peterborough Militia List, 1762

A List of the Men in the Parish of Helpston between the Age of 18 and 45 Years

Mr John Lawrence Farmer
Vincent Bellars Farmer
Thomas Bellars Farmer
Thomas Borrows Farmer
Mackerness Morton Farmer
Thomas Browton Baker
Thomas Clare Gardner 5 Child
John Winslow Taylor
John Clare Gardner
Thomas More Shoemaker
John Billings Shoemaker
John Bullemore Carpinter
William Balleram Taylor
Richard Riss Weaver
Richard Sharpe Baker
Thomas Riss Weaver
Francis Fell Masoner
Robert Wolborough Shepherd
James Namer Labourer
Richard Ross Labourer
William Bains Labourer
Francis Borrows Labourer Lame
William Oliver Labourer
John Spiers Labourer Lame
Thomas Gibbs Labourer
William Wiss Labourer
John Landon Labourer
Mathew Griffin Labourer
Thomas Yarrod Labourer

John Crowser Labourer
John Barker Labourer
John Bembs Labourer
William Wodde Labourer
Nestor Peake Labourer
Henry Woller Labourer
Francis Money Labourer
Giles Patrick Labourer 5ch
John Woodward Labourer
John Vins Labourer
Robert Boyal Sarvant
Thomas Cunington Sarvant
John Wiles Sarvant Lame
Francis Gregory Sarvant
John Skelley Sarvant
John Oliver Sarvant
John Burnam Sarvant
Richard King Sarvant
Robert Wils Pandman

December ye 11th 1762

Thomas Billing
Constable

Sworn before us 11 Dec: 1762
Wm Strong
Math: Whitbove
Pe 1376 ten

8 Helpston Militia List, 1762

2

THE
DAVENTRY TITHING BOOK
1700–1818

EDITED BY

R.L. GREENALL

INTRODUCTION

Amongst the parish records of Daventry is an unusual survival: a commonplace book kept by successive incumbents between about 1700 and the early years of the nineteenth century.[1] It consists very largely of observations on the parish and living set down for their own remembrance and the good guidance of their successors. Whilst at first sight fragmentary and apparently lacking in chronology, the Tithing Book in fact tells the story of how successive ministers of Daventry struggled to improve their conditions and income over more than a century. In doing so it reveals a good deal about the everyday realities of eighteenth century clerical life. It also contains much to interest students of the 'contentious tythe', and, with its listings of inhabitants, notes on religious practices, funeral customs, charitable bequests and other matters is a valuable source for local historians. Such books are not common, and whilst it can not be claimed that the Daventry Tithing Book is noteworthy in a literary sense, it is a welcome addition to our knowledge of the realities of the position of one class of the clergy of the Church of England in the eighteenth century. Its interest was recognised earlier this century by the distinguished ecclesiologist and historian, the Rev R M Sergeant, rector of St Peter's, Northampton, at whose expense it was repaired and rebound in 1914.[2]

The parish consisted of Daventry itself, one of the small boroughs of England, together with its hamlet of Drayton. The latter, although a mere appendage of Daventry, retained its own open fields separate from Daventry's until their parliamentary enclosure in 1753, Daventry's remaining open almost half a century longer. Overlooked by Borough Hill, a large flat-topped eminence encircled by a system of Iron Age ditches and ramparts, Daventry developed into a small market town and borough in the Middle Ages. In the fourteenth and fifteenth centuries it fell into a long decline, but revived with the population growth and expansion of economic activity of Queen Elizabeth's time. Situated on the great road to Chester, it began to prosper, receiving a new borough charter from the Crown in 1576. From that time until 1835 (with renewals of its charter in 1607 and 1675) Daventry was governed by a close corporation consisting of a Bailiff, thirteen Burgesses and Twenty Men of the Commonalty. Yet, despite flourishing markets and fairs, busy inns and a throng of wayfarers on the Chester road, eighteenth century Daventry never became very populous: at the time of the first census in 1801 its inhabitants numbered only 2,582. By modern standards the parish might not appear unduly large for a parson of normal energy to manage, though perhaps to eighteenth century clergymen comparison with a quiet country parish might have been more readily invoked. Be that as it may, the incumbents of early eighteenth century Daventry were decidedly unhappy with their lot. The first entry in

---

[1] N(orthamptonshire) R(ecord) O(ffice) 96P/94.
[2] Memorandum in Sergeantson's hand inside the cover. It seems it was he who first named it 'The Daventry Tithing Book' for this title appears nowhere else than on the front cover.

the Tithing Book, made by the Rev Charles Allestree, curate from 1687 to 1707, sets the tone. It declares roundly

The trouble and duty of exercising the ministerial function at Daventry is very great and discouraging and every man will find it so upon trial. I shall not therefore offer to describe what experience will teach every future minister so sensibly and so much to his vexation as it has instructed me.[3]

The living and its improvement

Although Allestree chose not to set down in so many words what made life unhappy for him at Daventry, the sources of his discouragement are clear enough from the pages of the Tithing Book, and from some inquiry into their background. They did not lie with troublesome Dissenters, as in some Northamptonshire places. There were and had been since the Great Ejectment of 1662 a body of Presbyterians (who later became Independents) numerous and well-organised enough to build their own chapel in 1722, and about that time, as the Parish Register records, Anabaptists who were inclined to dispute with the minister over such matters as burial in the churchyard.[4] But if Dissenters formed the 'opposition', in the political as well as religious sense, they were never numerous enough to upset the parson: Daventry was, from 1662, a thoroughly Church and Tory place. The deeper sources of unhappiness of the ministers lay more in a combination of relatively heavy parochial duties, ineligible status and unsatisfactory stipend, all compounded, one feels, by a sense of what might be, given that Daventry was a chartered borough, and that the patronage of the living was vested in a body that was the very epitome of all that was well-connected and aristocratic in the restored Church of England.

Perhaps because Daventry in the seventeenth century had been, like many a market town, a puritanical sort of place, with at least one tolerably famous divine as lecturer,[5] the 'trouble and duties' of the cure were fairly demanding. In the late seventeenth and early eighteenth century the minister was expected to read prayers every morning in the week, and morning and evening every Sunday. Some assistance in this daily routine was afforded under a bequest made by John Farrer in 1729,[6] and in the second half of the century the daily prayers were, it seems, discontinued or replaced by the institution of a regular Sunday afternoon sermon. In 1788 the parochial duties were described in the Tithing Book thus

There is a sacrament the first Sunday in every month, as well as on Christmas day, Easter day, and Whitsunday, and the Sundays that immediately follow these great festivals. The duty on Sunday:- prayers and sermon in the morning, except on sacrament days and then the sermon is omitted; and prayers and sermon in the afternoon, but this sermon is paid for by the parish. Prayers in the morning on Litany and Saints days, and in the afternoon preceeding a sacrament. Prayers morning and afternoon in Passion Week.

[3] See below p. 77.   [4] Parish Register 1700-1739, entry dated 23 Feb. 1721. NRO 96P/17.
[5] The Rev Timothy Dod was lecturer at Daventry from about 1640 and was apparently much esteemed. He refused to conform in 1662 and left the town, dying three years later. He was the son of a notable puritan, the Rev John Dod, minister at Fawsley. H. Isham Longden *The Clergy of Northamptonshire and Rutland from 1500*, iv. 109. See also W. J. Sheils, *The Puritans in the Diocese of Peterborough 1558-1610* (NRS, xxx, 1979), pp. 34, 86-7, 102.
[6] For an abstract of Farrer's will see NRO Butcher (Daventry) 52. An extract is given below p. 90-2.

The incumbent also noted that in 1788 there were 13 weddings, 79 baptisms, 67 funerals and that 'the calls for private baptisms, and visiting the sick are frequent'.[7] It seems fair to surmise that the trouble and duties of Daventry were the trouble and duties of a small but busy town parish where the minister was a man of standing, expected to be active, charitable and generous. A fundamental source of frustration for him was that the living carried neither stipend nor status commensurate with those expectations.

The minister of Daventry at this time was neither rector nor vicar. His title was the ineligible and legally uncertain one of perpetual curate, an 'inferior' title not abolished until the District Church Titles Act of 1868.[8] Perpetual curacies were attached either to the incumbencies of district churches, or of impropriate or appropriate rectories. The curacy of Daventry was of the latter kind, and its origins lay deep in the past. Medieval Daventry had been dominated by the presence of an Augustinian Priory, founded about 1090 at Preston Capes, whence it soon moved to Daventry.[9] Endowed with a considerable estate, the former demesne lands of the manor together with the tithes, the canons made arrangements to minister to the spiritual needs of the townspeople who used part of the priory church for worship. How the parish was served under the medieval priory had very long-lasting results. From at least 1209 until the time of Henry Harvey, who succeeded to the cure in 1435, there were a succession of vicars whose institutions were recorded in the episcopal registers of the Bishops of Lincoln. According to Baker, Harvey was the last vicar of Daventry so recorded. From the time of his successor the prior and monks adopted the practice of nominating one of their own number to serve the cure, and since he was disbarred by his vows from the personal enjoyment of the revenue of his benefice, it was thrown into the common stock of the convent.[10] As Baker remarks, 'This practice, thus established, operated as a precedent after the Dissolution'.[11] As late as the end of the seventeenth and the early eighteenth centuries, as the Tithing Book reveals, curates of Daventry were still uncertain whether or not they needed formal institution or induction by the bishop.[12] And the endowment of the living, subsumed by the medieval priory, long remained subsumed by its successors.

In the 1520s, when Cardinal Wolsey was preparing his great project of founding a college at Oxford to perpetuate his name for ever, his agents made demands upon the priory at Daventry for certain lands to endow the college. The canons refused, and Wolsey commanded the house to be dissolved and made over to his enterprise. A grant of the priory was made to him in 1526, but his fall and death occurring in 1530, the progress of the new college was arrested and the revenues appropriated to it were seized by the Crown. In 1532 the Cardinal's unfinished work was restarted by Henry VIII, and the priory of Daventry, with all its possessions, was included in the endowment, and continued annexed to it until the dean

---

[7] See below p. 105.

[8] Daventry became a rectory in the time of the Rev J. M. Collyns, who served in Daventry from 1867 to 1905. It was he who, in the words of H. Isham Longden, 'recovered the tithes', *Northants Clergy*, iii. 205. The living of Daventry was exchanged by Christ Church in 1879, along with those of Badby and Ravensthorpe, Northants, and Great Bowden and Market Harborough, Leics, for the living of Bluntisham, Hunts.

[9] J. Bridges *The History and Antiquities of the County of Northampton* (1791), i. 46-7, G. Baker *The History and Antiquities of the County of Northampton* (1822-30), i. 315-17.

[10] For a good account of the medieval vicarage and origin of the perpetual curacy, see Baker, i. 327.

[11] *Ibid.*, p. 328.   [12] See below pp. 77, 78.

and canons surrendered to the King in 1545, preparatory to the college being converted into a bishopric. In 1546 the college was revived for a third time with the title of 'the Cathedral Church of Christ in Oxford',[13] the dean and chapter of which became the possessors of a considerable estate in Daventry which consisted of the great and small tithes of the parish, sixteen yard lands in the fields of Daventry, a number of closes and pasture grounds, and certain houses and gardens in Daventry, including what was left of the now defunct priory, or Abbey House as it was usually called.[14] It was the practise of the dean and chapter to lease the whole of their Daventry estate to a single tenant, who then sublet.[15] From 1649 to 1751 the tenants of the college were successive members of a leading Daventry family, the Farmers.[16] In 1751 the tenancy passed to the Earls of Winchilsea, already possessors of a considerable estate in Daventry and the manorial rights, who held the Christ Church properties until 1793, when they passed to the Rev William Lucas Rose of Whilton and his successors.

The Tithing Book records the experiences of the curates of Daventry from the late 1690s to the early years of the nineteenth century. To fully understand their position it is necessary to dwell a little on what the conditions of their sixteenth and seventeenth century predecessors were. The history of the living, and in particular the question of how the dean and chapter of Christ Church related to their perpetual curates in Daventry, is not always very clear. What seems certain is that until 1666 the college took little direct interest in how the cure was served. And until 1751 the dean and chapter simply farmed the vicarage with the rest of the property and left it to the tenant to employ a curate. In 1535 the rectory and vicarage was let for £40 per annum.[17] In a valuation of the college property of 1588 the 'parsonage' was in lease for 13 years, apparently to a Richard Farmer, for £40 a year. Among the lessee's outgoings was £30 for the 'fyndinge of an hable curat'.[18] Another valuation made in 1597 records that the parsonage had the tithes of Drayton, being 36 yardlands, and of 18 yardlands in Daventry and was worth £80 a year to the lessee, which brought him a handsome profit, the salary of the curate that year being set down at a mere £18.[19]

The legacies of history outlined above—insecure status, poor stipend, delegated patronage—together with the non-provision of even a house to live in until 1788, combined to make the living of Daventry unattractive. These, and the absence of recorded institutions to the cure in the registers of the bishops of Lincoln and Peterborough, also make it difficult to arrive at a comprehensive list of successive curates of Daventry between the

13 Bridges, i. 46–7. Baker, i. 315–17.
14 In the year 1778 the estate consisted of 796 acres, of which 226 were in Drayton, and was valued at £899 per annum (Christ Church, Oxford, Estates MS 56, fo.142). It was estimated in 1772 the 16 yard lands in Daventry totalled 497a 0r 18p, i.e. 31a 0r 18p per yard land, ibid. fo.106.
15 In 1695 the value of Edward Farmer's leasehold was calculated thus: Great tithes of the parish £140; the 16 yard lands £109; rental of closes and pasture grounds £130 3s 6d; rental of houses £102 15s 6d; total £477 2s 2d. It was also noted that the 'House on the Abbey Hill fell down about 12 years ago. Chancel roof out of repair. Abbey House much in decay, and is used as a stable and pig sty. . . It is said that Farmer pays no taxes and does no repairs'. Ibid. fo.81.
16 It seems that the Farmers leased the parsonage before 1649 (see notes 18 and 22 below) and may possibly have had the whole estate. Between the time of one Isaac (or Isacke), who was the tenant in the 1590s, and 1646, it is difficult, in the absence of copies of the leases, to trace who the tenants of Christ Church in Daventry were.
17 Baker, i. 327.   18 NRO Thornton (Brockhall) 1666.
19 Ibid., 1671. Presumably the '18' yard lands was a mistake for 16.

Reformation and the Civil War. Certainly they were numerous.[20] Somewhat oddly two institutions to the 'vicarage of Daventry' occur in the Peterborough registers; one in 1623 and the other in 1631. The first notes that Nicholas Cartmell was instituted 'on the presentation of the king by lapse'.[21] However, in May 1630, Cartmell having either died or quitted Daventry, an agreement presumably about the finding of a successor is recorded in the Borough Assembly Book as follows

> Agreed by Mr Richard Farmer and Mr Dutton Farmer his sonne that theie will yearlie paie unto Mr James for his paines as curate of our parish church of Daventree £23 10s that is, from Mr Richard Farmer £19, from Mr Dutton Farmer for the churchyard 40s, for the redd wells 20s, for Bentlies howse 30s, this some of money theie and either of them doe hereby promise to Mr James quarterly every quarter for the time that theie or either of them shall injoie the vicaridg yf the said Mr James doe so long live. Alsoe that Mr James shall enjoy his three beasts commons and thirtie sheepes commons his fower lands on everie side of the field and alsoe marriadges christenings and buryings. [signed] Richard Farmer, Dutton Farmer.[22]

This agreement seems never to have become operative, for no curate of the name of James occurs. It shows, however, that the farming of the vicarage was still being practised in 1630. After Cartmell the names of three men— Robert Ladbroke, Simon Wastel and Thomas Easton—occur within a short space of time. Interestingly the latter was set down in the episcopal register as being instituted in 1631 to the 'vicarage of Daintre alias Daventree' on the presentation of the dean and chapter of Christ Church, Oxford.[23] Easton remained in the cure until 1635. It is also perhaps significant that his successor but one, William Loveledge, who occurs in 1638 and 1639, was a graduate of the college, and was sequestered in 1645 by the Westminster Assembly, though it is unlikely that he was then still curate of Daventry.[24] It does seem that for a time in the 1630s the college was taking a more direct interest in the cure than hitherto. If so, it was shortlived. In the time of the Great Rebellion local connections rather than the patronage of royalist Christ Church seem to have been more important to curates of Daventry. A Richard Farmer, probably the same person who was rector of Charwelton, was curate from 1639. He was buried in Daventry in 1649, but had been replaced by an intruder in 1647.[25] This was Samuel Crofts, the son of the schoolmaster of Daventry. Crofts was a survivor: he held on through all the changes of regimes which ensued and died in harness in Daventry in 1666.[26] As to the living, the parliamentary

---

[20] Isham Longden, working mainly from the evidence of which curates appeared as witnesses to the wills of local people in the period down to the early 17th century, arrives at a list of 21 men, from Sir William Mott who occurs in 1526 and 1528 to Richard Farmer, who seems to have been curate from 1639 to 1647 or 1649.

[21] Baker, i. 327.

[22] NRO ML 106, p. 9.

[23] Baker, i. 327.

[24] *Northants Clergy*, ix. 47.

[25] *Ibid.*, v. 14, *Baker*, i. 328.

[26] He was Cromwellian Registrar in 1653 and conformed in 1662. A graduate of Magdalen Hall, Oxford, he probably owed his position to the patronage of the Thorntons of Brockhall. Thomas Thornton was recorder of Daventry from 1618 to 1632, and Crofts was mentioned in the will of John Thornton made in 1637. He was then schoolmaster to the testator's sons and 'was to have the next advowson of Weedon Beck if he outlived Mr Smithe'. O. Barron, *Northamptonshire Families* (1906), p. 304.

commissioners in 1655 certified that it was worth £40 per annum in the patronage of Christ Church College in Oxford; that Samuel 'Craftes' was incumbent; that the church was near two miles distant from any other; and that they humbly conceived it 'convenyent' to have an augmentation granted to the minister, it being a great market town.[27]

It was not to be until after the Restoration that augmentation came, and when it came it was not to be from Parliament, but from a local quarter. In his will of 1662 Richard Farmer made arrangements for his heirs and assigns to pay an annual bequest of £20 to the curate, to which was added another £6 for the rent of a house, arising out of their income from the tenancy of the Christ Church property.[28] As was often the case with such bequests difficulties arose: the heir was a minor, and for several years the bequest was apparently not paid to the curate.[29] Nonetheless the Farmer bequest was an important turning point in the history of the living of Daventry. It improved the curates' financial position, and was certainly done with the college's approbation, which indicates that the college henceforth was to take a more direct interest in how its livings were to be served. Such matters are indicative of the new spirit abroad inside the Church of England after the Restoration. An era of recovery and sharp reassertion commenced. A bishop was restored in Oxford; Christ Church rapidly reestablished its position as the powerhouse of Stuart Anglican orthodoxy; clergy under its patronage naturally looked to the dean and chapter for aid and support in improving their position and prospects. The curates of Daventry certainly did. The difficulty was that the support they often sought was against the college's own tenant in Daventry, which often proved awkward for the dean and chapter, and frustrating for the curate.[30]

Commencing at the end of the 1690s the Daventry Tithing Book tells the story of how the curates there, ever conscious of the disparity between their felt aspirations and the terms and conditions of their position, struggled to improve them. They did not struggle in vain. It records how in the first place the Rev Charles Allestree fought a sharp engagement to prevent his stipend being eroded, and then how he and his successors gradually succeeded in augmenting and improving it. Down to about the 1750s the living was worth between about £100 and £120 per annum: by 1801 it had risen to about £165; by 1831 it had reached £344.[31] This process of successful augmentation and improvement was not at all unusual in the eighteenth century; it was a characteristic feature of the social history of rural England. It was one which however owed more to the effects of economic change than to the struggles of individual clergy. Nevertheless the experience of the curates of Daventry, as revealed in their Tithing Book, provides a good local example of what was going on in one parish in Midland England.

In the early eighteenth century the curates' stipend was derived from four principal sources. The first was the small tithes of the parish. These comprised the compounded tithes of the farmers' yardlands in the fields of Daventry and Drayton, tithes of sheep pastured on the town common on Borough Hill, of orchards and gardens of certain tenements in Daventry and customary tithe eggs due to the parson on Good Friday. In 1720 their

---

[28] NRO Butcher (Daventry) 52.
[29] See below p. 84.
[30] As in the case of the curate's house. See below pp.67–8.
[31] See *Report of the Commissioners on Ecclesiastical Revenues*, 1835 pp. 796–7.

value, in round terms, was £34. The second source consisted of Richard Farmer's bequest of 1662 of £20, with £6 for the rent of a suitable house (a sum raised in 1724 to £8). The third consisted of 'subscriptions', or quarterly contributions from parishioners which varied a little from year to year, but which came to about £25 in 1720. About the time the old church was pulled down and the new one built in the 1750s 'subscriptions' were replaced by the payment of a similar sum for a Sunday afternoon sermon from the curate. The fourth element was what the Tithing Book sometimes refers to as 'obventions', a miscellany of payments usually made up of 'Easter offerings' from the parishioners, the letting of the churchyard for grazing, a payment arising out of the town Malt Mill, and 'surplice fees'—sundry payments made for keeping the registers, reading banns, issuing marriage certificates and officiating at weddings and funerals. The yield from 'obventions' would vary from year to year, but in 1720 totalled just over £18, making an income of about £102 for that year.[32]

The first augmentation of the income and comfort of the curates of Daventry in the Tithing Book followed the bequest made by John Farrer in 1729. Farrer left £400 the income from which was to be divided between the schoolmaster of Daventry, if he was in Holy Orders (as he usually was), to read prayers in the parish church every morning, except Wednesday, Friday and Holy Days, when the curate was to perform this duty, and to assist in the administering of the sacrament. The testator's object was twofold: to augment the stipend of the schoolmaster, and to help the minister, because, as Farrer put it in his will, 'I think the Duty of the Place is too hard for one Minister to perform without prejudice to his Health'.[33] As a result the curate's burden was lightened and his stipend added to by £6 a year.

What really improved his income, however, was the parliamentary enclosure movement, which got under way in Northamptonshire in the middle third of the eighteenth century. In addition to the enclosure of land for the benefit of landowners and farmers a major objective of this process was to improve relationships between the latter and the church by replacing tithes with grants of land in lieu. Enclosure locally came in two stages, Drayton being enclosed half a century before Daventry. From 1752, the curate became the recipient of rents arising from a 51 acre estate in Drayton granted to him to compensate for the loss of the small tithes there.[34] The new arrangement was greatly to his advantage, and illustrates why the clergy were frequently amongst the most zealous advocates of parliamentary enclosure. The curate no longer had the bother and vexation of collecting his tithes from the farmers and townspeople with land or property in Drayton, and in the half century following, the value of the 51 acres there yielded a steadily increasing rental, rising from £37 10s in 1754 to £60 in 1796.[35]

It was not until the later part of the century that another long-standing vexation was removed. The lack of a parsonage house was a constant irritation, which Farmer's allowance in no way assuaged. Several curates recorded in the Tithing Book their continuing failure to persuade Christ Church to help. The Rev William Tayler chronicles one such attempt in 1723: 'But here I fail'd tho the college own many houses in this town. They

[32] See below p. 87.
[33] See below p. 91. In 1738 the trustees bought an estate at Newbold-on-Avon in Warwickshire with the Farrer bequest.
[34] 25 Geo III. c 25.
[35] See below p. 106.

did talk of repairing the old abby and fixing that uppon the minister, but that also dropt'.[36] The sticking point apparently was that successive lessees were unwilling to give up any of the tenements in the town to help the college in this matter. At last, in 1787, Mr Finch Hatton finally consented to allow the curate a cottage in High Street, with a garden and one acre of ground, which was usually let for £6 a year, on condition that the charge of £8 payable under Farmer's will was discontinued. The dean and chapter agreed, and donated £250 towards the reappointing of this dwelling (described as 'sufficient for a person of modest income'), raising the money from a sale of timber on their nearby estate of Thrupp.[37]

In 1796 the curate was the recipient of a windfall-gain resulting from the 'canal mania' of the time. To enable them to make a reservoir in Drayton to supply water to their canal from Braunston to London, the Grand Junction Canal Company compulsorily purchased a little over an acre from his estate, paying, as the Rev Samuel Smith recorded in his memoranda book, the goodly sum of £87 1s 3d for it.[38]

This entry is almost the last. The Tithing Book stops short of recording the final chapter in the story of the augmentation and improvement of the living, the enclosure of the open field of Daventry itself. Perhaps this was because, in contrast to the enclosure of Drayton half a century before, the curate was not a direct party. In the Daventry enclosure award of 1803 no apportionment was made to him for his loss of tithes.[39] However, the dean and chapter received due compensation for the ending of small tithes, and because they had hitherto allowed the curate to have the benefits in the tenant's lease, they now settled on him and his successors the allotments they received in lieu. They also arranged the exchange of the house in High Street for superior premises near the churchyard with 14 acres attached, making an interest-free loan for improvements.[40] As a consequence, the curate now became the possessor of an estate of some 127 acres in Daventry, in addition to his 49 in Drayton. Overnight his income doubled. At long last it became possible to afford a curate as a matter of course to ease the trouble and duty of exercising the ministerial function at Daventry.

The curates of Daventry, 1687 to 1833

Before the Restoration curates of Daventry were rarely, if ever, graduates of the college.[41] After the Restoration, or at any rate after the death of Samuel Crofts in 1666, they were invariably Christ Church men. The first of them was John Frauncis, curate 1667 to 1687, who despite an incumbency of two decades, remains an obscure figure.[42] His successor, Charles

---

[36] See below p. 85. Tayler was again unsuccessful seven years later when Christ Church renewed the lease, Christ Church, Estates MS 56, fo. 95.

[37] Memorandum by Rev Dr S Smith, *ibid.* fo.318.

[38] See below p. 108.

[39] The Enclosure Act (42 Geo III c. 79) says 'The Dean and Chapter of Christ Church ... are seised of the Rectory and Vicarage Impropriate of the said parish of Daventry, and in Right thereof are entitled to all Tythes, both Great and Small, annually arising, renewing and increasing (except within the Hamlet of Drayton in the Parish of Drayton aforesaid and except a certain Piece of Ground called Common Leys)': NRO Daventry collection 2574. Why the curate was a party to the enclosure of Drayton but not of Daventry remains obsure.

[40] Memo. by Rev Dr S Smith, as cited in note 37.

[41] The only one before 1667 seems to have been William Loveledge in the late 1630s. See above p. 65.

[42] Neither Baker (i. 328), *Northants Clergy* (ii. 117) nor J. Foster (*Alumni Oxoniensis*, i. 531) can add anything to the information that he was educated at Christ Church (BA 1651, MA 1654) and was curate of Daventry 1667 to 1687.

69
Allestree, was anything but. It is his trenchant memoranda that open the
Tithing Book and record some early exchanges in the long campaign to
improve the living. He too served in Daventry for twenty years, from 1687
to 1707. Born in 1654, the son of William Allestree of Derby, gentleman,
he was educated at Christ Church.[43] He was a kinsman of the important
college dignitary, Richard Allestree (1619–1681), who rose to be Provost
of Eton.[44] In 1685 the college presented him to the living of Cassington
near Woodstock (once held by Richard Allestree), and, two years later,
the curacy of Daventry. He remained incumbent of both places until his
death in 1707.

The incident which first caused Allestree to set down memoranda for his
successors seems to have been a sharp tithe dispute which arose in 1693.
The dean and chapter had leased the estate in 1688 to Edward Farmer,
Richard Farmer's nephew, and in Michaelmas 1693 Allestree brought a
Bill in the Court of Exchequer against several of Farmer's tenants for the
payment of three years' small tithes. The defendants answered that the 16
yardlands from which the tithes were claimed belonged to the rectory and
had never paid any small tithes to the vicar. To Allestree's chagrin the Bill
was dismissed in Hilary term 1694 because he had failed to prove he was
vicar of Daventry, which no doubt accounts for the notes he set down on
the subject of the legal position of the perpetual curacy of Daventry.
Thwarted in court, he took the matter up with the dean and chapter who
had granted him the small tithes when he had entered the cure in 1687, and
when Farmer's lease came up for renewal in 1695 the college desired him
to state why the 16 yardlands should not pay vicarial tithes.[45] It turned
out that though Farmer was entitled to the small tithes, he had never
received them, but the college ensured that henceforth his right passed to
Allestree and his successors,[46] which accounts for Allestree's triumphant
memorandum that

> I have rescued sixteen yard land from the power of an oppressor and
> made them tytheable as well as other parts of the field. And this matter
> is now inserted also into Mr Farmers lease for the prevention of any
> encroachment for the future. So that now the minister has a right to all
> the small tythes that arise in the parish and no body starts any pretended
> privilege or exemption.[47]

It is hard to resist the impression that Allestree was the first of a new type.
Often socially better-connected than their predecessors, they were men
sharper in asserting their rights, and fully expected their patrons in Oxford
to support them. And, in the manner of the times, it was to the practice of
pluralism that they turned as a way of improving their careers and prospects.

Allestree's successor, Samuel Hartman, who was curate of Daventry

[43] Northants Clergy, i. 49, Baker, i. 328. William Allestree had been Recorder of Derby
and MP for the borough 1640-43.
[44] Richard Allestree and Charles Allestree's father were cousins (Pedigree of the Allestree
family, Derbyshire Record Office). Charles Allestree, together with John Dolben, who became
Archbishop of York, and John Fell, later Bishop of Oxford, were a famous Christ Church
triumvirate of friends during and after the Civil Wars: a triple portrait of them by Sir Peter
Lely hangs in Christ Church. Under Dean Fell the college assumed its position in Oxford as
the centre of loyalty and devotion to the church of England and the Stuart dynasty after the
Restoration. Fell wrote a Life of Richard Allestree.
[45] Christ Church, Estates MS 56, fo.77.
[46] Ibid. fo.79.
[47] See below p. 77.

from 1707 to 1716, was also vicar of Badby from 1708. The son, apparently, of a German protestant emigré from the kingdom of Poland, Hartman was a graduate and petty canon of Christ Church, but the only reference to him in the Tithing Book is a dismissive note that 'he left only some confused papers which were of no use'.[48] The writer was William Tayler, minister for the next 34 years, whose experience illustrates how a clerical career in the early eighteenth century could be built from modest beginnings. For much of his life in Daventry, as well as being the curate, he was, like a few before him, master of the Free Grammar School, which was endowed with £20 a year. He therefore knew his predecessor at first hand. Tayler also pursued the paths of pluralism, becoming in succession vicar of Staverton (1723-26), vicar of Long Buckby (1730-38) and from 1728 rector of Malpas in Cheshire. Perhaps the latter preferment brought him to greener pastures: at any rate he gave up the Grammar School in 1732.[49] By then he certainly had a curate in Daventry,[50] though he did not live long enough to see the enclosure of Drayton which was such an important step in the augmentation of the living. It seems it is to Tayler that we owe the compilation of the Tithing Book in its present form. Into it he copied Allestree's notes, or at least some of them, adding numerous others of his own on a variety of matters including extracts from the wills of such benefactors as Richard Farmer and John Farrer, and notes on a variety of interesting, if minor local matters. No other contributor to the Tithing Book reveals as much about clerical life in eighteenth century Daventry.

In 1750 Tayler was succeeded by James Affleck, who was also to serve thirty four years in the cure of Daventry. Affleck, however, came from a different social rank. The fifth son of a country gentleman, his mother was a niece of Sir Gilbert Dolben, Bart. of Finedon, and two of his sons succeeded in turn to a baronetcy. In 1757 he was presented to the living of Finedon, and thereafter seems to have employed a curate in Daventry.[51] No doubt it is for this reason that his contributions to the Tithing Book are less extensive than some of his predecessors and successors. Yet in his time two events of considerable importance occurred, both mentioned in the Tithing Book. In 1751-53 Drayton field was enclosed and he and his successors became the possessors of an estate there in lieu of their extinguished tithe rights. As has already been noted, this produced a rental that increased in a very satisfactory manner as the century wore on. The other event was the complete rebuilding of the parish church. By the year 1752 the old one had become so badly decayed that it was too dangerous for public worship, and after the obtaining of an episcopal faculty it was demolished.[52] It was replaced by a fine new church in the fashionable 'Grecian' style, designed and built by the Warwick master-mason William Hiorne (or Hiorns) and completed in 1758. Paid for by public subscription, with a tower and spire modelled on that of St Giles-in-the-Fields in London,[53] it was a fine town church and made a handsome centrepiece in Daventry.

---

[48] See below p. 85. For Hartman see *Northants Clergy*, vi. 187.
[49] *Ibid.*, xiii. 157.
[50] See below p. 96 for Tayler's arrangement with Thomas Collis, his curate in 1743. In 1726 he had a curate by the name of Charles Powell, *Northants Clergy*, xi. 49.
[51] *Northants Clergy*, i. 29. Affleck also became prebendary of Southwell Minster, though Baker says 'of York' (i, p. 329).
[52] NRO Diocesan Records, Faculty Registers, no. 2, fos. 249, 251.
[53] I am indebted to Mr B. A. Bailey for this information. For the Hiorns see H. M. Colvin, *Biographical Dictionary of British Architects 1600-1840*, new edn (1978), pp. 419-21.

Affleck's long tenure was succeeded by two short ones in the eleven years following his death in 1784. Yet although Alexander Akehurst stayed only four years[54] he left some valuable notes in the Tithing Book on a variety of subjects, including the tracking down and collecting of the garden and other minor tithes. He also records his distribution of sacrament money amongst the poor of Daventry and the matter of opening the alms boxes in the church. There is also an account of what seemed to be the final chapter in the saga of securing a parsonage house, and his notes contain the draft of an 8 year lease of the Drayton glebe. Most interesting and valuable of all is a letter, apparently addressed to the college in 1788, containing the fullest account in the Tithing Book of the income of the living, together with the account of the religious duties of the place, already referred to above.[55] Akehurst's successor was Samuel Humfreys who died in 1794 at the age of 39 after only four years in post.[56] The only memoranda he set down refer to the costs of draining the Drayton property, and to another 8 year lease.[57] By the 1790s land improvement was clearly exercising the minds of the parsons of Daventry.

The last of the curates to make any contribution to the Tithing Book was Samuel Smith, in many ways the most distinguished of the incumbents in our period, or at any rate the one with the most successful ecclesiastical career. The son of a master of Westminster School he took his B.A. in 1786 and was appointed curate of Daventry in 1795, a living he continued in until 1833. Further preferments commenced in 1802 when he was appointed chaplain to the House of Commons, and thereafter he was canon of Christ Church in 1807, Doctor of Divinity in 1808, Treasurer of the college in 1813 and Dean 1824 to 1831. He was also rector of Dry Drayton, Cambridgeshire from 1808 to 1829. His career reached its peak when he was appointed to prebendal stalls at Southwell, York and Durham in 1830-31.[58] In his early days, before these preferments came his way he seems to have been as energetic as his predecessors in doing all he could to improve the living of Daventry, or so entries he made between 1794 and 1803 in the Tithing Book would seem to suggest. In 1794, with the instincts of a future treasurer of Christ Church perhaps revealing themselves, he set down his calculations on how the land 'belonging to the Revd. Mr Humfries' at Drayton, might, by a judicious outlay of capital on a division of the large close into four, and some draining of the other two, be made to yield an increased rental. And sure enough in 1818 he copied down a twelve year lease producing a rental somewhat in excess of his 1794 calculation.[59] Smith was lucky as well as shrewd and well-connected. The wars against the French inflated land values, and the canal boom of the 1790s resulted in a good price from the Grand Junction Canal Company for an acre of his land at Drayton for a reservoir.[60] Most fortunate of all was the fact that soon after he came to Daventry the rest of the parish was enclosed by parliamentary act. The Tithing Book closes on the eve of this event and on the eve of Smith's career taking-off with his appointment to the chaplaincy at Westminster. Soon a curate was installed in Daventry with a decent salary.[61] By the early years of the nineteenth century, the process of the

[54] *Northants Clergy*, i. 33.
[55] See below pp. 103-5.
[56] *Northants Clergy*, vii. 157.
[57] See below p. 106.
[58] Northants Clergy, xii. 327.
[59] See below p. 108.
[60] See above p. 68.
[61] £100. See *Rep. on the Eccles, Revs.*, 1835, pp. 796-7.

financial (and therefore social) transformation of the living of Daventry, started long before by Farmer's bequest of 1662 and Allestree's battles against an 'oppressor' in the 1690s, had been accomplished. Tithes had become a thing of the past and there was no further need, it would seem, for a memoranda book for the guidance of their successors.

The Curates of Daventry and their Parishioners

The Tithing Book would be a less interesting and useful document than it is if it dwelt exclusively on the concern of the curates with their stipend and working conditions. Happily it does not. In it there is a good deal on other matters, three of which are, perhaps, worthy of further scrutiny: other sources of friction between the curates of Daventry and the tenants of Christ Church; the relationships of the curates with the farmers and other payers of small tithes; and matters arising out of their day-to-day duties of ministering to their parishioners.

As to the first of these, the book has a certain amount to say on the shifting triangular relationships of parson, tenant and the townspeople, who seem to have looked upon the tenant as something akin to an over-bearing squire. In 1706 an incident arose which caused Charles Allestree to address a sharp letter to the tenant, which Tayler later copied down in the Tithing Book.[62] Farmer, apparently faced with the imposition of new taxes arising out of the War of the Spanish Succession, attempted to reduce his payment due to the curate under his uncle's will of 1662. In a charac-teristically combative manner Allestree not only set down the grounds why the tenant could not do this (having enlisted the support of the dean and chapter), but combined it with an elegant threat cushioned by an offer of friendship. The threat came by way of a suggestion that if Farmer persisted, Allestree might be obliged to draw the attention of the Tax Commissioners to 'a strict review of all the particulars of your assessment, which I am confident you would no more desire to have the discovery laid before the Commissioners, than I desire to have the trouble and necessity of making it'. (So much for life in a face-to-face society, with its lack of secrets.) However, this was followed, a sentence or so later, with concilatory words. 'If I might have redress willingly from you, I would make it my endeavours to assist and ease you doubly in all future taxes, because some of the Commissioners in this district are my particular friends, and will give a kind ear to any representation that I shall make to them'.[63] Friction occurred over other matters as well. Tayler noted rather tersely 'I have had several contests with the College Tenant about his encroachments upon my churchyard. 1st. With relation to the passage from the town to the upper Park. 2ndly. With relation to the cottages that bound my churchyard on the south side'.[64] From a letter surviving in Christ Church archives, written in 1709 by his predecessor Samuel Hartman,[65] it is clear that encroachment was not a new problem, but was one on which the curate could usually count on help from the townspeople against the tenant. Hartman's letter was in answer to a complaint to the dean and chapter from Farmer that the inhabitants had railed in the churchyard, preventing access to his tithe-barn in the Upper Park, to which there was a right of

---

[62] See below pp. 83–4.
[63] Ibid.
[64] See below p. 85.
[65] Christ Church, Estates MS 56, fo.91.

way through the churchyard. This had been done in response to the alleged destruction of graves by Farmer's tenants carting their tithe corn through the churchyard. It was also complained that 'another highway' for access had been made 'uppon sufferance', but that as a result pigs and dogs had opened graves. In an action at Northampton Assizes the parishioners had established that there was no legal way through the churchyard other than the footpath, and the churchwardens had then erected a line of poles and rails leaving only a pathway sixteen feet wide for carts. According to Hartman, Farmer was further annoyed because he could no longer encroach on the churchyard, in which cattle belonging to some of his tenants had been foddered a whole winter.[66] Evidently this matter did not rest there, but grumbled on. Years later, in 1723, Tayler records that, at last, he had succeeded in having restrictions on the lessee and his tenants as to the matter of churchyard encroachments and cottage nuisances inserted into the tenant's new lease.[67]

Hartman's letter of 1709 touched on other issues which illustrate just how unpopular the tenant on occasion could be with the parishioners of Daventry. Farmer had made complaints over the erection of certain pews in the church, but the proprietors of them had ignored his demands to have them removed. As Hartman observed, these were 'rich men, bent to stand it out' with Farmer. He also noted that the church was now so full of pews that a new gallery had had to be erected, and he further remarked that the chancel floor had been repaired, the communion table railed in, the chancel wainscotted 'as high as the pews', 'the walls whitewashed', and an altarpiece set up, all without so much as asking Farmer for sixpence. Meanwhile, he declared, Farmer 'will repair neither roof nor walls'.[68]

The Daventry Tithing Book was begun to record the result of the battle Charles Allestree fought in the 1690s to carry his point that the 16 yard lands of the Christ Church estate were titheable, and that he as curate, and no one else, should have the small tithes arising. Subsequently most of the farmers had agreed to compound at the rate of eight shillings per yard land (though in 1700 a few were still paying in kind). Thereafter, as several useful lists of farmers and their yard lands in the Tithing Book show, this rate became fixed and customary and never changed until the tithe itself was extinguished by the parliamentary enclosures. On this matter there was little or no friction between curate and tithe-payers in the eighteenth century. Compounders paid half yearly, and were apparently allowed to be quarterly in arrears with their Michaelmas dues. As Akehurst noted in 1789, the curate met the farmers at a public house on rent day and it was the custom to pay for their entertainment.[69] Over the small tithes on sheep and on gardens however no such unruffled acceptance of mutual obligations existed. As the curate was only too well aware, his parishioners strove to deny him the full value of the tithes due on sheep wintered on Borough Hill. In the 1720s, as Tayler reflected bitterly, though fully 500 sheep were grazed there, he received only nine or ten lambs a year and only a small quantity of wool.

The reason is because those that are not wintered there do pay only a rate tythe viz. half penny per sheep, and also because the several proprietors have some odd number which pay no tythe in kind

[66] Ibid.
[67] See below p. 85.
[68] Op. cit.
[69] See below p. 105.

Also, he added,

They reckon those only to be wintered upon the hill are found there on New Years day, at which time the sheppard brings me an account of them. I have often been defrauded by some in driving their sheep off and on a little before or after this time.[70]

The curate was also entitled to tithes of a few pence each from certain gardens in Daventry. Akehurst noted down in 1789 what must have occurred to some of his predecessors, when he remarked that only ten gardens paid: 'Why *they* pay so little, & why *others* pay nothing, might be worth inquiring'.[71] By then it was enshrined in custom and practice, and perhaps because enclosures were then very much on people's minds, nothing was done.

A third area of relationship between curate and parishioners illuminated is that arising out of the curates' ordinary religious duties. The detailed monthly accounts of his casual income left by Allestree for the year 1700 in particular throw much light on the day to day work of the curate, and on some of the customs of eighteenth century Daventry.[72] His surplice fees for marriages, christenings, churchings and burials are set out according to the principle of a moderate fee for those charged 'at the ordinary rate', whilst the grand and the well-to-do paid on a higher tariff. Christenings at home, for instance, were usually charged at one shilling, but for a private ceremony for Mrs Rawlins' child Allestree charged five. Similarly a churching at the ordinary rate cost 5d, but Mrs Jephcote's cost her 2s. Burials at an ordinary rate of 5d could rise to as high as 16s for a full funeral service with sermon, as in the case of Mrs Baker, in addition to which Allestree received a further 10s 9d for transcribing his sermon for her husband. The funerals of the richer burgesses and freemen also yielded gifts and mortuary payments. In 1700 Allestree lists four pairs of Cordovant gloves, a pair of white gloves, and a pair of shammy gloves and a hatband. Mortuaries were also graded; usually 3s 4d, William Rose's was 10s.[73] Sermons were required for special occasions as well as funerals, as on the occasion of the death of Queen Mary in 1695,[74] and an annual sermon was required for the inauguration of the Bailiff of Daventry each November, for which the curate received 10s.[75] So esteemed were sermons in the eighteenth century that in the 1750s the preaching of a regular Sunday afternoon sermon was instituted, for which the curate received an annual stipend of £20. Finally, on the subject of customary gifts and payments, Allestree reminded his successors in a memorandum that every time the sacrament was administered (then once a month) the minister was allowed a bottle of wine for his refreshment after the service.[76]

The administration of the sacrament was the occasion for the curate to raise money for the poor, for money collected at this service was periodically distributed as alms. Tayler set down how he distributed sacrament money, noting also that out of it he also gave the parish clerk and sexton five shillings each 'that they may better esteem me'. Prudent as always,

---

[70] See below pp. 85-6.
[71] See below p. 104.
[72] See below pp. 78-83.
[73] See below p. 82.
[74] *The Desire of all Men. A sermon preach'd at Daventry ... March 5, 1694/5 being the day of the internment of our late most gracious Queen etc*, London, 1695.
[75] See below p. 82.
[76] See below p. 77.

Tayler also noted 'I always set down in writing what I thus receive and pay to avoid clamours'.[77] Sixty years later, at a time of growing poverty, Akehurst recorded how he distributed sacrament money in 1786, 1787 and 1788, trying different methods of distribution on each occasion.[78] Just how necessary this particular form of charity was is perhaps revealed by Akehurst's account of the opening of the alms boxes in the church at this time. When he opened them for the first time for seven years in December 1786 he found they contained just 3s 9½d. In January 1788 all they yielded was five farthings, which, he records, 'were suffered to remain'. The following December the donations had grown by just 4d. These too were suffered to remain.[79]

In addition to the notes and memoranda outlined above the Daventry Tithing Book contains a number on other matters of some interest. Among these is a brief note about the smallpox in 1737,[80] extracts from the wills of certain benefactors which impinged on the living of the curates, and several listings of inhabitants of Daventry. Perhaps the most valuable among the latter are the lists of farmers for the years 1700, 1720, 1725, 1730, 1738, 1751, 1754, 1786 and 1789, together with the sums they were assessed at for tithe, and sometimes their yard lands.[81] For the local historian these chronologically well-spaced lists are most useful. As students of local communities in the eighteenth century will appreciate it is often surprisingly difficult to find out who, at particular points in time, the local farmers were, and what their holdings consisted of. Similarly, the listing of the inhabitants with their Easter offerings in 1732, graded according to wealth and status is also of interest.[82] It must, however, be allowed that much of this miscellaneous information may be of more direct use to the student of Daventry's history in the eighteenth century than to the student of English society more generally, though judgement on this particular point will vary from reader to reader. There is little doubt however, that overall the Daventry Tithing Book is an unusual local record. It is hoped that this edition of its text will prove of use to students of clerical and local life in the eighteenth century.

A note on editorial method

The original text measures approximately 15 inches by 6 inches (380 mm by 152 mm) and is bound in vellum. Its entries are not always chronological, and, as is often the case with such ledgers, are made not only from front to middle, but from the back to the middle with the book inverted. The pages have therefore been given numbers to follow this sequence, front to middle and then back to middle. Abbreviations are very extensive, and for this edition have been expanded and modern punctuation introduced. In the columns of accounts, for easier reading and clarity £ s d replaces l s d (as in £8 10s 6d instead of 081 10s 6d)

The principal editorial changes have been in the rearranging of entries chronologically in sections under the periods of the incumbencies of the succeeding curates of Daventry between 1687 and 1818. One difficulty which arises is that some entries were copied later from MS notes left by

---

[77] See below p. 86.
[78] See below pp. 102-3.
[79] See below p. 102.
[80] See below p. 96.
[81] See below pp. 78-9, 86-7, 90, 92-3, 96, 97, 99, 101, 105.
[82] See below pp. 95-6.

predecessors. This is so with Charles Allestree's memoranda, copied into the book by William Tayler, the first compiler of the book as it has come down to us. Another difficulty is that some entries were annotated later. It is usually obvious from the context where this has happened; where it is not, explanation is offered in a note in the text or in a footnote.

TEXT

[MEMORANDA OF THE REVD. CHARLES ALLESTREE, CURATE 1687 TO 1707][1]

[p. 5] A true Copy of a writing left by the Revrd Mr Charles Allestree, sometime Minister of this Parish of Daventry. The Preface giving an Account of the following Treatise.

The trouble and duty of exercising the ministerial function at Daventry is very great and discouraging, and every man living will find it so upon trial. I shall not therefore offer to describe what experience will teach every future minister so sensibly, and so much to his vexation, as it has instructed me.

But it will be reasonable that I should set down (for the benefit and information of my successor) the alleviation of expenses and the casual income of the place that he may depend upon for his invitation to undertake the charge and follow his employment here.

1. In the first place he will find at his admission to this cure, that as there is no need of institution and induction, so no fees are demandable either by the Bishop, or his officers (no, not so much as at a Visitation, either by himself or his Archdeacon) but only for a license to preach, which nevertheless I avoided because I had a license ad praedicandum per totam Angliam from the University of Oxford.

2dly. The Minister of this place is exempted from the payment of taxes to the King, and his small Tythes never come under any valuation so as to be charged with any debt to the Crown.

3dly. Whatever house he rents for his accomodation is, by the favour of the parishioners, freed from parish duties, or taxes to the poor.

4thly. Though I have struggled hard and met with great opposition yet I gained this point at last, that no abatements should be made in times of public taxing, of the twenty six pounds which Mr Farmer is bound to pay to the minister here. This matter is settled beyond dispute, and is inserted in his lease.[2]

5thly. Every time the sacrament is administered the minister is allowed a bottle of Tent wine for his refreshment after the Service is over.[3] And at every Visitation the church wardens pay the minister's charges and expense.

[p. 6] I might add that I have rescued sixteen yard land from the power of an oppressor and made them tytheable, as well as other parts of the field. And this matter is inserted also into Mr Farmer's lease for the prevention of any encroachment for the future. So that now the minister has a right to all the small tythes that arise in the parish and no body starts any pretended privilege or exemption.[4]

My successor will find in these papers such a scheme of things as will

---

[1] Written in the hand of the Rev William Tayler, curate 1716 to 1750.
[2] See Introduction above, p. 66, and below p. 83.
[3] Tent wine was a Spanish wine of deep red colour and of low alcoholic content often used as sacramental wine.
[4] See above p. 69.

prove a model for him to govern his expectations by. And more or less (that is to say within a very small matter) his annual income will be proportionable to this years increase and revenue. [*Signed*] Charles Allestree.

The above mentioned writing is scheduled 'a Preface to the Small Tythes at Daventry in the year 1700'.

[*Tayler comments*] My successor will find 2 mistakes in the writing above. 1st. That it says no fee is to be paid but only for a license to preach, whereas he will find himself obliged (as I did) by the act of Uniformity to subscribe before the Bishop of the Diocese, and to have a certificate of his subscription, which he must read at the same time with the Articles at his admission to this cure. For which certificate they made me pay £1 5s 0d, but I was ill used.[5] (For this, *videlicit* Clergyman's Vade-mecum, vol. 1, page 47.) Another mistake is that it supposes the University License ad praedicandum per totam Angliam sufficient to justify a man from taking a license from the Bishop of the Diocese, which I apprehend it will not, for this reason: because the University cannot give a license to serve a cure, although they can to preach in any part of England.

I made these 2 observations for the benefit of my successor and not out of the spirit of contradiction. November 15th 1718. [*Signed*] William Tayler.

The writing goes on and gives the following account of the income of the minister of Daventry for the year 1700.

[p. 7]   Stated Dues to the Minister

	£	s	d
Keeping the register at Lady Day		6	8
The Church Yard at four quarterly payments	2	0	0
Contributions raised quarterly	28	0	0
Tythe Eggs on Good Friday		10	4
Offerings at Easter	4	3	0
The Malt Mill paid every half year	1	0	0
For a house paid every half year	6	0	0
A Benefaction paid every half year	20	0	0

In all £62

Tythe of the Yard lands according
to agreement at 8s per yard land

1 Nicholas Stanton for four yard land and a quarter	1	14	0
2 John Stanton for three yard land and a half	1	8	0
3 Moses Stanton six yard land	2	8	0
4 Edward Basely for four yard land and a half	1	14	0
5 William Clarke four yard land	1	12	0
6 Samuel Capell three yard land	1	4	0
7 Humphrey Barker four yard land	1	12	0
8 Mr Maynard three yard land	1	4	0

[5] Of all the curates from the time of Easton (1631–35) to Smith (1795–1833), Tayler was the only one compelled to subscribe before the bishop. From Smith on all duly subscribed, see NRO, H. Isham Longden MS 59 no. 2.

	£	s	d
9 John Ward two yard land		16	0
10 Thomas Saunders for three yard land and a half	1	8	0
11 London Clarke four yard land and half	1	16	0
12 Richard Eaton two yard land and quarter		18	0
13 John Healey one yard land and half		12	0
14 William Smith three yard land and half	1	8	0
15 Samuel Tibbs three yard land and half	1	8	0
16 Edward Scotton three yard land and half	1	8	0

[p. 8]   In all £22 10s

What follows was taken up in kind without any agreement

1 From John Stanton		16	0
2 From James Smith		5	0
3 From Richard Slough		18	0
4 From Thomas Jefferys	1	1	0
5 From Edward Jeffreys		15	0
6 From Thomas Wright		3	10

In all £8 7s 6d

Humphry Barkers orchard	10	0
Mr Wares orchard (*now a close AD 1758*)[6]	4	0
Mr Sawbridges orchard (*afterwards Floyds now Hickmans and Mr Fraunces's, 1772*)	2	6
William Rogers orchard (*now William Caporn's orchard and pays the same, 1772*)	1	6
Sampson Moors orchard (*now Bull's orchard*)	1	0
Staverton windmill	4	0
Welton water mill	3	0
Rate tythe from Burrough Hill	14	0
For eight pigs	16	0
For William Pains garden *now called Burdock Close*	5	0
For Widow Lyddals garden	6	0

In all £3 7s 0d

January 1700

For two marriages abroad	5	0
For two christenings at home	2	0
For Joseph Bryans funeral sermon and buriall	11	0
Consulting the register twice	1	0
For William Hobs burial and funeral sermon	1	0
Four churchings at the ordinary rate	1	8
Two burials at the ordinary rate	10	10

In all £1 12s 6d

[p. 9]   February 1700

A Pew entered into the register	2	6
Churching Mrs Jephcote	2	0
Christening William Kents child	1	6

[6] The words in italics here and below were added at a later date, and are in the hand of the Rev James Affleck.

	£	s	d
Christening Mr Coddal (a Troopers) child		2	0
Christening at home		1	0
Registering an Anabaptist's child			6
A burial with prayers in the Church		1	0
Three burials at the ordinary rate		1	3
Five churchings at the ordinary rate		2	1
Two certificates for burying in Woollen[7]			8

14s 6d

March 1700

	£	s	d
A funeral sermon for Mrs Barker		16	0
Transcribing the sermon for her Husband		10	9
A pair of Cordovant gloves at her funeral		2	0
Christening William Wells his child		2	0
Christening Sam Smiths child		2	6
A Christening at home		1	0
Registring two Anabaptists children		2	0
Four certificates for burying in Woollen		1	4
Burying John Jops a stranger		2	6
A buryall with prayers in the Church		1	0
A strangers marriage with license		5	0
William Muddimans marriage with banns		3	0
Five burialls at the ordinary rate		2	1

£2 14s 8d

April 1700

	£	s	d
Christening Lieutenant Leeds child		10	0
A Strangers marriage with license		5	0
For a marriage abroad		2	6
Consulting the register once			6
A burial with prayers in the church		1	0
Five burials at the ordinary rate		2	1
Three churchings at the ordinary rate		1	3
Three certificates for burying in Woollen		1	0

£1 3s 4d

[p. 10]   May 1700

	£	s	d
Christening Mr Rawlins child		5	0
Christening Edward Daniels child		2	0
Two burials with prayers in the church		2	0
A strangers marriage with license		5	0
A marriage with banns		2	6
Five burials at the ordinary rate		2	1
Three churching at the ordinary rate		1	3
Three certificates for burying in Woollen		1	0

[7] Under the Act of 1678 which stipulated that 'no corpse of any person (except those who shall die of the plague), shall be buried ... in any stuff or thing, other than what is made of sheep's wool only'. W. E. Tate, *The Parish Chest* 1946, pp. 66-7. It was a protectionist measure.

	£	s	d
Consulting the register once			6
Mrs Winstons quarterly present		7	6

£1 8s 10d

June 1700

A marriage with license		5	0
A christening at home		1	0
Three certificates for burying in Woollen		1	0
A stranger's marriage with license		5	0
Five churchings at the ordinary rate		2	1
Three burials at the ordinary rate		1	3
Consulting the register twice		1	0

16s 4d

July 1700

Mrs Winstons quarterly present		7	6
Christening Mr Obediah Smiths child		2	6
Christening Mr George Checkly's child		2	6
Christening Mr Edward Spencers child		2	6
Two other christenings at home		2	0
A marriage with Banns		2	6
Two burials with prayers in the church		2	0
Four burials at the ordinary rate		1	8
Two churching at the ordinary rate		10	0

£1 4s 0d

August 1700

A christening at home		1	0
Consulting the register			6
For two marriages abroad		5	0
[p. 11] A funeral sermon and burial of Mary Powel		11	0
A burial with prayers in the church		1	0
Six churchings at the ordinary rate		2	6
Five burials at the ordinary rate		2	1

£1 4s 1d

A pair of white gloves

September 1700

Mrs Clarks funeral Sermon and burial	1	1	6
Opening a grave for her in the Chancel		10	0
A pair of Shammy gloves and hatband		6	0
John Woddalls marriage with banns		2	6
A christening at home		1	0
Four churchings at ordinary rate		1	8
Michael Stantons funeral sermon		15	0
Six burials with prayers in the church		6	0
Two pair of Cordovant gloves at two funerals		4	0

	£	s	d
Eleven burials at the ordinary rate		4	0
Churching Mrs Prior		10	0

£4 2s 3d

October 1700

	£	s	d
Mrs Winstons quarterly present		7	6
Christening Mr Matthew Arnolds child		2	6
Churching Mrs Knight of London		10	0
William Rose his funeral sermon & burial		11	0
John Ganderton's marriage abroad		2	6
Thomas Jacksons marriage		3	6
A Mortuary for William Rose		10	0
Consulting the register			6
Two certificates for burying in woollen			8
A Funeral Sermon for Mrs Elizabeth Stanton		11	0
Three churchings at the ordinary rate		1	3
Four Burials at the ordinary rate		1	8
Four Burials with prayers in the church		4	0
A pair of Cordovant gloves		1	8

£3 6s 6d

[p. 12]   November 1700

	£	s	d
An Inauguration Sermon for Mr Bayliff [8]		10	0
Christening William Currals child		2	0
Christening John Kinnings child		1	0
Christening Mr Rootes child		5	0
A mortuary (at the lowest rate) for John Wood		3	4
Patrick Ravens marriage abroad		2	6
Christening Mr Kenwricks child		5	0
Two burials with prayers in the church		2	0
Six burials at the ordinary rate		2	6
Three churchings		1	3

£1 14s 7d

December 1700

	£	s	d
Registring an Anabaptist's child			6
Consulting the register twice		1	0
Samuel Edwards his marriage		2	6
Seven churchings		2	11
Two burials with prayers		2	0
Four burials at ordinary rate		1	8
Henry Cooks marriage with banns		2	6
Mrs Winstons quarterly present		7	6

£1 0s 7d

	£	s	d
1 For obventions	21	1	6
2 For Tythes of all sorts	34	6	6
3 For quarterly collections	28	0	0
4 For benefactions	26	0	0
5 Bakehouse and churchyard	3	0	0
[6] Offerings and eggs at Easter	5	0	0

[8] The Bailiff was the equivalent of a Mayor in the borough of Daventry.

The summ of this years dues to me was about £117. I paid out of this for the hire of a house and for the Window Dutys £7 10s.

[p. 13] The writing that follows is a copy [*made by William Tayler*] of a letter from Mr Allestree to Mr Farmer who is now Tenant to the College:
Good Sir,
     Having this letter from the Treasurer of Christ Church to convey to your hands, I think fit to accompany it with another of my own, as I suppose, upon the same subject

1. You may please to take notice that by your cousin Farmer's will, the whole estate which he left you here, is chargeable with the payment of £30 per annum to the Bayliff and the 3 Senior Burgesses of Daventry. So that it is a great mistake to think that the said sum is to be raised out of the great Tythes of the parish. If therefore you are considered in the bulk of your estate, and lessened in your taxes a great deal more than the sum comes to (as I believe it will be found so) then you've no reason to make any abatement out of my share of the payment, or deduct any taxes at all for it.
2. But if I am chargeable by the Act[9] with taxes, it must be in proportion to what your whole estate is assessed at (as the very words of the Statute run, page 14.). And this will require a strict review of all the particulars of your assessment, which I am confident you would no more desire to have the discovery laid before the Commissioners, than I desire to have the trouble and necessity of making it, for it lies solely in your breast to adjust and settle this proportion. But you demand the whole extent and rigour of the law from me. And though there are allowances made to you, yet you still require the payment of the utmost farthing from me.
3. You may find, Sir, that the sum of £30 is but one gift, and made payable to Mr Bayliff & the 3 Senior Burgesses in trust, and they and not you are appointed by the will to make a division of it to the parties concerned in the [p. 14] legacy. And I am to have expressly, by the very words of the will, two parts in three upon the division of what shall be delivered to Mr Bayliff.
4. You may see by the testator's vehement urging and entreating the College of Christ Church to be assisting his charitable intention, and conjuring[10] them by some binding clause in future leases to secure the said sum, that it was his design the payment should be perpetual at the usual times, without any abatement. For by constituting them the judges in the matter, he took the most effectual method that could be devised for settling the sum entirely and without deduction upon the legatees, because they had formerly allowed (antecedently to his bene-faction) the same annuall stipend to the minister here. And as they could not be supposed in times of the highest taxing even to abate any part of your allowance, so they must be supposed to provide for the security of the same in the like manner without charges at all upon it, because they themselves and not the minister here have received the whole benefit of your cousins bounty to this place. But I know not what they have determined in this matter, it is a secret reserved for your

---

[9] Probably that of 1705, 'An Act for granting an Aid to her Majesty by a Land Tax, to be raised in the year 1706 ...', 4 Anne cap. 11. At this time land taxes were levied every year or so to pay for the wars against France and Spain.
[10] i.e. appealing solemnly or earnestly to.

discovery at the opening of this letter enclosed.[11] I have fairly laid things before you and if the subject matter do not give offence I am sure my words cannot. If I might have redress willingly from you, I would make it my endeavours to assist and ease you doubly in all future taxes, because some of the Commissioners in this district are my particular friends, and will give a kind ear to any representation that I shall make to them.

I am your must humble servant, and I hope shall be your most obliged one too,

Charles Allestree. December 18 1706.

[*Upon which Tayler comments*] By the foregoing letter it plainly appears that the College did formerly allow £20 per annum to their minister here, and that they withdrew this allowance upon Mr Farmers benefaction. So that the College received the benefit of the benefaction entirely, and not the minister, which surely should induce them to favour the minister here as much as possible.

[*Upon which Alexander Akehurst later commented*] This postscript is contradicted now at College. It is said there that Mr Farmer's benefaction was at first contested by his representative, that the Chapter allowed an equivalent from the time it ought to have taken place 'till it actually did take place, and that then, and only then, the College withdrew their payment.

A. A. May 18 1787.

[p. 15] An Abstract of Mr Richard Farmers Will [*of 1662*] containing only the 2 paragraphs that relate to his double benefaction both to the Poor and Minister of Daventry Page 4, line 1.

I do will and devise, that my said executors shall immediately from and after her decease pay unto the Bayliff of Daventry and his successors, and the 3 senior Burgesses of the said Corporation, the sum of thirty pounds by the year, and that they pay the same at the 2 usual Feasts in the Year, (that is to say) at the Feast of the Annunciation of the Blessed Virgin Mary, and at the Feast of St Michael the Archangel, by even and equal portions. The first payment thereof to begin at either of the said Feasts, which of them shall first happen after the decease of my said Aunt, Mrs Dorothy Norwood, to the use and in trust, that they, the said Bayliff and Burgesses, shall within one week after they shall receive the same, pay two parts thereof to the Minister of Daventry and his successors, and distribute the other third part thereof among the poor of the parish of Daventry aforesaid according to their discretions.

[Page 5, line 31 and so over the leaf] And I do will and devise that the aforesaid conveyance and assignment so to be made by my executors as aforesaid, be made in trust for the payment of the said thirty pounds per annum to the said Bayliff of Daventry and the 3 senior Burgesses in manner as aforesaid. And likewise I instruct and desire the said College of Christ Church in Oxford to be as much as may be assisting to this my charitable intention, and that when ever they shall make any new lease or grant of the said premises, or of any part thereof, they would by way of trust or

---

[11] What the college wrote to Farmer has not survived. It seems that in this, the last of his struggles over his curacy, Allestree prevailed.

condition, or by some other way, as they shall think most apt and convenient, provide that the said premises, and every part thereof, may be charged with the payment of the said £30 per annum to the said Bayliff and 3 senior Burgesses of the said Corporation to the uses and trusts aforesaid. And I do likewise desire and intreat the said Bayliff and Burgesses and the rest of the parishioners of Daventry that they will not at any time hereafter shorten their allowance to the poor, by reason of this my gift, but rather enlarge the same, so that what I do hereby give may be according as I intended it, for the poor and not the rich.[12]

[MEMORANDA OF THE REVD. WILLIAM TAYLER, CURATE 1716 TO 1750]

[p. 13] So far Mr Allestree, to whom I think myself much obliged for the foregoing writing. After him succeeded Mr Hartman[13] who left only some confused papers which were of no use.

July the 8th 1716 I took possession of this cure. I have now been possessed of it above six years, whereby I am the better able to give a particular account of the profits of it, and to make some reflexions and observations as I hope may be for the benefit of my successor for whose use I intend them, and I desire that this book may be given to him.

[p. 16] I have had several contests with the College Tenant about his encroachments upon my churchyard[14]

1st. With relation to the passage from the town to the Upper Park.

2ndly. In relation to the cottages that bound my churchyard on the south side.

In February 1723 when the Tenant was treating with the College about renewing his lease, I went up to Oxford and complained to the Chapter and obtained this grant from them viz.

1st. That the Tenant by his lease should be obliged to remove the nuisances or muckhills in the churchyard that lie before the doors of the said cottages, and not to suffer the like again.

2ly. Not to make any more door places to open into the churchyard.

3ly. Not to use any cart-way or horse-way, by or through the churchyard great gates to the little tenements in the churchyard, or to or from the Upper Park, only for carriages of materials for necessary repair of the tenements.

4ly. Not to hinder any burial in any part of the churchyard.

At this time I also petitioned the Chapter that a house might be settled upon the minister here for ever instead of the £6 per annum, which the Tenant pays. But here I failed, though the College own many houses in this town. They did talk of repairing the old Abbey and fixing that upon the minister, but that also dropped. However, I prevailed so far as to get an addition to the salary, and the tenant is now obliged to pay £8 per annum, whereas he paid but £6 before for the hire of the ministers house.

[p. 17] Burrough Hill tythe I take in kind, but though there is 500 sheep kept upon the Hill yet I usually have no more than 9 or 10 lambs and about

---

[12] For Farmer's will, see PCC 17 Juxon. Mrs Norwood died in 1694: NRO, 3rd ser. wills, S. 75.
[13] Curate of Daventry 1707 to 1716.
[14] See above p. 72.

3 or 4 Tod of Wool. The reason is because those that are not wintered there do pay only a rate tythe *viz.* half penny per sheep, and also because the several proprietors have some odd number which pay not tythe in kind.

They reckon those only to be wintered upon the hill are found there on New Years day, at which time the sheppard brings me an account of them.

I have often been defrauded by some in driving their sheep off and on a little before or after this time.

It has been my usual way to collect those tythes I receive in kind by my clerk and to give 10s per annum for his pains.

At every sacrament I divide the money given with the churchwardens and bestow it as I think fit among the poor. I generally keep some in my hands to give the poor families in distress, and always every sacrament I give out of the money to my clerk and sexton 5s to each. By this means the poor do the better esteem me, and my clerk and sexton are the more ready to assist me. But I always set down in writing what I thus receive and pay to avoid clamours.

[p. 52]   12 September 1720

Memorandum I have agreed with all the farmers in my parish to pay me according to the Rate of eight shillings for a yard land for their Small Tythes, John Clarke only is excused half a yard land in Daintree field.

The following writing is an exact account of what each man pays or ought to pay every half year *viz.* at May day and at Martlemas

	£	s	d
John Clarke	1	14	0
John Thomline	1	5	0
Samuel Mobs	1	3	0
Mrs Masters	1	1	0
Henry Dolton		19	0
Moses Stanton *x read Mrs Stanton*[15]		18	0
John Stanton		18	0
Thomas Pinkard		18	0
Samuel Pinkard		14	0
Nicholas Stanton		14	0
Richard Marriot		14	0
John Pen		13	0
Mrs Basely		12	0
Thomas Easom *x read Mr Parsons*		12	0
Richard Easton		9	6
Thomas Wright *x*		9	0
John Parrot		8	0
John Healy		6	0
Roger Moor *x read Linnel*		12	0
Samuel Tibs		4	0
Matthew Lucas *x read John Dunkley*		4	0
Thomas Saunders		14	0
	16	1	6

[15] The annotations to this list are in Tayler's hand and were added at a later date.

1722

The following alterations are made in the above mentioned payment. *Viz.*
Mrs Masters quitts 2 Yard land to M. Stanton & John Parrot and Thomas
Wright all his to John Pen so that the payment stands thus, besides N.
Stanton has quitted all to John Stanton who pays

	£1	12s	0d
Mrs Masters		13	0
Mrs Stanton	1	2	0
John Parrot		12	0
John Pen	1	2	0

[p. 53]   Stated Dues 1720

Mr Farmers benefaction	20	0	0
For the hire of a house	6	0	0
Contributions by subscription paid quarterly	24	19	0
Easter offerings	8	11	9
The church yard	2	0	0
The malt mill	1	0	0
Keeping the register		6	8
	62	17	5
For Burrough Hill tythe	2	12	0
Tythe eggs on Good Friday		5	5
Surplice fees	6	4	0
Tythe compounded	29	7	2
Sum Total	101	6	0

tythe of Orchards omitted 19s.
[so sum total is] one hundred two pounds and five shillings

1721

Mr Farmers benefaction	20	0	0
For the hire of my house	6	0	0
The church yard	2	0	0
The malt mill	1	0	0
Keeping the register		6	8
Tythe compounded	32	3	0
Contributions	24	10	6
Easter offerings	10	19	0
Surplice fees	8	4	6
Tythe for orchards and gardens		19	0
Burrough Hill tythe	3	0	0
	109	2	8

Memorandum there is half a years payment due for the malt mill [*crossed out*] [p. 54] Received 1722

	£	s	d
Tythe eggs on Good Friday in money		6	0
In eggs	120		
Easter offerings	10	3	4
Cowes and calves		6	0
April dues and surplice fees		15	1
May dues and surplice fees	2	9	3
June dues and surplice fees		8	6
July dues and surplice fees		6	7
August dues and surplice fees		2	11
September dues and surplice fees		5	0
October dues and surplice fees		7	11
November dues and surplice fees		17	2
December dues and surplice fees	3	0	6
January dues and surplice fees		9	8
February dues and surplice fees		5	8
March dues and surplice fees		4	8
Received as above for 1722	20	8	3
Due for my benefaction	20	0	0
for Tythe compounded	32	3	0
for contributions	24	10	0
for hire of a house	6	0	0
The church yard	2	0	0
The malt mill	1	0	0
Orchards and gardens		19	0
Keeping the register		6	8
Burrow Hill tythe compounded at	3	0	0
Licenses	4	8	0
	114	14	11

Memorandum I have received nothing for the malt mill this year [*crossed out*]

[p. 55] Received 1722

	£	s	d
For Midsummer subscription	6	6	6
For Mr Farmers benefaction 1 half year	10	0	0
For hire of a house	3	0	0
1 Payment of Tythe compounded due on May 3	16	1	6
1 Payment of Tythe compounded due at Martlemas	16	1	6
Michelmas subscription	6	6	6
Christmas subscription	6	6	6
Lady days subscription	6	6	6
For the hire of a house	3	0	0
Keeping the register		6	8
Church yard in my own hands	2	0	0
Easter offerings, tythe eggs cowes and calves	10	15	4
Surplice fees	9	12	11
Orchards and gardens		19	0

	£	s	d
Burrow hill Tythe computed	3	0	0
Licenses	4	8	0
The malt mill not paid	1	0	0
Benefaction last half year not paid X	10	0	0
	114	10	11

Memorandum I have received nothing for the malt mill this year. [*Crossed through*]

[p. 56]   1723

Tythe eggs and Easter offerings	10	15	2
Benefaction	20	0	0
For a house hire	6	0	0
Tythe compounded at 8s per yard land	32	3	0
Contributions	24	15	0
Church yard	2	0	0
Malt mill	1	0	0
Orchards etc		19	0
Keeping the register		6	8
Burrough Hill Tythe computed	4	12	7
Surplice fees	10	5	4
Licenses	3	8	0
This years profits	116	4	9

Memorandum I have received nothing for the malt mill this year. Memorandum I have received £2 of Mr Townsend for the malt mill so that there is only one half year behind due last Lady day.
[*dated and signed*] 30 June 1724. William Tayler

1724

Tythe eggs and Easter offerings	9	15	0
Benefaction	20	0	0
For the hire of an house	8	0	0
Tythe by 8s per yard land	32	3	0
Contributions	24	14	6
Surplice fees	7	19	7
Church yard	2	0	0
Malt mill	1	0	0
Orchards and gardens	1	3	0
Keeping the register		6	8
Licenses	3	2	0
Burrough hill tythe	3	18	0
This years profits	114	1	9

Memorandum I have received nothing for the malt hill this year.

[p. 57]   8 May 1725

The half years payment for my small Tythes at 8s per yard land stands thus with the farmers

Yard lands[16]	Names	Money £	s	d
$8\frac{1}{2}$	John Clarke	1	14	0
8	John Stanton X	1	12	0
$6\frac{1}{1}$	Tomeline	1	5	0
6	Mrs Stanton	1	4	0
$5\frac{1}{1}$	Mobs	1	3	0
$5\frac{3}{2}$	John Pen X	1	2	0
$4\frac{1}{1}$	Dalton		19	0
$4\frac{3}{2}$	Thomas Pinkard X		18	0
$3\frac{1}{2}$	Saunders		14	0
$3\frac{1}{2}$	Marriot X		14	0
$3\frac{1}{2}$	S Pinkard X		14	0
$3\frac{1}{1}$	Mrs Masters		13	0
3	Parsons		12	0
3	Basely		12	0
3	Parrot X		12	0
3	Linnel X		12	0
2	Easton X		9	6
1	Tibs X		4	0
1	Dunkley		4	0
1	Ashburn		4	0
[Total = 78][17]		16	1	6

[p. 22] The following Writing is a Copy of Mr Farrers Will [of 1729] so far as it relates to the Minister and Schoolmaster of Daventry[18]

Item, I do hereby direct and my will is that my executors do and shall, within one year after my decease, pay to the said Benjamin Fraunces, Edward Sawbridge, John Watters, and Thomas Smith, and to Thomas Matthew of Daventry aforesaid gentlemen (trustees for the purpous hereafter mentioned) and to the survivors of them four hundred pounds. And which said four hundred pounds I do give to my same trustees and to the survivors or survivor of them, upon trust that the same trustees and the survivors and survivor of them, and the heirs of such survivor, do and shall, with the said £400, as soon as may be after the receipt thereof, purchase lands of inheritance (but not houses), which lands I direct shall be conveyed to my same trustees and the survivors of them, their heirs and assignes upon trust nevertheless, that the said trustees their heirs and assignes do and shall at all times for ever hereafter, pay and apply the rents

[16] The notation below of yard lands with fractions is somewhat idiosyncratic. With yard lands given in whole numbers, or with halves there is no difficulty. However, where ¼ or ⅓ is used it seems that the denominator refers to shillings. Thus, at a compounded tithe of 8s. per yard land per year, 6¼ amounts to £1 5s., i.e. one half of 6 at 8s. plus 1s.: 5½ for a half year amounts to £1 3s., i.e. half of 5 at 8s. plus 3s. It seems possible the extra shillings were arrears.

[17] In medieval Daventry there were 88 yard lands of arable: 44 in Drayton and 44 in Daventry, ex. info. A. E. Brown. The Drayton enclosure Act of 1751 says that there were then 43½ yard lands in the field. See 25 Geo. 111 c. 25. Perhaps the list of farmers given here is not complete, or some yard lands were exonerated from small tithes.

[18] See above p. 67.

and profitts of the lands so to be purchased as aforesaid, to the school master of Daventry aforesaid for the time being (if he shall be in holy orders) upon this express condition nevertheless, that he shall at all times for ever hereafter read morning and evening prayer every Sunday in the year (though an holy day) and also read every morning of every Monday, Tuesday, Thursday and Satturday in the year, (unless which Mondays, Tuesdays, Thursdays and Satturdays shall be holidays) Morning prayer in the Parish Church of Daventry aforesaid, according to the usage of the Church of England prescribed by the book of Common prayer. And upon this express condition also that such school master do and shall at all times for ever hereafter assist the minister of Daventry aforesaid for the time being [p. 23] in administering the holy sacrament as often and when ever such minister shall think fitt to administer the same. But if there shall be no such school master or such school master shall not be in holy orders, or shall neglect or refuse to read prayers, or assist in administering the holy sacrament as aforesaid, then my will is that my same trustees, their heirs and assignes during such time as there shall be no such schoolmaster, or such school master shall not be in holy orders, or shall refuse or neglect to read prayers, or assist in administering the holy Sacrament as aforesaid, find and provide such person or persons as they shall think fit to read prayers and assist in administering the holy sacrament as aforesaid. And that they do during such time as such person or persons shall read prayers and assist in administering the holy sacrament as aforesaid pay him or them the whole rents and profits of the said lands so to be purchased as aforesaid my will being that prayers be read in the Church of Daventry in manner aforesaid. The minister of Daventry aforesaid reading prayers there on all holidays, Wednesdays and Fridays, and that the salary of the school master be augmented there, and the minister there be in some measure eased, in regard I think the duty of the place is too hard for one minister to perform without prejudice to his health. And I do direct after my executor shall have paid the said £400 to my said trustees that they do put out the same at interest, till they can purchase land as aforesaid. And that they in the mean time pay the interest thereof as the same shall be from time to time received for the same uses as I have directed the profits of the land [p. 25] to be purchased as aforesaid to be applied. And my will is that when any 3 at most of my said trustees, or any other person or person hereafter to be elected trustee or trustees for the purposes aforesaid shall dye, that then the survivors of them shall elect more persons inhabitants of the parish of Daventry aforesaid within six months after such deaths to be trustees in the room of them so dying as they shall think fitt, so as such trustees do never exceed 5 in number, and so as such person or persons so to be elected trustee or trustees, for 3 years next before his or their election hath or have received the holy Sacrament according to the usage of the Church of England, and during that time hath or have not been at any other place or meeting of besides the Church of England. And my will is that such person or persons so to be elected trustee or trustees shall have the same powers to all intents and purposes whatsoever as the trustees appointed by this my last will. And which said hereditaments so to be purchased as aforesaid shall, within six months after such election of the new trustees, be by the surviving trustees granted to the use of the surviving trustees and of such persons so to be elected trustees and of their heirs and assignes for the purposes, and upon the trusts aforesaid. The charges whereof I direct shall be paid out of the profits of the land so to be purchased as aforesaid. And I do hereby direct that the said trustees, their heirs and assignes shall be paid out of the profits of the same lands all their costs and charges which they shall lay out, expend or be put unto about the trust aforesaid. And that they shall not be charged or chargeable for any more money than what every one shall severally and actually receive. Nor shall be answerable or chargeable the one for the other, nor for the acts, deeds, receipts [p. 24] defaults or miscarriages of the other, nor shall be liable to make good and pay any money that shall be by them, or any of them, be lost, or put out at interest on any insufficient or deficient security or securities.

[p. 18]   An Account of the Profits of my Curacy of Daventry as they were paid in the year 1729

	£	s	d
Tythe eggs on good friday		3	8
Easter offerings	8	13	0
Tythes compounded at 8s per yard land	32	3	0
Paid by Mr Farmer	28	0	0
Bake house and malt mill	1	0	0
Orchards and gardens	3	8	6
Burrow hill tythe	3	0	0
Contributions about	16	0	0
Surplice fees about	5	0	0
Keeping the register		6	8
Church yard	2	0	0
	99	14	10

[p. 58]   18 November 1730

The half years payment of my small tythes compounded at 8s per yard land stands thus

Yard lands	Names	Sum		
11	John Clarke	2	4	0
8	John Stanton	1	12	0
4	Mr Tomeline		16	0
2½	Mrs Tomeline		9	0
5½[19]	Mobs	1	3	0
5½	John Pen	1	2	0
4½	Henry Dalton		19	0
4½	Smith		18	0
4½	Widow Marriot		18	0
4	Seawell		16	0
3½	Samuel Pinkard		14	0
3¼	Mrs Masters		13	0
3	Mrs Stanton		12	0
3	Mr Parsons		12	0
3	Mrs Basely		12	0
3	Linnel		12	0

[19] See footnote 16.

		£	s	d
$2\frac{1}{1}$	Richard Easton		9	6
2	Samuel Tibs		8	0
2	John Adams		8	0
1	John Dunkly		4	0
		16	2	6

[p. 60]   1731

Tythe compounded stands as last year, except Widow Marriot who has
parted with 1 yard land to Mr Hindes

in all	32	5	0
120 Eggs on good Friday in money		6	0
Easter offerings	8	3	6
Orchards and gardens	2	15	0
Burrough hill tythe besides stock	3	14	4
Michaelmas Mr Farmers money	14	0	0
Subscriptions	15	15	6
Surplice fees	9	2	8
Lady Day Mr Farmers money	14	0	0
Church yard	2	0	0
Malt mill not paid	1	0	0
Licenses	4	5	0
Keeping the register		6	8
	107	13	8

[p. 62]   Easter Book 1732

Tythe eggs on Good Friday in eggs – 100, in money   6   0
Easter Offerings received

of Mr Walford, Bayliff	1	0	Mr Watters	1	0
Mr Beeten, Justice	1	0	Mr Thompson	0	3
Mr Matthew	2	6	Mr S Wyment	2	6
Mr Wyment senior	2	6	Mr Rawlins junior	1	0
Mr Rawlins senior	1	0	Mr James Smith	2	6
Mr Sawbridge	2	6	Mr Armstead[20]	1	0
Mr Harris	1	0			

Dr Adams	1	3	0	Mr Hiccock	1	0
Mrs Barker		5	0	Mr Rose	1	0
Mr John Sawbridge		2	6	Mr Philips	1	0
Mr John Smith		2	6	Mr John Adams	1	0
Mr Thomas Smith		2	0	Mr Westley	1	0
Mr Attwell		2	6	Mr Such	1	0
Mr Nathaniel Root		5	0	Mr Jephcote	1	0
Dr Theed		2	6	Mr Cue	1	0
Mr R Edwards		2	6	Mr Johnson	1	0
Mr Wildgoose		1	0	Mr Henry Smith	1	0
Mr Calcut		1	0	Mr Web senior[21]	1	0
					4	6	3

[20] These names seem to be those of the Bailiff and Burgesses, the equivalent of an
aldermanic bench in Daventry.
[21] The rest of the corporation of Daventry, principally the Twenty men of the Commonalty.

[p. 64]   Easter Offerings 1732

	£	s	d		£	s	d
Lady Combes and				Mrs Lucas		1	0
sister	1	1	0	Mrs Nicholson		1	0
Mrs Yalden		11	6	Mrs Obediah Smith		1	0
Mrs Bankes		5	0	Mrs Basset		1	0
Mrs Fraunces		5	0	Mrs Avery		1	0
Mrs Sparkes		2	6	Mrs Clarke senior		1	0
Mrs Theed		2	6	Mrs B Arnold		1	0
Mrs Bromwich etc		2	6	Mrs Crofts[22]		0	6
Kitty Marriot		2	6				
Mrs Brooks		2	0				
Mr Reynolds		1	6	Robert Chambers			6
William Brown		1	0	Mrs Durrard			6
Mr Wilson		1	0	Charles Easton			6
William Capon		1	0	William Darnell			6
Widow Leddy		1	0	Matthew Bryan			6
William Welch		1	0	Thomas Saunders			6
Mr Shen			9	Mr Parsons			6
Purcel			9	Mrs Stanton			6
Thomas Barnel			6	Mr Web junior			6
William Butcher			9	Mr Neal			6
					3	16	3

[p. 6]   Easter Offerings 1732

		John Clarke	9	Richard Easton	3
		William Easton	8	John Clarke junior	3
		Mrs Wright	6	Nathaniel Glen	3
		John Watkin	6	William Watts senior	3
		G Leeson	6	Thomas Evans	3
		Joseph Charlesworth	6	G Checkly	3
		Mr Prat	6	Miles Stonely	3
		Mr Thomas Wyment	6	M Rogers	3
		Widow Robinson	6	Shaw	3
		Mr Avery	10	Ryland	3
		George Warnham	3	Robert Claridge	3
		William Kennerd	3	John Easton	3
		Thomas Turner	3	William Peters	3
		S Tibs	3	Thomas Church	3
		Richard Smith	3	John Pen	3
		H Dalton	3	Seawell	3
		John Stanton	3	Richard Bunting	3
		Christopher Smith	3	Thomas Marriot	3
		John Clarke senior	3	Thomas Brooks	3
		Mrs Marriot	3		13 0

[22] This appears to be a list of the substantial widows of the borough.

[p. 68]   Easter Offerings 1732

	£	s	d		£	s	d
Thomas Rogers			6	John Luck			3
Thomas Makepeace			6	John Keck			3
S Pinkard			3	John Evans			3
Thomas Parrot			3	Henry Brooks			3
John Parrot			3	Nathaniel Buswell			3
Richard Marriot			3	Matthew Lucas			3
Anthony Adams			3	John Cole			3
William Watts junior			3	Wright			3
Widow Easton			3	Edward Earle			3
John Thompson			3	Thomas Crofts			3
John Thornton			3	Hindes			3
Widow Kenning			3	John Falkner			3
Widow Gudgings			3	Peter Newberry			3
S Cole			3	Thomas Ganderton			3
Thomas Wynns			3	Bentom			3
Thomas Pratt			3	Richard Linnel			3
John Warren			3	Widow Judkins			3
John Town			3	Richard Lee			3
Samuel Edwards			3	Robert Litchfield			3
Moses Bates			3	Evans senior			3
						10	6

[p. 70]   Easter Offerings 1732

	d		d
Edward Wawman	3	Thomas Ward	3
Richard Moor	3	William Mobs	3
John Jeffery	3	T Tomeline	3
John Barrett	3	Mrs Tomeline	3
John Wright	3	Joseph Simons	3
Widow Lockington	3	Joseph Walker	3
John Powel	3	Benjamin Noon	3
Little	3	Thomas Wilson	3
James Bawcut	3	John Falkner junior	3
Rapier	3	John Bass	3
John Bromwich	3	John Simcock	3
Valentine Clare	3	John Wyment	3
Benjamin Pratt	3	S Chater	3
William Sladin	3	H Barker	3
John Wood	3	Briggs	3
Thomas Smith	3	Richard Burnham	3
John Stockin	3	Richard Thornton	3
William Freeman	3	John Faux	3
William Mole	3	Edward Robinson	3
Richard Grub	3	John Leet	3
			10 0

[p. 69]   Easter Offerings 1732

	£	s	d		£	s	d
John Boughton			3	John Dunkley			3
William Dunkley			3	Mr Chaly			3
				brought over		11	0
						10	6
						13	0
					3	16	3
					4	6	3
				total	9	17	0

[p. 71] In the Year 1737 we were much visited with the the Small Pox and I received three mortuaries

For Joseph Clarke shepperd	10	0
For Mr Walford a Burgess	10	0
For Mrs Cole	10	0

[p. 19] An account of the half yearly payment of the farmers as it stood May 1738

John Clarke senior	1	14	0
John Stanton	1	12	0
Mobbs	1	3	0
Henry Dalton		19	0
Thomas Radbourne		18	0
John Leagh		18	0
Thomas Rawbone		18	0
John Adams		16	0
Thomas Thomeline		16	0
Joseph Bull		16	0
Samuel Pinkard		14	0
John Clarke junior		14	0
John Parsons		17	0
Robert Arnold		13	0
Mrs Tomeline		13	0
Anthony Wrighton		12	0
Widow Shaw		12	0
Charles Easton		9	6
Richard Penn		8	0
	16	2	6

[p. 72] I reckoned with my curate Mr Thomas Collis 2nd July 1743. I allow him the quarterly subscriptions, surplice fees and tythes of orchards and gardens, and Easter dues and paid him nineteen shillings and four pence over and above to make up his years salary to Midsummer.[23]

[Signed] William Tayler.

[23] Despite this memorandum it remains unclear what Collis's salary amounted to; it seems about £40.

[MEMORANDA OF THE REV JAMES AFFLECK, CURATE 1750 TO 1784]

[p. 26] Composition for small Tythes at 8s per Yard land 1751. And the names of the compounders

	£	s	d
Thomas Clark	1	16	0
Edward Clark	1	4	0
Thomas Rawbone	2	12	0
Mrs Stanton	2	8	0
William Bull	2	8	0
J. Wodhams	2	4	0
J. Leigh	1	8	0
Thomas Radbourne	1	16	0
Thomas Tomlin	3	4	0
Robert Andrew	1	8	0
J. Clark	1	8	0
Thomas Stephens	2	2	0
Anthony Wrighton	3	14	0
Mrs Bliss		19	0
John Stanton		16	0
Mrs Parsons	1	16	0
Widow Wood	1	2	0
	£32	5	0

[p. 27]   An account of the profits of my curacy of Daventry
1751

Tythe eggs		3	9
Easter offerings	8	4	0
Compounded tythes	32	5	0
Paid by Lord Winchilsea[24]	28	0	0
Part of the benefaction for reading prayers	6	0	0
Afternoon sermon[25]	27	4	0
Garden tythes and malt mill	2	17	0
Burrough hill tythe	2	2	0
Mortuaries	2	0	0
Other surplice fees about	9	10	0
Churchyard	1	0	0
Keeping the register		6	8
	£119	12	5

[Signed] James Affleck

[24] The new tenant of Christ Church. Until the enclosure of Daventry, when new arrangements were made, the terms of Farmer's bequest of 1662 were written into the tenants' leases by the college.
[25] Instituted that year.

An account of the Profits arising from the Cure of Daventry within the
Year 1752

Tythe eggs		3	11
Pigs		15	0
Afternoon sermon	26	16	0
Compounded Tythes	32	5	0
Lord Winchilsea's payment	28	0	0
Benefaction for reading prayers	6	0	0
Mortuaries and other surplice fees	13	0	0
Easter offerings	7	16	0
Garden Tythes and mill Tythes	2	18	6
Borough hill	2	2	0
Keeping the register		6	8
	120	3	9

The church this year being rebuilding I had no advantage from the church
yard.[26]

[p. 28] The following is a Particular of the Plot in Drayton Field awarded
by Act of Parliament to the Minister of Daventry in lieu of Small tythes.

Quantity			Price	Value		
Acres	Roods	Poles	Per Annum	£	s	d
0	3	9	£17		13	$8\frac{1}{4}$
10	2	0	14	7	6	$11\frac{3}{4}$
18	2	19	12	11	3	$4\frac{3}{4}$
14	1	10	10	7	3	$1\frac{1}{2}$
6	2	17	8	2	12	10
50	3	15		29	0	$0\frac{1}{4}$

[p. 29]   Memorandum April 26 1753

The Award for the inclosing the hamlet of Drayton in the parish of
Daventry (in persuance of an Act of Parliament obtained for that purpose)
was signed by the commissioners this day. In which there is allotted to the
vicar or curate of Daventry for ever in lieu of the sum of £16 16s 0d (the
annual consideration received by my predecessors and myself for the small
Tythes) a plot of ground lying in the North East Field containing 50 acres
3 roods 15 perches adjuged by the commissioners according to an agreement made between me and the several Impropriators to be of the yearly
value of £29 0s 0d. The fence round the said plot already made and must
be maintained by the adjoining proprietors as the commissioners have
allotted. Note, there is the following clause in the Act of Parliament which
is also recited in the Award.

And it is further enacted and declared that the [p. 31] said plot and
parcel of ground herein before directed and appointed to be assigned, laid
out and allotted unto the said James Affleck and his Successors, shall be in
lieu and full satisfaction and compensation of and for all manner of Tythes
whatsoever, growing arising and belonging to the said James Affleck, and

[26] See above p. 70.

his successors, Ministers, Vicars, or Curates, from and out of all and every the messuages, lands and grounds in the said Hamlet of Drayton, and also from and out of such gardens and orchards as shall hereafter be made in or upon any part of the said common fields and common grounds so intended to be inclosed, and of and for all other dues and duties what-soever, due or payable to the said James Affleck and his successors from and out of the Hamlet of Drayton, save and except oblations, mortuaries and Easter offerings, and except garden-pence, tythes, and dues for the gardens and orchards now made or hereafter to be made in or upon the present Homesteads or the present Home-closes in Drayton aforesaid, and except also marriage, churching and burial fees, and other surplice fees [p. 33] all which shall remain due and payable to the said James Affleck and his successors in the same manner as before the passing of this Act.[27]

Memorandum

The above plot was let (as soon as inclosed) to William Wood of Drayton for a term of three years upon a grazing rent of £37 10s per annum by me James Affleck.

1756 February 28

William Wood's term being expired at Lady-day, and it appearing that he had suffered by his bargain, I was obliged to lower the rent 1s per acre, and we agreed this day that he should hold the above Ground for three years more at £35 per annum.

[p. 34] Since the foregoing Alteration the Composition for the remaining small tythes is as follows.

	£	s	d
Anthony Wrighton	2	8	0
Mrs Tomalin	3	4	0
J Wodhams	2	4	0
William Bull	1	12	0
Thomas Clark	1	16	0
Thomas Rawbone		16	0
John Stanton		16	0
Nicholas Stanton		16	0
Mr Parsons		12	0
Edward Clark		8	0
Mr Andrew		8	0
William Wood		6	0
Mrs Bliss		2	0
John Clark		6	0
	15	14	0

Copied by Alexander Akehurst [after 1784] from a Memorandum of the Revd James Affleck

[27] 25 Geo 111 cap 25, pp. 4–5.

[p. 35]   An Account of the Profits of the Curacy of Daventry for the
Yeare 1754 [*also in Akehurst's hand*]

	£	s	d
Eggs		3	7
Easter offerings	8	2	7½
Compounded Tythes	15	14	0
Part of the land in Drayton Field	37	10	0
Lord Winchilsea's payment	28	0	0
Afternoon sermon	25	16	0
Share of the benefaction for reading prayers	6	0	0
Garden tythes and malt mill	3	3	6
Borough hill tythe	2	2	0
Mortuaries	2	0	0
Pigs and surplice fees	12	13	0
Signing the register		6	8
	141	11	9½

N.B. The surplice fees are heightened about £4 yearly by my acting as a
surrogate and granting licences.
Copied by Alexander Akehurst from a Memorandum of the Revd James
Affleck
  [*A further memorandum added later by A A*] The Garden tythes *now* are
£1 11s 6d—the malt mill £1 1s 0d and Bland's water mill 2s—making in all
£2 14s 6d I cannot account for the difference between this sum, and that
stated above by Mr Affleck.
  Query. Has any Garden Tythe been lost by neglecting to claim it—or
has any ground, that was then garden, been converted into pasture, and so
been exonerated from this payment?
  Mr Affleck either did not receive the two Visitation fees (10s) or has
forgot to state them or else includes them in the surplice fees. The rent of
the church yard is omitted in the above account. Perhaps the church yard
was not let this year, as the church was unfinish'd.

[p. 65]   Form of a Certificate of the Publication of the Banns of a
marriage

This is to certify that Banns of Marriage between John Smith, of the Parish
of Girton, in the County of Cambridge, and Mary Hughes, of the Parish
of Hartford, in the county of Hunts, were publish'd in the Parish Church
of Girton aforesaid, on the three Sundays underwritten; that is to say, on
Sunday eighteenth day of March, twenty fifth of March, first of April and
no impediment alleged. As witness my Hand,
                                            Jeremiah Pemberton, Minister.
Girton April 1st, 1776
To the Minister of the Parish of Hartford, Hunts

[p. 67]   Certificate of a Person's having been buried in Woollen

[Town of Cambridge] I Elizabeth Mortimer, of the Parish of St Michael,
in the town of Cambridge, make oath, that the body of Henry Godfrey, of
the Parish of All Saints, was not wrapped, or put in any sheet, shirt, shift,
or coffin, lined, faced, or covered with any materials contrary to the late

Act of Parliament; nor with any thing but what was made of sheep's wool only, As witness my hand,

Elizabeth Mortimer

Sworn in the said town, this 1st day of January, 1776, before me W. Weales, Mayor.

[MEMORANDA OF THE REV ALEXANDER AKEHURST, CURATE 1784 TO 1789]

[p. 4] Alexander Akehurst held this curacy from the 21st of November 1784 to the 5th of January 1789. He had no license from the Bishop, nor was he required to take one out, though he had attended an Episcopal Visitation at Towcestre.

[*Signed*] Alexander Akehurst

The usual fee for exhibiting letters of Orders at the Visitation was paid by Alexander Akehurst. (On the subject of License, see Grey's *System of Ecclesiastical Law*, pages 227-312, 2nd edition, 1732.)

[p. 74]   The names of the Compounders February 21st 1786

	£	s	d
Mr Thomas Adams	3	4	0
Mr Wodhams	2	4	0
Mr Thomas Clarke	1	16	0
Mr Tomelin	1	12	0
Mr Richard Rawbone	1	12	0
Mr Richard Stanton	1	12	0
Mr Bull		16	0
Mr Masters		16	0
Mr Roberts (Whelton)		12	0
Mrs Andrew		8	0
Mr Clarke		8	0
Mr John Adams		6	0
Mr Blount		2	6
	15	15	0

[p. 73] Deduct for Land tax ½ year	1	2	0
—for collecting eggs		1	0
—for ditto at the *Horse Shoe*		11	0
—for ditto garden tithes		1	0
—for land tax ½ year	1	2	0
—for collecting the churching fees		10	0
—for collecting the subscription		10	0
Necessary outgoings	3	17	0

[p. 75]   Garden tythes

John Lyddal—home garden	6	0
Ditto—Tippet's near Daventry Wood	2	6
Mr Wilcox	1	0

Ditto—Bumbler's Close	6	0
Mrs Peter Freeman	5	0
Mrs Cadman	2	6
Mrs Watkins	2	6
Mr Hickman of Newnham	2	6
Mrs Marshall	2	0
Capron's Orchard	1	6
	1 11	6

The Clerk has one shilling for collecting these tythes; and receives for Bland's mill 2s.

In the account which Mr Slade gave me of these tythes there was a garden mentioned, called the *Green Garden*, charg'd 6d, which never paid me anything. [*Initialled*] A. A.
This composition is due at Michaelmas and is usually collected the first week in the January following

[p. 2]   [*Memoranda about alms boxes and charity money*]

December 9th 1786. On this day the alms-boxes in the church were opened. Present A. Akehurst, Peter Freeman, churchwarden, and William Simcock, clerk and Thomas Crofts, whitesmith. There were found in them the sum of three shillings and ninepence half-penny, which Mr Freeman had to distribute to the poor. They had not been opened for seven years.

January 7th 1788. On this day the alms-boxes were opened and five farthings found in them, which were suffer'd to remain. Present A. Akehurst, John Morgan, church warden.

December 4th 1788. On this day the alms-boxes were opened and five pence and one farthing found in them, which are suffered to remain. Present William Simcock, clerk, Richard Morton, sexton.
    Alexander Akehurst. Witness William Simcock, Richard Morton.

[p. 3] January 6th 1786. Distributed the sacrament money this time in small sums to each person by the hands of William Simcock, clerk.

at sundry times	£3	11s	0d
January 6th	£11	1s	10d
	£14	12s	10d

January 3rd 1787. Disposed of it this time in bread and meat by the hands of Mr P Freeman, churchwarden and William Simcock, clerk.

at sundry times	£5	2s	4d
January 3rd	£9	2s	6d
	£14	4s	10d

January 17th 1788. Disposed of it this time in bread only, on the last two Tuesdays in 1787. This appeared the most eligible plan. The bakers which I employed were Mrs Birch, Mrs Rogers, James Brompton, Thomas Butlin, Richard Cole, William Cole, and William Bucknell, who delivered

89 sixpenny loaves every Tuesday for five weeks to 89 persons, who, upon strict enquiry seem'd to be most in want.

at sundry times	£2	16s	0d
January 17th	£10	19s	0d
	£13	15s	0d

January 12th 1789. Disposed of it this time in bread the last week in 1788 to 85 persons and the first two weeks in 1789 to 113 persons each time

85 loaves	£2	2s	6d
113 ditto	£2	16s	6d
113 ditto	£2	16s	6d
Given at sundry times	£4	13s	9d
	£12	9s	3d

[*Signed*] Alexander Akehurst

[Leaved between pp 40 and 41]
    Mr Akehurst's Account of the Curacy of Daventry [*c. 1787*][28]

Dear Sir

I was sorry to find that it was inconvenient to you to visit Daventry at present, as a personal inspection would have been much more satisfactory to you than any account that I can send by letter. However all that I can do is much at your service. First, let me thank you for inquiring about the letter (which arrived last Sunday) and for examining Hownam's account. I think that I paid for disputations in Michaelmas Quarter, which made me wonder at another sconce coming so soon.[29] Will you be so obliging as to make a memorandum just to ask about this when you return to Oxford?

The Dean asked me, when last in College, to send some account of this Curacy to be inserted into the Students' book. I do not think the whole of what follows fit for that purpose, but I leave it to your discretion to make any extracts from it, which may appear to you of any moment.

	£	s	d
1. A house, with something more than an acre of land, worth about twenty guineas per annum	21	0	0
2. Almost fifty acres of land, let for fifty pounds per annum. No deduction, except £2 4s for land tax. This rent will perhaps bear some advance.	47	16	0
3. Farmer's benefaction	20	0	0
4. Good Friday sermon	1	0	0
5. Tithe of Borough Hill, two guineas, out of which the shepherd has one shilling	2	1	0

This payment remains as I found it; but as it has varied some years back from this sum up to £4 12 7 I apprehend more might be made of it than is now paid.

---

[28] The heading is in the handwriting of the Rev Dr Samuel Smith, Akehurst's successor but one.

[29] In eighteenth-century Oxford 'disputations' were still much the same series of syllogistic exercises which had constituted the 'examination system' of the medieval university. John Fell was responsible for many reforms of the old 'schools' system during his Vice-Chancellorship, but it was only in the nineteenth century that the modern examination system was introduced, and that remained largely an oral system until well into the century, 'Sconcing' in Christ Church was a system of fines payable to the censors. From the context they seem to be a penalty for non-payment of fees in this particular case. *Ex inf.* Mrs June Wells, Assistant Archivist, Christ Church, Oxford.

6. Composition for small tithes at 8 shillings per yard land—fifteen guineas—at pay day the farmers are treated so that I put down only fifteen pounds. **15 0 0**
An old book in my possession speaks of this composition as commencing about the beginning of this century, and gives an account of eight sums (amounting to £8 7s 6d) which arose from articles *'taken in kind, without any agreement'*. If the tithe of hay does not belong to the curate, this composition is even then too low. If it does (and this is the opinion of the best informed people in the Parish) it is much below par   **106 17 0**

[verso]

7. Composition for two mills   **1 3 0**
8. Garden tithes one pound eleven shillings and sixpence. One shilling for collecting   **1 10 6**
This tithe is paid only for ten gardens. Why *they* pay so little, and why *others* pay nothing, might be worth enquiring.
9. Rent of church yard one pound eleven shillings and sixpence. This let for forty shillings half a century ago, and then was not so large by a third   **1 11 6**
10. Two visitation fees, five shillings each, and signing the register, six shillings and eightpence   **16 8**
These are certain payments

111 18s 8d

11. A pew in the church, and three sittings. These would let, as I am informed, for two pounds
12. Share of a benefaction for reading prayers   **6 0 0**
13. Afternoon sermon, twenty pounds, deduct for collecting 10s   **19 10 0**

	1785			1787			medium		
	£	s	d	£	s	d	£	s	d
14. Eggs		6	1½		6	11		6	6
15. Easter offerings	4	16	7	5	3	0	4	19	11
16. Sacramental wine	3	8	0	4	14	0	4	1	0
17. Silk and gloves	2	11	0	3	10	0	3	0	6
18. Pigs		7	6		12	0		9	9
19. Mortuaries	2	0	0	3	10	0	2	15	0
20. Vaults, gravestones etc	4	6	10	5	6	10	4	16	10
21. Extracts from register		3	0	1	2	0		12	6
22. Weddings	9	8	0		14	0	7	12	6
23. Banns		13	0		14	0		13	6
24. Funerals	5	9	3	6	3	0	5	16	0
25. Churchings	2	0	0	1	14	6	1	17	3
							174	9	11

There is a sacrament the first Sunday in every month, as well as on Christmas day, Easter Day, and Whitsunday, and the Sundays that immediately follow these great Festivals. The duty on Sunday:- Prayers and Sermon in the Morning, except on sacrament days and then the sermon is omitted; and prayers and sermon in the afternoon, but this sermon is paid for by the parish. Prayers in the morning on Litany and Saints Days, and in the afternoon on Saturday preceding a sacrament. Prayers morning and afternoon in Passion Week.

In 1788 there were thirteen weddings, seventy nine baptisms, sixty seven funerals. The calls for private baptism, and visiting the sick are frequent.

[p. 20]   [*Memoranda about a parsonage house*]

After many fruitless applications had been made at College for a house at Daventry for the curate, the Dean and Chapter at length determined to comply with so reasonable a request, and in the spring of 1787 Mr Pywell (the Steward of Mr Hatton, the College Lessee) gave John Ward notice to quit his house and the land belonging to it on the North side of the High Street at Lady Day 1788. He accordingly surrendered the premises to me on the 7th of April in that year. William Cole, builder, had contracted with the College to take down the old house, and to build a new one according to a plan delivered, and to complete by the 31st of October in the same year. His terms were to have the materials of the Old House, and £350. To raise this sum the Chapter cut down wood on their estates at Thrupp to the amount of about £250.

(This house is not yet finished January 5th 1789. A. A.)

I was in Oxford about the time the house ought to have been finished, according to the contract, and represented to the Dean and some of the Canons the unfinished state of the house and the insolent treatment I had at various times received from the contractor. In consequence of my representations a builder was sent from Oxford to view what had been done: and Mr Cole, in conversation with him, expressed his opinion that all might be completed by St Thomas 1788, and he solemnly promised him that by that day all should be done. (The house is still unfinished this 6th day of March 1789. A. A.)

[p. 76]   Compounders February 21 1789

	£	s	d
Mr John Adams's executors	1	0	0
Mr Thomas Adams	3	12	0
Mr Blount		2	6
Mr Clarke (Judkins)	1	16	0
Mr Bull		16	0
Mr Masters		16	0
Mr John Rawbone malt mill	1	1	0
Mr Richard Rawbone	1	12	0
Mr Robert Rawbone of Welton		12	6
Mr Stanton	1	12	0
Mr Tomalin	1	12	0
Mr Wodhams	2	4	0
	16	16	0

A. A. has received to the 5th of January 1789.

This Composition is usually allowed to be a quarter of a year in arrears. The Curate meets the compounders at a public house and pays for the entertainment, about 1s each person. A. A.

[p. 49] [*Memorandum of an undated lease of the glebe in Drayton.*]

	£	s	d
Rent of 32 acres 2 first years at 2.2.0 per acre	134	8	0
Rent of ditto 3rd and 4th at 1.11.0	103	4	0
Rent of 19 acres for 4 years at £1.0.0. per acre	76	0	0
Rent of all the land for the last 4 years at 52.0.0 per annum	210	0	0
	523	12	0

A lease for eight years. Four crops of corn, one Summer's fallow, then laid down with oats or barley. No straw or hay to be carried off the premises. Five pounds off the rent for the first four years to be allowed the tenant towards neccessary buildings, the rent to be paid quarterly.

[MEMORANDA OF THE REV SAMUEL HUMFREYS, CURATE 1789 TO 1794]

1794

[p. 36] In the month of October this year I began to drain the two lesser portions of the glebe and finished on Christmas Eve. The work was very tedious and heavy, and much impeded by the frequent falling in of the ground. In the upper part of the portion farthest from the high road the drain is very deep, extending nearly the breadth of the close in a right line of ten foot depth. The same depth is continued in a rectangular line from the transverse section down the middle of the close for several yards. In consideration of the expense which hereby I incured I advanced the rent of the whole to £60 Mr Richard Staunton being still my tenant

	£	s	d
Paid Mr Hart the contractor of the work	6	16	6
For stones	2	11	6
For labor	18	18	0
	28	6	0

[*Signed*] Samuel Humfreys, minister.

[p. 47]   [*Undated memorandum of an 8 year lease of the Drayton Estate*]

	£	s	d
Rent of 32 acres. 2 first years at £2 2s per acre	134	8	0
Rent of ditto 3rd and 4th at £1 11s 6d	103	4	0
Rent of 19 acres for 4 years at £1 per acre	76	0	0
Rent of all the land for the last 4 years at £52 10s per annum	210	0	0
	533	12	0

A lease for 8 years. 4 crops of corn. One Summer's fallow. Then laid down with oats or barley. No straw or hay to be carried off the premises. 5 pounds of the rent for the first 4 years to be allowed the tenant towards necessary buildings. The rent to be paid quarterly. The expense of the lease to be joint.

[Interleaved between pp. 44 and 45]
1794 An Estate at Drayton belonging to the Revd Mr Humfries[30]

	£	s	d
The condition the land is now in for a farmer to rent is not worth more than 20s. per acre, but being near Daventry probable it may be let for 24s per ditto, and if 51 acres, at the last price, will bring	61	4	0

But suppose the largest close was divided into four, and the other two were drained (expence of which will be about £66) it's likely the land would let to different tenants (such as inn holders or trader people) for the prices at under (viz.) 20

	£	s	d
acres at 35s	35	0	0
And suppose 20 acres at 31s	31	0	0
The remaining 11 acres at 20s	15	8	0
brings a yearly rent of	£81	8	0

For laying out the above sum brings an income of twenty pound a year and being in small lots will be much better managed

[MEMORANDA OF THE REV SAMUEL SMITH, CURATE 1795 TO 1833]

[p. 1] This book was given into my hands in the mutilated state in which it now is, and I have reason to believe that it was so mutilated by Mr Akehurst

[*Signed*] Samuel Smith

[leaved between pp. 44 and 45]
[*A letter to the Rev Mr Smith*]

Searazens Head Inn Daventry
August 17 1795

Dear Sir,
    Being employed by the Company of Proprietors of the Grand Junction Canal to value and agree for the purchase of such lands as they want for the said Canal, its towing paths etc. etc., I hereby inform you that a plan of an intended reservoir in the parish of Daventry was put into my hands yesterday evening in which said plan I perceive there is about an acre of your land which is intended to be purchased by the said Company, and as I am going to view the said reservoir this morning should be obliged if you can make it convenient to appoint some person to attend me on your behalf to settle the price of the same.

I am, Revd Sir,
Your most Obedient Servant,
William Collisson.

Am going to look over some damage in Daventry Field this morning after which I shall look over the said reservoir, the principal part of which belongs to Mr Richard Stanton of this town and the Revd Mr Rose, and I understand Mr Penn of Norton is to meet me on their behalf.

---

[30] In the hand of Samuel Smith, who succeeded Humfreys in 1795.

[p. 37]   1796

On the third day of December this year the Company of Proprietors of the Grand Junction Canal paid me the sum of £87 1s 3d as the price of 1a 0r 39p of land taken from the estate in the Hamlet of Drayton belonging to the curate of this parish, for the purpose of making (with other lands) a reservoir for the use of their canal.

Samuel Smith, curate of Daventry.

Of this was paid to Mr Penn for his valuation of the land £1 1s.

1800

The land tax charged on the house and premises belonging to the curate of this parish, and the estate at Drayton was redeemed and the said premises and estate and all the profits of the curacy were exonerated from the land tax charged thereon, from the 25th of December 1799. The sum paid upon this account was £70 5s to be deducted from the above £87 1s 3d.

[p. 51]   [*Memorandum about a monument in the church*]

Mrs Clay returns compliments to Mr Smith, and she wishes the monument to be placed in that part of the church which Coxe[31] who made it thinks best calculated for it. The inscription Mrs C supposes Mr S can have no objection, as 'tis only a plain one, but if Mr S will take the trouble to call on Coxe he may see the monument as it is there finished.

Any fee Mr S requires, Mrs C will not scruple to pay

Daventry January 5th 1803

The fee was five guineas, with four of which I bought the Communion table book. S. S.

[p. 38]   1818

On the first of January this year the plot of ground in Drayton belonging to this curacy containing 49a. 2r. 16p. or thereabouts was lett to Mr William Wilkins for the term of twelve years at a rent of £84 per annum if I so long continue curate of Daventry. And I hereby recommend to my successor if I should cease to be curate within that time to continue Mr Wilkins tenant on the above terms which I believe to be fair and equitable, he having been at considerable expense in improving the land by banking and draining it

[*Signed*] Samuel Smith, Curate of Daventry

[31] Samuel Cox the younger of Northampton and Daventry, 1767–1851, one of a dynasty of Northampton stone masons: R. Gunnis, *Dictionary of British Sculptors 1660–1851*, rev. edn (1968), p. 115.

3

NASSABURGH MILITIA LISTS 1762

EDITED BY

VICTOR A. HATLEY AND
BRIAN G. STATHAM

INTRODUCTION

Series of militia lists for Northamptonshire exist for 1762, 1771, 1774, 1777, 1781 and 1786; there are also lists, some of them undated, for many parishes from the period of the Revolutionary and Napoleonic Wars with France. The series for 1777 was reproduced by the Society in 1973, but unfortunately the lists from Nassaburgh Hundred (Soke of Peterborough) for that date are missing. The only surviving lists from Nassaburgh are those for 1762, and these are reproduced in this volume.[1]

The English militia was a force raised for the defence of the realm against invasion or rebellion. It was not liable for service overseas. Under the Militia Act of 1662 all owners of property were charged with the provision of horses, arms and men, in accordance with the value of their property, but this liability was removed from the individual to the parish by the Militia Act of 1757, itself modified by a series of subsequent acts. Each county had now to contribute a quota of men for militia service, 640 in the case of Northamptonshire; elsewhere the quota ranged from 1,600 each for Devonshire and Middlesex, 1,240 for the West Riding of Yorkshire and 1,200 for Lincolnshire, down to 240 each for Monmouth and Westmorland, and only 120 for tiny Rutland. Responsibility for raising the militia and providing it with officers lay with the lord lieutenant of each county and his deputies.

Liability to serve in the militia rested on able-bodied men between the ages of 18 and 45 years. However, peers of the realm, clergymen (including dissenting ministers), articled clerks, apprentices, seamen and parish constables were exempt. So also were poor men who had three or more children born in wedlock, a number which was reduced to one in 1786. Service in the militia was for three years and determined by ballot, but any man whose name was drawn had the right to provide a substitute. In the opinion of the late Professor J. R. Western, the most thorough historian of the eighteenth century militia, few men whose names were drawn in the ballot actually served in person.[2] Those who could afford to pay for a substitute usually did so; moreover, statutory powers were available for parishes to provide volunteers in place of drawn men (who, if they served, might have dependents, the responsibility for whose subsistence would fall on the parish itself), and groups of individuals would sometimes raise by mutual subscription a sum of money sufficient to indemnify any of their number who were unfortunate in the ballot. Indeed, it was stated with pride in 1763 that most of the men who were serving in the newly-enrolled Northamptonshire militia regiment 'were Substitutes and procured by

---

[1] The 1762 militia lists for Nassaburgh Hundred are held in the Northamptonshire Record Office (hereafter cited as NRO). Vol. XXV in the main series of the Northamptonshire Record Society's publications was edited by Victor A. Hatley under the title of *Northamptonshire Militia Lists, 1777* (hereafter cited as *Militia Lists, 1777*). The introduction to Vol. XXV has been drawn upon extensively for the introduction to this section of Vol. XXXII.
[2] J. R. Western, *The English Militia in the Eighteenth Century* (1965), chapter x ('Raising the Men'), esp. pp. 255-64.

Messrs. Cook and Co. [agents at Northampton], whose Engagements in this Concern have been everywhere punctually perform'd, and given the highest Satisfaction to the Deputy-Lieutenants and Justices, as well as the County in General'.[3]

Militia men were trained and exercised for a period of 28 days annually, when they were billeted in public houses and paid according to a scale laid down by Act of Parliament. For the Northamptonshire militia this usually took place at Northampton during May and June, although in 1771, because of an epidemic of smallpox in Northampton, the men were divided between two detachments, one stationed at Wellingborough and the other at Kettering.[4] It was customary for the regiment to celebrate the birthday of King George III, which occurred on 4 June, by assembling in Northampton's spacious market square and firing three volleys of blanks. It was not embodied for prolonged service away from the county until April 1778, a month after the declaration of a state of war between Great Britain and France, the latter having given material assistance to the thirteen North American colonies which had proclaimed their independence in July 1776.

The militia in each county was raised by the lord lieutenant and his deputies who, to quote Professor Western, 'used what was in effect the ordinary machinery of local government. The general and subdivisional meetings which directed the work were simply military equivalents of the quarter and petty or local sessions respectively; justices of the peace could attend and do most of the business provided at least one deputy lieutenant was present.'[5] The subdivisions consisted, in practice, of two or more of the hundreds, rapes, lathes or wapentakes into which the county was divided. (Nassaburgh in 1762 was an exceptional case, for, alone among the twenty hundreds of Northamptonshire, it formed a subdivision by itself.) At the first general meeting, held on the last Tuesday in May or October, a precept was issued to the chief constable of each hundred requiring him to produce 'fair and true lists, in writing, of the names of all the men usually and at that time dwelling within their respective parishes, tythings and places, between the ages of eighteen and forty-five years, distinguishing their respective ranks and occupations ... and which of the persons so returned labour under any infirmities, incapacitating them from serving as militia men...'.[6] This task was performed at parish level by the parish constable or, in some cases, the constable for a certain district within the parish. Before being delivered to the first subdivisional meeting, each list had to be displayed on the door of the parish church for the space of a Sunday morning. Any person who considered that his name ought not to be included, or that the name of some other person had been wrongly omitted, was entitled to appeal at his subdivisional meeting. The lists, amended where necessary, were now passed to a second general meeting at which was determined the number of men to be raised from each hundred. At the same time copies were made of the lists, and these were sent to second subdivisional meetings which determined the number of men to be raised from each parish or group of parishes. The next step was third subdivisional meetings at which the balloting took place; these

---

[3] *Northamptonshire Mercury*, 28 Feb. 1763. See also 27 Dec. 1762 and 7 Feb. 1763.
[4] C. A. Markham, *The History of the Northamptonshire & Rutland Militia* (1924), p. 13. This is the standard work on the Northamptonshire militia.
[5] Western, p. 247.
[6] 2 Geo. III, cap. 20, s. 42 ('An Act to explain, amend, and reduce into one Act of Parliament, the several Laws, now in being, relating to the Raising and Training the Militia, within that part of Great Britain called England'). The Militia Act of 1762.

meetings had to be held within three weeks of the second subdivisional meetings. The men whose names were drawn in the ballot were informed of this by their parish constable, and they, or their substitutes, were required to attend fourth subdivisional meetings at which they took an oath of allegiance to the king, and their names were entered on the militia roll. This roll was returned to the county authorities, and at a third general meeting the militia was organised into regiments, battalions and companies, according to the number of men available. The minimum size of a militia regiment was eight companies of 60 to 80 men each, from which it may easily be calculated that Northamptonshire was able to provide one regiment for the defence of Great Britain in time of war. The colonel commanding the Northamptonshire militia raised in 1762-3 was Henry Yelverton, third Earl of Sussex, who lived at Easton Maudit, and who held the appointment from 10 January 1763 to 18 March 1784.

Nassaburgh Hundred contained the only parish in Northamptonshire where the men were not liable for service in the county militia. This was St Martin's, Stamford Baron, which lies immediately to the south of Stamford (Lincolnshire), and includes Burghley Park, seat of the Marquess (Earl to 1801) of Exeter. For militia purposes, St Martin's was reckoned a part of Lincolnshire, although its hamlet of Wothorpe, which is situated west of the turnpike road which bisected the parish (the modern A1), was included with Northamptonshire.

The names of 1,286 men appear on the Nassaburgh Hundred militia lists for 1762. Table 1 shows the number of men recorded in each parish (including the City of Peterborough), and in each hamlet which, having its own constable, submitted a separate list to the militia authorities. These hamlets have been grouped with their mother parishes (e.g. the hamlet of Deeping Gate which lies within the parish of Maxey), although the figures for the latter do not include the figures for the hamlets. Also included, for the sake of comparison, are figures for the population of each parish and hamlet as recorded at the first decennial census in 1801, together with the male population, all ages, in 1801.

The Nassaburgh lists of 1762 are similar in form and layout to those of 1777 for the rest of the county. The names of farmers and other substantial inhabitants usually appear first, followed by men of lesser status and ending with labourers and servants. The last-mentioned were mostly 'servants in husbandry', young unmarried men (with perhaps a few older bachelors) boarding with the farmers who employed them.[7] Some of the lists carry details of the subdivisional meeting at which appeals against militia liability could be made. For Nassaburgh in 1762 this meeting was held on 11 December at the Angel Inn in Peterborough, the landlord of which was William Elger, an enterprising man who, among other things, was concerned during the 1760s with the provision of stage coaches between Peterborough and London.[8] His name appears on the main list for Peterborough, although his occupation is, for some reason, omitted.

The standard of literacy displayed on the lists varies, as would be expected, from high to very low. Quite the worst list, taken all in all, is from Castor, which is extremely difficult to transcribe. Sometimes the list was made out by somebody other than the constable, as at Deeping Gate, Dogsthorpe, Southorpe, Werrington and Wittering where the respective

---

[7] For the boarding of agricultural servants by their employers, see James Donaldson, *General View of the Agriculture of the County of Northampton* (1794), pp. 44-6.
[8] E.g., *Cambridge Chronicle*, 10 Mar. and 13 Oct. 1764.

Table 1: Men recorded in each parish and hamlet, Nassaburgh Hundred, 1762; all inhabitants and all male inhabitants, 1801.

	a		b	c
Bainton	26		134	65
Barnack	43 ⎫			
Pilsgate	16 ⎬ 74		613	322
Southorpe	15 ⎭			
Borough Fen	25		116	58
Castor	66		475	251
Ailsworth	28		154	83
Sutton	13		110	59
Upton	5		76	37
Etton & Woodcroft	16		95	49
Eye	85		501	256
Glinton	50		314	159
Helpston	48		301	155
Marholm	14		109	56
Maxey	52		313	152
Deeping Gate	18		143	64
Northborough	32		192	89
Paston	10		55	26
Gunthorpe	5		30	15
Walton	20		126	64
Werrington	64		372	191
Peakirk	24		132	64
Peterborough and hamlets				
St John the Baptist	397 ⎫	410	3,449	1,571
Minister Close Precincts	13 ⎭			
Dogsthorpe	39		276	146
Eastfield & Newark	30		160	78
Longthorpe	34		190	94
Stamford Baron, St Martin's				
Wothorpe	2		34	17
Thornhaugh	23		214	118
Ufford	20		120	63
Ashton	16		96	55
Wansford	16		148	76
Wittering	21		194	85
	1,286		9,242	4,518

Key
a = Number of names on militia list, 1762
b = All inhabitants, 1801
c = All male inhabitants, 1801

constables attested themselves by making a mark. The spelling of very many names is erratic and on some lists may reflect local pronounciation, e.g. John Yorwoord (Yarwood) at Bainton, Samuel Skirrit (Skerrit) at Maxey, and Edwood Tarpe (Edward Thorpe) at Wittering. A few have been mangled beyond recognition. Would it be possible to guess that William Hislbeu (Sutton) was really William Aislaby? The correct form of his surname (hopefully) is known only because somebody crossed out Hislbeu and above it wrote Aislaby. Several of the lists carry entries which have been similarly corrected (e.g. Ailsworth, Peterborough, Wittering), although sometimes the amendment is itself inaccurate, by later standards at least. Occasionally a name is cancelled, only to be written in again in identical form.

Undoubtedly the constable at Longthorpe had problems in compiling his list, because two of the men refused to tell him their names. 'Farmer Hichcock's man' may have known that he was not liable for militia service, for he was exempted at the subdivisional meeting. 'Thomas', servant to Sir John Bernard, who lived at Thorpe Hall, was liable, and his surname was later discovered and duly inserted on the list. So was the surname of 'Mathey y groom' at Castor. However, at Maxey 'William Addye's servant' and 'William Addye's shepard' remained anonymous. At Glinton there is the intriguing mystery of the three 'runaways'. Had they absconded from the parish in an attempt to avoid being included on the militia list? Or, hired for annual service, were they the victims of an intolerable master? Or even, having engaged in criminal activities, were they now fleeing from well-merited legal retribution? It is unlikely now that the truth will ever be known about them. Samuel Nuton (Newton), 'labourer in prison' from Dogsthorpe, was obviously non-resident when the list there was compiled; nevertheless, the constable included his name perhaps because the other men in Dogsthorpe would have felt aggrieved if 'Nuton' had been omitted from the ballot.

Not all the men listed by the constables of Nassaburgh were physically or mentally fit enough to bear the strain of marching and drilling, let alone the rigours of camp life if the militia had been embodied for prolonged service. Since each list was displayed on the door of the parish church, it may seem rather hard that Robert Collinge, who kept a public house at Marholm, should have been described as having 'remarkable crooked legs', especially as this unflattering disability did not earn him an exemption. The most frequent cause for exemption was, of course, being a 'poor man' with more than two legitimate children. Numerically, the family record in the Nassaburgh lists was held by two labourers at Pilsgate, each of whom had nine offspring. Exemption was also granted to men who had already been ballotted in another county. Again at Pilsgate, two of Lord Exeter's servants had 'stood the ballot' for Lincolnshire, probably with the men from Stamford Baron, while another of his servants had been ballotted for Rutland. At Gunthorpe, John Jarvis, a cobbler (presumably he repaired shoes but did not make them), was already enrolled as a militia man for the Isle of Ely; no doubt he was serving as a substitute.

Out of 1,286 men recorded on the militia lists for Nassaburgh Hundred in 1762, the occupation or status (i.e. esquire or gentleman) of 1,224 was recorded by the parish constables. Table 2a sets out the occupations of the men in all the parishes and hamlets except the City of Peterborough, and Table 2b the occupations of the men in the City of Peterborough. It should be borne in mind that the constables were not working to an agreed schedule of occupations, and that in the construction of these tables, and in Tables 3a and 3b which follow them, like has sometimes been grouped with like in order to produce a single entry. In Table 3a, for example, 'servant' includes farm servants, farmers' men and the gentleman's servant, and 'farmer' includes graziers and husbandmen.

Analysis of the militia lists shows that most of the men aged between 18 and 45 years in Nassaburgh Hundred in 1762 were employed either in agriculture or in occupations readily associated with an agricultural community. Nowhere, not even in the City of Peterborough, did any form of

Table 2a: Occupations in Nassaburgh Hundred (excepting the City of Peterborough)

'Ailding' (?)	1	Grazier & farmer	1	Shoemaker	19
Alehouse keeper	1	Grocer	1	Surgeon	1
Alekeeper	1	Hemp-dresser	4	Tailor	20
Baker	11	Herdsman	2	Turnpike/turnpike	
Blacksmith/		Horse rider	1	gatekeeper	2
smith	12	Husbandman	4	Victualler	7
Blacksmith &		Innholder	1	Waterman	1
freeborough	1	Joiner	1	Weaver	14
Boatman	1	Keeper	1	Wheeler/	
Butcher	17	Knacker	1	wheelwright	5
Cadger	1	Labourer	287	Woodman	1
Carpenter	29	Labourer &			835
Clothier	1	freeborough	1		
Cobbler	2	Labourer in			
Cooper	2	prison	1		
Cottager &		Maltster	2		
labourer	1	Mason	14	Apprentice	4
Drover	1	Merchant	1	Churchwarden	1
Farm servant	2	Miller	11	Clerk of the	
Farmer	88	Miller's man	1	parish	2
Farmer &		Park-keeper	1	Headborough	1
headborough	1	Plough-wright	1	Lodger	1
Farmer's man	2	Printer	1	No details given	
Farmer's son	10	Sand man	1	or illegible	18
Gardener	10	Schoolmaster	2	Poor man	10
Gelder	2	Servant	182	Poor man &	
Gentleman's		Servant &		parish clerk	1
servant	1	shepherd	1	Runaway (sic)	3
Grazier	7	Shepherd	36		876

manufacturing industry exist comparable with industry established in certain other parts of Northamptonshire, such as shoemaking at Northampton and Wellingborough, or weaving at Kettering, Rothwell and district.[9] By the early years of the eighteenth century the extensive Fenland in eastern Nassaburgh had been drained and was being used for pasturage and crop production.[10] Open field agriculture was practised throughout the hundred; except for an Act of 1749 confirming an agreement to enclose an unspecified acreage of land in Wittering, the parliamentary enclosure movement did not get under way in Nassaburgh until the 1790s.[11]

A few comments on several of the occupation categories on the lists are offered below.

Shepherds: there was a higher proportion of shepherds recorded in rural Nassaburgh in 1762 than in any of the nineteen other hundreds of Northamptonshire in 1777. 4.4 per cent of the men appearing on lists other than those for the City of Peterborough were shepherds (1762) compared with

[9] *Militia Lists, 1777*, pp. xviii, 106-10, 170-2; Victor A. Hatley and Joseph Rajczonek, *Shoemakers in Northamptonshire, 1762-1911* (Northampton, 1971), pp. 15-17.
[10] John Morton, *The Natural History of Northamptonshire* (1712), pp. 8-9.
[11] W. E. Tate and M. E. Turner, *A Domesday of English Enclosure Acts and Awards* (1978), pp. 191-9. John Barrell, *The Idea of Landscape and the Sense of Place, 1730-1840* (1972), contains a challenging appendix, 'John Clare and the enclosure of Helpston', which throws much light on the effect of enclosure on Helpston and several other villages in Nassaburgh.

Table 2b: Occupations in the City of Peterborough

Apothecary	1	Gentleman	6	Saddler	3
Attorney	2	Glazier	3	Schoolmaster	1
Baker	11	Glover	7	Servant	25
Barber	10	Grocer	6	Shoemaker	21
Blacksmith/		Hatter	1	Sieve-maker	1
smith	12	Heckler	6	Slater	12
Boat-wright	2	Hosier	1	Staymaker	2
Brazier	1	Hostler	5	Surgeon	3
Brewer	2	Innholder	1	Sweep	1
Butcher	17	Joiner	3	Tailor	15
Cadger	1	Knacker	2	Tanner	1
Carpenter	16	Labourer	77	Thatcher	1
Carrier	1	Limner	1	Tinker	1
Chair-maker	1	Maltster	3	Upholder	1
Confectioner	1	Mason	11	Watchmaker	1
Cooper	2	Mat-maker	1	Waterman	9
Currier	1	Merchant	3	Weaver	8
Cutler	2	Miller	3	Wheeler	2
'Docr' (?)	2	Musician	1	Whittawer	2
Draper	4	Net-maker	1	Wool-comber	14
Esquire	3	Organist	1		391
Exciseman	3	Painter	1		
Farmer	4	Patten-maker	1	Lodger	1
Fellmonger	2	Pipe-maker	1	No details given	17
Founder	1	Porter	6	Workhouse	1
Gardener	11	Publican	2		410

3.4 per cent in Higham Ferrers Hundred (1777), 3.0 per cent in Orlingbury (1777), 2.7 per cent in Wymersley (1777), and, at the other end of the scale, 0.5 per cent in both Nobottle Grove and Towcester (1777), 0.3 per cent in Greens Norton (1777), and no shepherds at all in Chipping Warden (1777).[12] John Morton in 1712 observed that Northamptonshire heathland, which he located in Nassaburgh at Stamford St Martin's, Wittering, Barnack, Helpston, Thornhaugh and Ufford, 'yields a sweet and cleanly Herbage, which feeds a Breed of small Sheep, whose Flesh is usually much commended and esteem'd'.[13] More than a hundred years later William Cobbett, travelling on the turnpike road between Huntingdon and Stamford (the modern A1), which crossed western Nassaburgh, stated that 'Here as all over the country (sic) everlasting fine sheep'.[14] In 1762 more shepherds were recorded at Castor and its hamlets than in any other parish in Nassaburgh, 7 in all. Castor lies between Morton's heathland and the River Nene, and contains much pasturage, including river meadow. John Stimson, maternal grandfather of John Clare, the poet, was a shepherd at Castor, and his name appears on the Castor militia list. Clare referred to him as having been 'a town shepherd as they are called, who has care of all the flocks of the village . . .', confirmation that sheep had a prominent place in the agricultural economy of Castor during the eighteenth century.[15]

[12] *Militia Lists, 1777, passim.*
[13] Morton, p. 10.
[14] William Cobbett, *Rural Rides* (Everyman edn. 1912), ii. 236.
[15] Edmund Blunden, ed., *Sketches in the Life of John Clare written by Himself* (1931), p. 45.

Graziers: 7 graziers and 1 farmer and grazier were listed in rural Nassaburgh in 1762. 4 of the graziers were dwelling on Borough Fen; 2 at Peakirk, which included part of North Fen; 1 at Paston; and the farmer and grazier at Marholm. The drained Borough Fen, according to John Morton, was 'justly accounted one of the richest Parcels of Feeding-Land in the Kingdom'.[16]

Flax- and Hemp-Dressers: among the crops grown on the reclaimed Fenland were flax and hemp.[17] Hence it is not surprising to find 6 'hecklers' (flax- or hemp-dressers) listed at Peterborough in 1762, 3 hemp-dressers at Northborough, and 1 hemp-dresser at Glinton. Glinton and Northborough are adjoining parishes, both bordering on the Fenland. Robert Mugliston, draper, who is listed at Peterborough, was probably the Robert Mugliston who was proprietor of a flax- and hemp-dressing business at Peterborough at this period. It lasted for many years, certainly into the mid-1780s.[18] A typical Mugliston advertisement, taken from the *Northampton Mercury* of 14 November 1768, is as follows:—

To all Dealers in HEMP and FLAX
ROBERT MUGLISTON & Co. beg leave to acquaint them, that they have lay'd in a large Assortment of HEMP and FLAX, both of Foreign and Home Growths, and the Produce of Lincolnshire and the Isle of Ely, at their Warehouse in Bridge Street, Peterborough; where all Dealers therein may be served wholesale, upon the lowest Terms, by
Their humble Servants,
ROBERT MUGLISTON *and* Co.
N.B. Will also undertake to procure Heckles [combs used for dressing hemp and flax] of any Size to any Degree of Fineness, and such as are allowed by experienced Judges to be as complete-made Tools as any in England, and at moderate Prices.

Gardeners: compared with the Northamptonshire militia lists in 1777, rural Nassaburgh in 1762 had almost three times the percentage of gardeners to all men whose names and occupations were recorded by the constables. The figure for Northamptonshire is 0.7 per cent (1777), and that for rural Nassaburgh is 1.8 per cent (1762). 2.8 per cent of the men listed at Peterborough were gardeners (1762), against 1.4 per cent at Northampton (1777).[19] Most of these men would have been engaged in market-gardening rather than the cultivation of flowers. John Clare, himself a member of a family of gardeners (p. 122), stated that at Helpston, his native village, 'flower gardens are but little store set bye, as the taste of Farmers turns entirely on profit'.[20] Market gardeners at Northampton later became an important sub-occupational group, comprising 159 men aged 20 years and over in 1851, 2.1 per cent of all the male inhabitants who were within this age category.[21] Figures for Peterborough are not so readily available; never the less, it would be interesting to know whether market-gardening, which was obviously well-established there in 1762, developed further during the next hundred or so years.

---

[16] Morton, p. 8.
[17] Daniel Defoe, *A Tour through the Whole Island of Great Britain* (Everyman edn. 1974), ii. 100; H. C. Darby, *The Draining of the Fens*, 2nd edn (1956), *passim*.
[18] The firm of Muggleston (*sic*) & Bladwin is listed as 'Hemp and Flax Merchants, and Drapers' at Peterborough in *Bailey's British Directory ... for the Year 1784*, ii (1784), p. 429.
[19] *Militia Lists, 1777*, pp. xxii–iv, 176.
[20] Blunden, p. 60.
[21] *Printed Census Schedules, 1851*.

Wool-Combers and Weavers: according to John Morton, 'the poorer Sort [at Peterborough] are usually employ'd in the Carding, Spinning, or Knitting of Wooll, and many others in the Combing and Weaving it; so much the Woollen Manufactures have of late taken Place in this City.'[22] This was in 1712; fifty years later it is clear from the militia lists that wool-combing and weaving were no longer of prime importance in the pattern of employment at Peterborough. Only 14 men were described as wool-combers and 8 as weavers, while there were no framework-knitters. Taking the Nassaburgh lists as a whole (i.e. the City of Peterborough and the rural parishes), there were 36 men listed who were either wool-combers or weavers; this represented 2.9 per cent of all the men whose occupations or status were noted by the constables. It compares with 12.2 per cent for the rest of Northamptonshire in 1777 (a figure which includes framework-knitters), with much higher proportions being recorded in 'textile' hundreds such as Corby, Guilsborough, Huxloe (which contains Kettering) and Rothwell.[23]

Shoemakers: the proportion of shoemakers to all men on the militia lists for the City of Peterborough is 5.4 per cent, or slightly more than one man out of every twenty. This is high enough to suggest that the city was a local centre for making shoes, probably for people living in the neighbouring districts. It should be compared, however, with 17.8 per cent for shoe-makers at Northampton in 1777, and 27.7 per cent at Wellingborough.[24] For rural Nassaburgh in 1762 the proportion of shoemakers was 2.3 per cent. This was lower than in any of the Northamptonshire hundreds in 1777, including those where shoemaking was still a local craft and not part of a nascent wholesale industry.

Slaters: in the Northamptonshire militia lists for 1777, 'slater' is the term generally used to denote a man who quarried 'slate' (i.e. fissile sandy limestone as at Collyweston and Easton on the Hill), and 'hilliard' or 'hillier' a man who fixed 'slates' or tiles on a roof.[25] Hence it is surprising to find 12 slaters listed at Peterborough in 1762, because the existence of 'slate' quarries within the boundaries of the city and its outlying hamlets is unproven.[26] Even if these men were roof-coverers rather than quarry-men, 12 seems a large number to appear on the lists for so small a town, especially as there were only 11 masons recorded by the Peterborough constables. Northampton had six hilliards listed in 1777, and that town was about twice the size that Peterborough had been in 1762. No explan-ation for the slaters of Peterborough is known to the editors of these lists. However, it may be noticed that no fewer than 5 slaters are shown at Peterborough in a trade directory published in 1798.[27] Two of the names, James English and John Jamblin[g], are the same as names on the 1762 lists. Moreover, two of the surnames of slaters in the 1798 directory are the

---

[22] Morton, p. 24. See also W. D. Sweeting, ed., Fenland Notes & Queries, iv (1900), pp. 115–17, for an interesting account, taken from The Post Boy, 2 June 1713, of the proclamation in Peterborough of the Peace of 1713. Wool-combers, who represented 'the principal manu-facture of the place', took a prominent part in the celebratory procession.
[23] Militia Lists, 1777, p. xviii.
[24] Hatley and Rajczonek, pp. 16–17.
[25] According to Anne E. Baker, Glossary of Northamptonshire Words & Phrases, i (1854), p. 324, a 'Hillyer' is 'One who covers houses with slate or tile, or any material but thatch.'
[26] Limestone outcrops at Peterborough are of higher geological horizons than those at Collyweston and Easton on the Hill, and are not known to contain Collyweston type 'slate'.
[27] The Universal British Directory of Trade, Commerce & Manufacture ... Volume the Fourth (1798), 190–2.

Table 3a: Occupations in which ten or more men were recorded
(Nassaburgh except the City of Peterborough)

'Labourer'	289	34.6 per cent
'Servant'	187	22.4
'Farmer'	101	12.1
Shepherd/servant & shepherd	37	4.4
Carpenter/joiner	30	3.6
Tailor	20	2.4
Shoemaker	19	2.3
Butcher	17	2.0
Mason	14	1.7
Weaver	14	1.7
Blacksmith/smith	13	1.6
Miller/miller's man	12	1.4
Baker	11	1.3
Farmer's son	10	1.2
Gardener	10	1.2
'Innkeeping'	10	1.2
	794	95.1
All occupations plus esquires and gentlemen	835	100
No occupation or status given	41	
Total names	876	

Table 3b: Occupations in which ten or more men were recorded
(City of Peterborough)

Labourer	77	19.7 per cent
Servant	25	6.4
Shoemaker	21	5.4
Carpenter/joiner	19	4.9
Butcher	17	4.3
Tailor	15	3.8
Wool-comber	14	3.6
Blacksmith/smith	12	3.1
Slater	12	3.1
Baker	11	2.8
Gardener	11	2.8
Mason	11	2.8
Barber	10	2.6
	255	65.2
All occupations plus esquires and gentlemen	391	100
No occupation or status given	19	
Total names	410	

same as surnames of slaters appearing on the lists at Collyweston and Easton on the Hill in 1777 (Mitchell [Mishal] and Cotton). Is this coincidence of surnames significant? The slaters of Peterborough are a subject for further investigation.

Watermen and Turnpike Employees: Peterborough stands on the River Nene, and its status in 1762 as a minor inland port is attested by the 2 boat-wrights, 9 watermen (boatmen) and 6 porters (who probably earned a living by loading and unloading boats and wagons at the wharf) who appear on the main list for the city. With one exception, a waterman, they are all bunched close together towards the end of the list, which suggests that the constables compiled it district by district, and that this section carries the names of men who lived near the river. By 1762 the River Nene was navigable all the way to Northampton, sixty miles upstream from Peterborough. A waterman is listed at Maxey, and a boatman at Deeping Gate; these men would have been employed on the River Welland, which was navigable as far as Stamford.[28]

'Mr Brickwod' at Castor, who is described as 'turpik', was doubtless connected with the road between Leicester and Peterborough (*via* Uppingham and Wansford: now the A47), which passed through Castor and had been turnpiked by Act of Parliament in 1753-4. In view of the handle to his name, he must have been a person of local importance, perhaps a surveyor. A turnpike keeper (who collected tolls at a gate) will be found on the list at Wansford, where the Leicester to Peterborough turnpike crossed the Great North Road (now the A1), the Wansford to Stamford section of which had been turnpiked in 1748-9. Wansford lies on the River Nene, and was thus a link point between two important roads and a navigable river. The appearance of Mr Pank Meadmore, merchant, on the Wansford list, together with two maltsters (who may have been employed by him), suggests that the village had become a centre for the reception and distribution of road and river freight, with coal and grain probably in substantial quantities, over a wide area of the surrounding countryside.

Links with John Clare

Several persons whose names are included on the militia lists deserve individual mention because of an association with Nassaburgh's most famous son, the poet John Clare, who was born at Helpston in 1793.

THOMAS CLARE (Helpston): great-uncle of the poet. Son of John Clare and Alice Gorge, who were married at Helpston on 18 January 1724-5. Thomas, their fourth child, was baptised there on 23 January 1730-1. His sister 'Ailce' (Alice), baptised on 14 August 1737, was the poet's grandmother. She was buried at Helpston on 4 January 1820 aged 82 and not 86 as stated in the burial register, and also by her grandson in one of his autobiographical fragments.[29] Thomas Clare married Anne Garfet

---

[28] Defoe, *Tour*, i. 73.

[29] Parish registers of Helpston (NRO). John and Alice Clare of Helpston had a daughter, baptised Alice on 22 July 1733, and buried 26 July 1733. Four years later they had another daughter, baptised Ailce (her mother is described as 'Ailce Clare' in the register entry) on 14 August 1737, who survived. It is this little girl who became the grandmother of John Clare, the poet. When Alice (Ailce) Clare was buried on 4 January 1820, the parson, not knowing her age, must have looked back through the Helpston baptismal register and found the entry for the earlier Alice Clare who was baptised in 1733. However, he cannot also have examined the burial register, hence his error in describing Alice Clare as 86 and not 82. Alice Clare herself had probably been quite unaware how old she was. On the evidence of her journal (entry for 13 July 1825), John Clare, her grandson, did not know his exact age (J. W. and Anne Tibble (ed.), *The Prose of John Clare* (1951), p. 155).

(Garfot or Garfoot) at Helpston on 22 October 1752. The registers of that parish show that they had 5 children baptised between 1754 and 1761, which agrees with the number recorded by the Helpston constable in 1762, thereby gaining Thomas, a 'poor man', his exemption from militia liability. He is described on the list as a gardener, which is in accord with his great-nephew's statement that 'all I can make out [about my ancestors] is that they were Gardeners...'[30]

JOHN CLARE (Helpston): probably the son of John Clare and Rachel Whitaker, who were married at Helpston on 13 December 1724; if so, he was baptised on 4 May 1729. His family's relationship with the family from which the poet was descended is not established, but they were undoubtedly kinsfolk. Like Thomas Clare, John Clare was listed as a gardener in 1762. He does not appear to have married, or if he did the ceremony was not at Helpston, prior to 1762.

JOHN CLARE (Northborough): perhaps a great-uncle of the poet. John and Alice Clare had four sons baptised at Helpston with the name of John between 1725 and 1741-2, but only the last of these boys appears to have survived infancy. He was baptised at Helpston on 24 January 1741-2. If it is this John Clare who was the servant at Northborough in 1762, he would then have been twenty years of age and probably unmarried, living with the farmer who employed him in the traditional manner of 'servants in husbandry'.

JOHN STIMSON (Castor): maternal grandfather of the poet. John Stimson married Elizabeth Daves at Castor on 5 November 1750; he was a shepherd who has already been noticed in the section on shepherds in Nassaburgh.[31] His daughter Ann, who was baptised at Castor on 17 April 1757, married Parker Clare of Helpston, but not at either Castor or Helpston and the whereabouts and date is not known (1982). John Clare the poet was their son.

JOHN CEW (more modern spelling Kew) (Ufford). 'Ailce' Clare, who never married, was seduced c. 1764 by a travelling Scottish schoolmaster calling himself John Donald Parker. The result was Parker Clare, the poet's father. According to John Clare: 'This I had from John Cue of Ufford, an old man who in his young days was a companion and confidential to my run-a-gate of a grandfather; for he [Parker] left the village [Helpston] and my grandmother, soon after the deplorable accident of misplaced love was revealed to him...'[32] John Cew, servant, on the Ufford list in 1762, is surely the John Cue who, many years later, spilled the beans to the young John Clare about the latter's paternal grandfather. It is tempting to wonder whether Cew, like his erstwhile friend, John Donald Parker, had been an amorously irresponsible character in his time!

FRANCIS GREGORY (Helpston): the father of Francis Gregory, smallholder and proprietor of the Blue Bell Public House at Helpston, who employed John Clare for a year when the latter was in his mid-teens.[33] Francis Gregory senior married Ann Bland at Helpston on 11 October 1768, their son Francis being baptised on 30 May 1769.

Francis Gregory junior was a bachelor who lived with his mother; he suffered from ill health, and died soon after Clare left his service. It is obvious from Clare's comments on Gregory that he was a kind master

---

[30] J. W. and Anne Tibble, *John Clare: a Life*, new edn (1972), p. 5.
[31] Parish registers of Castor (NRO).
[32] Blunden, pp. 45-6. There is no entry for the baptism of Parker Clare in the Helpston registers.
[33] *ibid.* p. 55.

whom the youthful poet respected. Francis Gregory senior was buried at Helpston on 21 April 1796, Francis Gregory junior on 31 January 1811, and Ann Gregory on 15 October 1819. Mrs Gregory's age was recorded in the burial register as 77.

Several other men appearing on the Nassaburgh militia lists of 1762 had surnames which are the same or very similar to those of persons who, forty or fifty years later and at the same places, were part of John Clare's early life. They include William Bains, John and Thomas Billings and John Bullemore (Bullimore) at Helpston, John and William Bellars (Bellairs) at Etton and Woodcroft, James and William Joyce at Glinton, and John Porter at Ashton. John Turnell (Turnill) at Northborough should also be noticed. The genealogical links between these men and the generation known to Clare remain to be demonstrated.

Note on Editorial Method

The militia lists are, on the whole, straightforward documents, some of them neatly and carefully written and laid out, others just the reverse. We have tried to edit them so that the character of the original is maintained as far as possible. Spelling remains the same as on the lists, but capitalisation has been adapted to modern usage. As far as possible the original punctuation on the lists has been maintained—many have no punctuation at all, and some are punctuated in the wrong places—but certain additions and alterations have been made to assist the reader. Of these the most important is that where names are followed by an occupation, status or some information, the surname has been separated from the next word by a comma. A name enclosed by ⟨   ⟩ indicates that it has been crossed off the list, the man concerned being exempted from liability for militia service. Other words enclosed by ⟨   ⟩ have also been crossed off the list. Corrections to names have been indicated by italic type, e.g. from the Wittering list:

Edwd. Lee

⟨Edwood Luee⟩ sarvent

Where the correction was itself crossed off, it too has been enclosed by ⟨   ⟩. All the lists, with the exception of those from Peterborough, carry the signatures of one deputy lieutenant and two justices of the peace before whom, at the first subdivisional meeting, the constables made a statutory verification upon oath that their returns were accurate; these signatures, which are the same for each list, have been omitted from the transcription. Thus the signatures of Matthew Wyldbore, a deputy lieutenant, William Strong and the Rev. William Brown, justices of the peace, appear on the list for Helpston (Plate 8).

GLOSSARY

This glossary includes explanations of technical terms, and a few of the many variant spellings which will be found in the lists.

Ailding. Ale house keeper (?)
Aprents. Apprentice
Blmacks. Blacksmith
Bossher. Butcher
Cadger. Tramping beggar (AEB); carrier or hawker (SOED)
Cager. Cadger (q.v.)
Cartpinder. Carpenter
Cloather. Clothier; one who sells cloth or men's clothes (SOED); in this context, perhaps a dealer in second-hand clothes.
Cordwainer. Shoemaker
Cupper. Cooper
Founder. Metal caster (?)
Freborow. Freeborough (q.v.)
Freeborough. Deputy Constable
Gadner. Gardener
Graser. Grazier
Headborough. Deputy Constable[1]
Heckler. Flax-dresser (SOED); also a hemp-dresser
Huck bone. Hip- or haunch bone (huckle = hip or haunch: SOED)
Juner. Junior
Knacker. Dealer in horse flesh (SOED: the alternative 'harness maker' seems less likely by 1762)
Labear. Labourer
Laber. Labourer
Laem. Lame
Malster. Maltster
Meler. Miller
Milner. Miller
Myellier. Miller
Patin maker. Patten maker (Patten = overshoe of wood and iron worn to raise the ordinary shoes out of mud and wet: SOED)
Seaner. Senior
Taler. Tailor
Turpik. Turnpike
Upholder. A dealer in or maker of small wares, furniture, etc. (SOED)
Viller. Victualler
Weeler. Wheelwright (SOED as 'wheeler')
Well rite. Wheelwright
Whitawer. A man who taws skin into whitleather (Whittawer)

AEB = Anne E. Baker, *A Glossary of Northamptonshire Words and Phrases*, 2 vols. (1854).
SOED = *Shorter Oxford English Dictionary.*

[1] In some districts this term was used as synonymous with that of constable: W. E. Tate, *The Parish Chest* (1960), p. 307.

ERRATUM: VOL. XXV

The late Mr Harold Clifton of Long Buckby was kind enough to point out that the two flat-makers at Towcester in 1777 were making baskets, not shoes (*Militia Lists, 1777*, p. 196). According to Miss Baker, a flat was 'a straight-sided shallow basket made of peeled osiers with a flat lid, whence the name; used principally for carrying butter to market, and frequently called a "butter-flat".' (Anne E. Baker, *Glossary*, i. 240). There is an interesting reference to these baskets in the report of a riot just south of Northampton in 1795 when several wagons carrying provisions 'were attacked near Queen's Cross [Hardingstone] by a numerous body of people, who immediately proceeded to cut open the butter-flats, the contents of which, as well as a quantity of meat, they carried off, and brought part of it into the town in triumph' (*Northampton Mercury*, 11 April 1795).

The total number of shoemakers in the 1777 lists should therefore be reduced from 705 to 703 (Tables 5 and 6), although the proportion of shoemakers to all men whose occupations or status were recorded by the constables remains at 5.9 per cent (Table 5). Shoemakers in Towcester hundred are reduced from 24 to 22, and the proportion to all men from 6.2 to 5.7 per cent (Table 5).

NASSABURGH HUNDRED

BAINTON

A lest of all persons betwen the ages of eighteen and forty five years. Richard Garner, constable of Benton.

1. ⟨Mr. William Barker⟩ farmer
2. John Canwell, farmer
3. Thomes Nottingham, farmer
4. Edward Nottingham, farmer, his not in parsh at present
5. Samuel Garner, bossher
6. ⟨W. Calesdine, poor man⟩ three children & pended
7. Matthew Jackson, poor man
8. Robert Flower, plowrite
9. ⟨Edward Gadsby, poor man⟩ three children
10. John Falconer, well rite
11. ⟨Frances Digdike⟩ printer
12. ⟨William Kew⟩ poor, fore children
13. Natel Alling, poor man
14. ⟨William Jesson, poor man⟩ three children & clark
15. John Smith, poor man
16. Richard Jackson, poor man
    Chris.
17. ⟨Cate⟩ Blads, a savent
18. William Boyfield, a savent
19. William Smith, a savent
20. ⟨John Yorwoord, massner⟩ five children
21. ⟨Nekles Lown, poor man⟩ three children
22. ⟨Richard Palmer, poor man⟩ three children
23. William Shefeld, a savent
24. John Pendard, a savent
25. John Clark, a sarvent, one eyes
26. James Horning, blacksmith & freebrogh

The meeting his on Saturday eleventh day of December at house of William Elger in Peterborough to bee thare by nine of the clock in forenoon that all persens think themselselves thereby agrived may then appeal and no peale will be afterwardes received.

BARNACK

Barnick list.

John Sisson, farmer
Moses Sisson, farmer
William Burbide, farmer
Juner, Moses Sisson, farmer
Richard Sims, cartpinder
Richard Dolby, laber
⟨Thomas Low, blacksmith⟩
  3 children
⟨Thomas Pridmore, shewmacker⟩
  5 children
⟨Thoms Page, shewmacker⟩
  4 children

David Jeson, tayler
⟨Thomas Draycote, laber⟩
  4 children
Gorge Dolby, laber
John Smith, laber
Lucass Jaxson, laber
⟨David Bullimer, cartpinder⟩
  apprentice
Robert Hays, bacor
John Rudkin, shewmacor
⟨Edward Lenton, shewmacor⟩
  7 children

James Coal, shepperd
John Tasker, laber
⟨John Gamble, masner⟩ and
    ⟨freborow⟩ peace officer
William Smithergale, sarvent
William Earle, shepperd
Francis Gamble, bblacksmith
⟨William Gamble, masner⟩
    apprentice
Samewell Andrew, tayler
Joseph Younger, laber
William Burbige, buther
John Maulsbuary, laber
⟨Samewel Wing, shepperd, bad of
    eyfightsit⟩ blind

Richard Smith, sarvent
Francis Redin, sarvent
William Backor, laber
Robart Canner, sarvent
⟨Robart Barrow, sarvent⟩
John Morris, myellier
John Tayler, sarvent
Toby Brown, shepperd
Larans Gilbart, cartpinder
John Yarwood, laber
Samuel Jaxson, sarvent
William Lewes, sarvent
⟨George Ward, lame⟩

Cunstobels
Richard Boor
John Gambol

PILSGATE

Pilsgate. December ye 11th. 1762. A list of the inhabitants to be drafted on the militia.

William Molshin, labourer
Robart Twelvetree, do.
John Scotney, shephard
John Tabner, servant
Thomas Mapasey, do.
Thomas Pears
James Smithringale
⟨William Ashley, labourer⟩ 5 children
⟨Thomas Chatbourn⟩ do. 9
⟨Mathew Burbidge⟩ do. 9
⟨William Jesson⟩ do. 6
⟨John Pridmore⟩ shoemaker, do. 3
⟨John Allin, farmer⟩ & headborough, do. 4 children
⟨Jos. Harrison, a servant to the Earl of Exeter his family repoes at Pilsgate
    and he stood the ballot for Lincolnshire⟩
⟨Peter Hill, servant to do. and stood the ballot for do. then his family
    resided at Saint Martens [Stamford Baron] but since removed to
    Pilsgate⟩
⟨John Lilley, sarvant and stood the ballot for Rutlandshire⟩

Thomas Pears
John Lowe
Constables

SOUTHORPE

Southarpe list. William Barker, cunstable

John Sweby, mason
John Allin, farmer
⟨Willm. Allin, heardborough⟩
Thos. Allin, farmer

Willm. Scotney, shepard
John Hurd, farmer man
⟨Willm. Goodyer, fore children⟩
    labour

⟨George Sisson, fore children⟩
labour
Stiles Beaver, farmer
Willm. Sharp, farmer man
⟨Thos. Roberson, not capable⟩ an
idiot

⟨Edward Cunnington, fore
children⟩ labour
Peter Beaston, milner
Abraham Batts, milner man
John Hays, gardiner

Wm.
The mark X of sworn
Barker

BOROUGH FEN

A list of persons names dwelling and living in Borough Fen in the liberty
of St John Baptist Peterborough in the County of Northampton from the
ages of eighteen to forty five years taken this thirteenth day of Decr. 1762.

John Cole, farmer
Christopher Jarvis, servant
Frans. Foareman, labrour
Thos. Porter, graizer
John Wolton, do.
Thos. Griffin, do.
Ezekel Jackson, servant
Thos. Allen
⟨Thos. Allen, do., lame⟩
Isaac Pickaver, do.
Hugh Wych, butcher
Wm. Ridley, servant
⟨Wm. Preston, labrour⟩ 3 ch.

Charles Moore, graizer
Thos. Moore, labrour
Saml. Watson, servant
Thos. Kitchings, do.
Millecent Gunton, victualer
Wm. Bennington, servant
Wm. Speeckly, farmer
Peter Grummell, servant
⟨Wm. Allen, farmer, infirm'd⟩
⟨Thos. Sims, labrour⟩ 3 children
Thos. Gray, servant
Phillip Henson, do.
John Dunmore, do.

CASTOR

A list of the inhabitance and servents in Castor wit Milton that is qualified
to serve one the melishe for the parrish above menched for Northamptonshire as folrith. December ye 3, 1762.

		Number of children. Each famleys
1.	Mr. Wright Serjent, ferm.	
2.	Mr. Wm. Wright, surgon	
3.	Mr. John Peeter, fermer	
4.	Mr. Tho. Bate, fermer	
5.	Mr. Wm. Wolgrave, fermer	
6.	Mr. Rob. Laxton, fermer	
7.	Mr. Clem. Tompson, fermer	
8.	Mr. Knotton, gardner	4 children
9.	Mr. Crow, park keeper	8 dit.
10.	⟨Nat. Guding, miller⟩	3 dit.
11.	⟨John Shelston, carpend.⟩	3 dit.
12.	⟨Tho. Chapel, blmacks.⟩	3 dit.
13.	⟨Wm. Shelston, bacor⟩	btc.
14.	⟨Tho. Brown, taler⟩	btc.
15.	John Darby, juner, weellrigh	6 dit.
16.	James Stanger, shumaker	2 dit.
17.	⟨John Ashby, viller⟩	
18.	Tho. Porders, blmacks.	

19.	Edward Serjant, bacor		btc.
20.	Mr. Wm. Serjant, farmer		
21.	John King, laber	2	dit.
22.	⟨Wm. Smith, taler⟩	3	dit.
23.	Wm. Suton, laber	1	dit.
24.	Tho. Dolby, shepard	2	dit.
25.	⟨Wm. Cope, laber⟩	5	dit.
26.	⟨Tho. Liming, shomaker⟩	4	dit.
27.	⟨Wm. Hill, laber⟩	3	dit.
28.	⟨Wm. Chamberling, bucher⟩	6	dit.
29.	⟨Tho. Shelston, carpindr.⟩	6	dit.
30.	⟨Tho. Judson, laber⟩	7	dit.
31.	⟨John Stimson, shepard⟩	5	dit.
32.	John Broten, laber	2	dit.
33.	Tho. Serjeant, laber	2	dit.
34.	James Willkson, carpinder		wid.
35.	Mathe. Boland, laber	2	dit.
36.	Tho. Bate, backer		bct.
37.	Wm. More, laber		
38.	Wm. Edwards, laber		
39.	⟨Tho. Dawkens, wever⟩	3	dit.
40.	⟨John Burbig. laber⟩	4	dit.
41.	⟨Wm. Herson, laber⟩	4	dit.
42.	Tho. Snel, laber	2	dit.

Newman

43.	Edward ⟨Numon⟩ laber	1	dit.
44.	⟨Gorg. Green, laber⟩	4	dit.
45.	John Hale, masner		
46.	John Dunston, laber		

Twelv

47.	⟨Tho. Tweltrees, laber⟩ *Thos. Twelvetrees*	
48.	John Woddell, laber	
49.	Robt. Cuper, serven	
50.	⟨Mr. Brickwod, turpik⟩	
51.	John Parrish, serven	
52.	Robt. Peper, dit.	
53.	Robt. Ex, shepard	
54.	Wm. Sandfild, dit.	
55.	Wm. Rowell, dit.	
56.	Robt. Gregry, dit.	
57.	Gabril Core, dit.	
58.	John Traton, dit.	
59.	Wm. Quiner, dit.	

Wilkinson

60.	Mathey ⟨y groom⟩ dit.		
61.	Richard Hudson, sheprd.		
62.	Wm. Lenton, dit.		
63.	Tho. Gilby, dit.		
64.	Wm. Cobley, laber	6	dit.
65.	Wm. Dolby, sheprd.		
66.	Wm. Leading, servent		

Robt. Wright, custable

Notes

(1) bct. = bachelor
     btc. = bachelor
     wid. = widower

(2) Nos 54–60 and 62–3 have been counted as servants and not as shepherds in Tables 2a and 3a. If nos 54–60 had been shepherds, it would have been unnecessary for Robert Wright, the constable, to indicate that no 61 was also a shepherd. Moreover, 'Mathey y groom' is more likely to have come into the category of servant rather than shepherd. Nos 62 and 63 are more difficult to place. If they were shepherds this would mean that, out of 66 listed men, seven (10.6 per cent) were employed in looking after sheep. This is an exceptionally high proportion compared with other occupations, even at Castor where sheep were numerous (p. 117). (One shepherd is also recorded at each of Castor's two hamlets, Ailsworth and Sutton.) Moreover, it will be seen from the table of 'Number of children. Each famleys' that Wright was quite unreliable in his use of the abbreviation 'dit' (ditto).

AILSWORTH

Decm. 11 1762. A lest of the in habants and sarvents of Alesworth from the aedge of 18ten to the aedge 45.

Willm. Briggs, farmer
John Briggs, farmer
Danoll Baet, farmer
     r   *mason*
John Ganer, ⟨masner⟩
⟨Thos. Searieant, carptner⟩ laem
Willm. Braken, labear
Thos. Masan, woodman
⟨John Brown, shapard⟩ por man,
     3 childrn
Thos. Gunton, sarvent
     Gabriel Sapten
⟨Garboll⟩ Sapten, sarvent
Thos. Poap, sarvent
John Shalsten, carpenter
Clapol Cober, blacksmeth
⟨Robt. Stapoll, meler⟩ 6 chiln
Thos. Pamer, meler

⟨Will. Clapol, labear, poeer man,
     4 children⟩
⟨Willm. Satcholl, bucher⟩
     Turner
John ⟨Toner⟩, bucher
Charls Smeth, gadner
Robt. Scalet, labear
John Edwards, carptner
Wm. Sutton, searvent
     Eaton
Wm. ⟨Etean⟩, seavent
Hanery Daws, searvent
Willm. Gunell, wearver
Sam. Bryan ⟨h⟩aleceeper
     Jucob
⟨Juckobt⟩ Gunsey, labear
Wm. Lasbey, labear

Willm. King, cunstabell

SUTTON

December 5, 1762. Sutton. A list of the names of the inhaberts and servants between the ages of eighteen and forty five years.

Mr William Hopkinson, farmer
Mr John Parkinson, farmer
John Dots, servant
William Avary, servant
William Hillard, servant
William Hardey, cordwainer
Thomas Featherston, butcher

⟨John Read⟩ cupper, lame
⟨Thamas Brawn⟩ shapard, 3 child.
James Gardner, labour
⟨Richard Bagley⟩ labour, 3 child.
Isaac Cant, labour
     Aislaby
William ⟨Hislbeu⟩ labour

This is to give nodice that thers names will be given in on Saturday next eleventh day of December by nine of the clock in the forenoon at William Elyer, Peterborough, and aney man may appeal that day and no appeals will be afterwards.

Thomas Hardey, constable

UPTON

Disembr 11, 1762. Upton in the County of Northamptonshire. A trew list of the men from eighteen years to forty five.

John Patman. labour
Fransis Basbay, labour
Sails
John ⟨Salls⟩ sarvent

John Colman, sarvent
William Sharman, farmar

John Sharman, cunstable

ETTON & WOODCROFT

A list of the mens names of Etton and Woodcraft all under 45 and a bove 18

William Bellars, farmers son
John Bellars, farmers son
Thomas Smith, servt.
⟨Thomas Dale⟩ lame
Frances Bloodworth, labourer
Henery Young, farmer
William Person, weaver
John Homes, labourer
William Hill, labourer

⟨Frances Thather⟩ 3 children
Thomas Barefoot, labourer
John Green, servt.
William Frier, servt.
Thomas Bland, servt.
George Hardy, servt.
⟨George Chamberlin, farmer⟩ lost an eye

Vincent Bellars, constable
Decr. ye 8th 1762.

EYE

A list of persons names dwelling and being in the parish of Eye in the County of Northampton from the ages of eighteen to forty five years taken this fourth day of Decr. 1762 by me, Ricd. Forster, constable.

Edwd. Green, labrour
Wm. Chesterfield, do.
⟨Jeremiah Presgrave, do., lame⟩
Edwd. Wright, labrour
John Tooley, servant
⟨Frans. Cook, labrour⟩ 3 children
Griffin Ricraft, churchwarden
⟨John Hill, labrour⟩ 4 children
Thos. Short, do.
⟨John Brown, cordwainer⟩ three children
Wm. Eldered, victuler
Joseph Skieff, labrour
Wm. Reedshaw, farmer's son
Stephen Ervin, junr., butcher

John Alben, junr., farmer son
Robt. Skieff, labrour
John Hyde, do.
Thos. Harryson, junr., cordwainer
John Brakes, junr., carpenter
⟨Robt. Brown, labrour, 4 children⟩
Thos. Harryson, do.
Daniel Brakes, do.
Thos, Pennell, grocer
John Moore, butcher
⟨Wm. Barson, carpenter⟩ 50 yr. old
⟨Thos. Sawfoard, victuler⟩ 3 children, infirmed in speech
Ralph Perkins, labrour

Wm. Cliff, baker
John Smith, aprentis to a baker
⟨John Chadbord, tayler⟩
David Edis, servant
John Henson, farmer
Abel Cunnington, miller
Wm. Askew, servant
⟨Thos. Youles, weeaver⟩ 3 children
Jos. Little, farmer son
James Batterham, junr., labrour
Richd. Horspole, farmer
⟨John Whithead, labrour⟩
    4 children
⟨John Harryson, do., lame and
    3 children⟩
Henry Shivers, labrour
⟨John Sutton, do., 3 children⟩
Saml. Dolby, shephard
John Barnet, lodger
George Paul, farmer
John Thompson, servant,
Michael Miller, drover
Wm. Harryson, servant
Thos. Rooding, labrour, lame
Wm. Bassingham, farmer
John Leeach, labrour
⟨Stephen Morris, wheelwright⟩ one
    eye
John Woodward, cordwainer
⟨Saml. Smith, labrour⟩ 45
Thos. Pack, do.
Robt. Norman, do.

⟨Wm. Scotney, do.⟩ 4 children
⟨Richd. Moore, servant⟩ one eye
Daniel Porter, blacksmith
John Pank, farmer
Wm. Roades, servant
Daniel Briggins, do.
Thos. Batterham, labrour
John Baxter, farmer
Daniel Miller, junr., farmer son
Wm. Ervin, cloather
⟨Thos. Love, carpenter⟩ 6 children
Millecent Brown, do.
Robt. Allen, labrour
⟨Edwd. Richardson, gardener⟩
    4 children
Wm. Turner, junr. shephard
Thos. Dixey, labrour, lame
⟨John Peal, clark of the parish⟩
    3 children
Joseph Eat, labrour
James Haddon, do.
⟨John Lewin, servant⟩ under age
Robt. Roe, do.
⟨John Sprigs, do.⟩ lame
Richd. Pepperdine, do.
Benjamin Bonner, labrour
⟨Wm. Forster, do.⟩ 5 children
Thos. Lewis, servant
Thos. Young, blacksmith
Lawrence Stocks, labrour
Saml. Eaten, a servant

N.B.   That if any persons in this list thinks themselves agreeed they are
to appeal on Satuerday next being the eleventh of this instant Decr. at the
Angel Inn in Peterborough by ten o clock of the fore noon of the same day
that no other appeals will be afterwards heard.

GLINTON

A true list of all the men now or usually dwelling in the parish of Glinton
in the County of Northon. as per act of Parliament, tober the 5th 1762.

Thomas Skerrit, servant
Robert Sutton, servant
Thomas Ankley, servant
James Joyce, farmer
William Chambers, servant
Wm. Muse, labourer
Zachariah Bradfield, servt.
⟨John Smith, farmer⟩
Robert Jones, labourer
John Giddens, shephard
John Hudson, butcher
Thomas Walker, farmer

Jno. Quince, servt.
⟨Jno. Horsepole, labourer⟩
Wm. Hardy, carpeter
Wm. Joyce, farmer
Jno. Clark, farmer
Seth Williamson, schoolmaster
Thomas Johnson, servt.
Jno. Gray, victular
Jno. Bains, taylor
Hen. Bothways, taylor
Robt. Tyers, weaver
Joseph Hughs, baker

⟨Joseph Etherly, weaver⟩
Sam. Barret, labourer
Matthew Hudson, labourer
Wm. Howett, carpenter
Matthew Burgess, labourer
Jno. Birtch, servt.
Jno. Webster, farmer
Wm. Munton, servt.
Jno. Holmes, servt.
Robt. Lambert, labourer
Thos. Bell, runaway
Jno. Munton, servt.
James Stanley, servt.

Robt. Smith, labourer
Thos. Elvidge, runaway
Wm. Tyers, runaway
John Day, labourer
Stephen Day, labourer
Zachariah Decan, mason
Wm. Birtch, labourer
Thos. Baseley, labourer
Wm. Tyers, farmer
Nichollas Muse, servt.
Benj. Smith, shepherd
⟨Wm. Ashby, hempdresser⟩
⟨Henry Robertson, labourer⟩

Thos. Scott, constable

HELPSTON

A list of the men in the parish of Helpstone betwene the age of 18 and 45 years.

Mr John Lawrence, farmer
Vincent Bellars, farmer
Thomas Bellars, farmer
Thomas Borrows, farmer
Mackerness Morton, farmer
Thomas Browton, baker
⟨Thomas Clare, gardener⟩ 5 childn
John Winslow, taylor
John Clare, gardener
⟨Thomas More, shoemaker⟩
John Billings, shoemaker
John Bullemore, carpinter
⟨William Batteram, taylor⟩
Richard Rise, weaver
Richard Sharpe, baker
Thomas Rise, weaver
Francis Fell, masoner
⟨Robert Molborough, shepard⟩
James Pamer, laborou
⟨Richard Rose, labourou⟩
⟨William Bains, labourou⟩
⟨Francis Borrows, labourou, lame⟩
⟨William Oliver, labourou⟩
⟨John Spiers, labourou, lame⟩

⟨Thomas Gibbs, labourou⟩
William Wise, labourou
John Landon, labourou
Mathew Griffin, labourou
Thomas Yarrod, labourou
⟨John Crowson, labourou⟩
⟨John Barker, labourou⟩
⟨John Bowls, labourou⟩
⟨William Woods, labourou⟩
Peeter Peake, labourou
⟨Henry Wells, labourou⟩
Francis Money, labourou
⟨Giles Patrick, labourou⟩ 3 chn
John Woodward, labourou
⟨John Vine, labourou⟩
Robert Boyal, sarvant
Thomas Cunington, sarvant
⟨John Wiles, sarvant, lame⟩
Francis Gregory, sarvant
John Skelley, sarvant
John Oliver, sarvant
John Burnam, sarvant
Richard King, sarvant
⟨Robert Wiles, sandman

December ye 11th 1762.
Thomas Billings, constable

MARHOLM

Decr. 2d 1762. A list of all persons in the parish of Marholm liable to serve in the militia for the County of Northampton.

Jos. Chamberlin, grasiers and
    farmer

Robt. Collinge, victualar,
    remarkable crooked legs

Aug. Foster, cottager & labourer
⟨Adam Cook, labourer⟩ 3 children
James Wright, do.
Miles Stanyon, do.
⟨Wm. Sayles, junr., do.⟩ 3 childn.
⟨Wm. Griffin, do.⟩ 3 childn.

⟨John Pacey, do., very full
    shouldered⟩
Saml. Chapman, servt.
Hen. Baxter, do.
Edwd. Lincoln, shepheard
Wm. Allen, shepheard
Richd. Bell, do.

Benj. Bull, constable

MAXEY

Northamptonshr. A list of the names of all the men usually at this time dwelling within the parish of Maxey between the ages of eighteen and forty-five years, and their occupations.

Peter Andrew, junior, carpenter
John Smith, baker
⟨Anthony Garfoot, labourer⟩
    3 children
Francis Dixson, labourer
Martin Lambert, servant
⟨Edward Farrow, labourer⟩
    3 children
John Crowson, labourer
John Berrige, labourer
William Brumley, servant
John Roberts, servant
William Burton, servant
Charles Smith, servant
⟨Samuel Skirrit, gelder⟩ 5 children
⟨Richard Whitehead, shepard⟩
    3 childn.
⟨Robert Green, labourer⟩ lame
George Dixson, junior, labourer
Thomas Dixson, labourer
⟨William Cluff, labourer⟩ lost an
    eye, infirm
Roger Avery, labourer
Francis Green, servant
William Addye's servant
William Addye's shepard
Charles Bonner, servant
William Mason, servant
Daniel Webster, farmer
George Searl, servant

John Osborne, butcher
John Addinton, servant
⟨William Bollands, labourer⟩
    3 children
Henry Green, weaver
William Green, carpenter
John Style, taylor
William Morris, farmer
William Halley, servant
Edward Smith, labourer
⟨Thomas Bollands, taylor⟩ lame
⟨John Searl, labourer⟩ 3 children
William Swanson, servant
⟨William Berrige, labourer⟩
    3 children
John Dixson, labourer
⟨Edward Harris, labourer⟩
    3 children
⟨Francis Stanyan, labourer⟩ lame
Peter Peach, shepard
Richard Gillson, junior, butcher
Thomas Bellars, farmer
Thomas Baggarly, servant
Richard Cimberley, servant
John Browning, servant
⟨John Lenton, labourer⟩ lame
⟨John Audlin, gardiner⟩ lame
Henry Smith, waterman
Moses Young, servant

Thomas Sanderson, cunstuble

DEEPING GATE

The constable of Deepingate his bill.

⟨Willm. Smith, laborer⟩ 4 chiln.
Tho. Randle, laborer
Willm. Wade, shepherd

John Hinson, laborer
Tho. Corner, laborer
Tho. Hoggard, farmer

Walter Collens, laberer
Mathew Wise, a farmers son
Tho. Measure, farmer
Willm. Horsley, sarvant
Henery Eldered, boatman
John Ward, laberer

Edward Sutton, laberer
Frances Adason, horse rider
⟨Robt. Leaton, laberer⟩ 5 children
John Farrow, laberer
⟨Willm. Answel, servant, fits⟩
⟨Joseph Marrat, laberer⟩ 3 childeren

John Wright, constable
John
The mark of   X
Wright

NORTHBOROUGH

Decebr. 10th 1762

A list of the names between the ages of eighteen & forty five now dwelling in the parrish of Northborow.

Willm. Bellas, farmer
James Preston, herdsman, commandly cald feen (*sic*) Reaves
Robert Preston, herdsman
⟨James Woolley, carpinder, lame of his right hand⟩
⟨John Sharman, carpinder⟩ aprentes & 3 years to serve
John Smyth, labouerer
Thos. Royston, do.
⟨James Riddington⟩ blacksmith, infirm,d
⟨Joseph Browton⟩ a poor labourer & 4 chilldren
⟨Joseph Dickins⟩ a poor labourer & 3 chilldren
⟨John Thorp⟩ a poor labourer & 4 chilldren
⟨Robt. Swift⟩ a poor sheepard and 6 chilldren
Thos. Rowson, sheepard
Willm. Bland, labourer
James Seffton, do.
John Seffton, hempdresser
Willm. Masson, labourer
Gyles Young, farmer
John Turnell, bucher
James Cole, bucher
⟨Francis Cade, hempdresser⟩
Edward Wikes, do
Robt. Larrat, farmer
⟨Willm. Rowson, labourer and 3 chilldren⟩
John Charity, taylor
Willm. Cole, weeler
James Cole, masson, suposed to be aprentes & a year to serve
⟨Willm. King, labourer⟩ and 4 chilldren
Robt. Resling, servant
James Sarson, a servant
Thos. Lewing, a servant
John Clare, a servant

Joseph Clark, constable of Northborough
Francis Cade, headborrow

PASTON

December ye 10 1762: the nams of the inhabentence of Paston

John Forman, ⟨garser⟩ farmer
William West, labourer
Edward Cross, ⟨graser⟩ graser
Robert Hide, ⟨logger⟩ labourer
⟨William Bornham, labourer⟩

Bates
John ⟨Bats⟩, labouerer
William Dixson, labourer
⟨William Hide, carpenter⟩
John Smith, labourer
Jeremiah Cross, labour

Jeremiah Cross, constubele

GUNTHORPE

The men of Gunthorpe

William Bodger, labourer
⟨William Reed, labourer⟩ 5 children
Richard Clarksom, servant

Daniel Ellam, labouer
⟨John Jarvis, cobler⟩ militia man for
Isle of Ely

Wm. Smith, constable
December 11

WALTON

A lisst of the inhabbitants of Walton to be return'd to His Majesty's duputy lieutenants and justices of the peace at their subdivision militia meeting.

Mr John Landon, farmer
Frans. Lowe, ditto
John Sharp, ditto
⟨George Rudd, junor, labourer⟩
⟨Mark King, labourer⟩
⟨Frans. Greefin, labourer⟩
Robt. Manton, labourer
Hen. Willsworth, clark of the
parish
Joseph York, blacksmith
⟨Peter York, carpinter⟩
Willm. Brightman, labourer

⟨Sam. Stock, cordwaner⟩
⟨Thos. Barnit, labourer⟩

Servants

⟨Thos. Benton, lame⟩
Edward Hare
Frans. Gambol
⟨John Ward, lame⟩
Willm. Crowson
Richd. Yeats
Willm. Hooper

Hen. Ruff, constable

WERRINGTON

A trew list of the inhabitants of Werrington that are able to serve the military betwixt the age's of eighteen and forty five years.

Richd. Whitwell, farmer
John Pepper, sarvant
⟨Tho. Hadcin, aprentis⟩
Tho. Whithead, farmer
Benjman Bland, laber
Abraham Elsham, mason
Henery Pits, bacer
John Buckworth, laber and freeborough

Children

⟨Francis Paul, weelright⟩   4
⟨John *illegible*, laber⟩
  Richd. Cunington, miller
  Steven Cunington, miller
  Adam Jones, weever
  Thos. Willson, laber
  Joseph Green, laber, lame
  Tho. Horsley, taler
  Wm. Crafts, laber
  John Lord, laber, lame
  Robt. Blesseid, butcher
⟨John Smithagel, laber⟩   6
  Edward Darley, farmer
  Edward Corby, laber
  John Vine, sarvant
⟨Wm. Balding, laber⟩   4
⟨John Hays, laber⟩   4
  John Trusil, nacker
⟨Joseph Spencer⟩ aprents.
  John Holman, laber
  Edward Holman, laber
  Wm. Holman, cordwinder
⟨Abram Pits, dito⟩ rupturd
⟨John Hall, aprents⟩
  Wm. Jefferson, laber
  Wm. Ashby, farmer
  Tho. Bean, sarvant
  Daniel Pepper, sarvant
⟨John Tilley, laber⟩ lame
  Gorg. Beever, laber
  Tho. Lee, sarvant
  John Edis, sarvant
  John Hays, butcher
  John Pits, laber
  Mathew Gibson, carpanter
  Tho. Gilbort, dito
  Tho. Watson, cooper
  David House, laber
  John Young, shepard
  John Somes, sarvant
  Henery Somes, sarvant
  Mathew Shelston, sarvant
  John France, laber
⟨Wm. Berridg, laber⟩   4
⟨Gorg Spires, laber⟩   3
⟨Gorg Cornwell, laber⟩
  Abram Ashby, shepard
  Booros Boothway, laber
⟨Edward Hill, taler⟩   4 childn.
  John Hodghes, smith
  John Born, laber
⟨Kellham Right, cobler⟩ lame
⟨Wm. Gilby, laber⟩   3

Tho. Haley, laber
Tho. Cox, laber
⟨John Hull, aprentice⟩

The mark   Matthew X   of constable sworn
          Deny

PEAKIRK

A list of the names of the inhabitants of Peakirk betwixt the age of eighteen and fortyfive.

Mr Thos. Brecknock, graizer
Wm. Landen, grazer
John Gyles, farmer
⟨Wm. Bailey⟩ victualler
⟨Robt. Tyers⟩ labourer
⟨Jno. Sutton⟩ cordwainer
Jno. Tabiner, labourer
⟨Jos. Wakefield⟩ labourer
⟨Abal Vine⟩ sheepard
⟨Robt. Edas⟩ shepherd
Henery Foot, labourer
⟨Robt. Foot⟩ labourer

⟨Jno. Tyers⟩ labourer
Lenord Thorpe, tayler
Geo. Featherstone, labourer
Thos. Quincey, labourer
Wm. Sutton, labourer
⟨Step. Woolley⟩ blacksmith
⟨Robt. Louth⟩ farmer
⟨Robt. Smith⟩ sarvant & shepherd
Wm. Scoot, servant
Heny. Woods, servant
Thos, Pirkins, servant
Cristr. Jarvis, sarvant

Richd. Perceval, constable
Decr. 1762

PETERBOROUGH: St John the Baptist

A list of persons names in Peterborough liable to serve in the militia.

Joseph Beale, grocer
Philip Cole, butcher
⟨Chas. Bingham, baker, infm.⟩
Willm. Biggot, labr.
Willm. Wallis, carpenter
Saml. Silverwood, baker
John Richards, servant
Barthw. Herson, servt.
Thos. Dexter, labr.
Ben. Branston, labr.
⟨Wm. Simpson, labr.⟩
⟨Wm. Wright, carpenter⟩
Mattw. Green, wheeler
Thos. Cave, weaver
⟨Richd. Skinner, weaver⟩
Henry Love, labr.
⟨John Everett, workhouse⟩
⟨Saml. Hopkins, labr.⟩
Thos. Seaton, butcher
Hen. Cole, carpenter
George Bond, labr.
⟨Moses Moseley, smith⟩

Saml. Cockett, gard'ner
James Leay, comber
⟨Fras. Tompson, labr.⟩
Wm. Stricklin, labr.
Richd. Dickins, labr.
⟨John Britain, mason⟩
Jas. Batteram, labr.
John Frear, farmer
⟨Joseph Annables, labr.⟩ infirm
⟨John Johnson, shoemaker⟩
Richd. Johnson, shoemaker
Jas. Bull, carpenter
Thos. Hillam, labr.
⟨Chrisr. Strickson, gardener⟩
Richd. Holland, labr.
⟨Solo. Holmes, labr.⟩
⟨Richd. Rowell, miller⟩
John Rippon, slater
Thos. Moseley, weaver
John Wiggins, smith
Mark True, comber
Mattw. Smith, labr.

Thos. Simkin, farmer
⟨Gabl. Rose, shoemaker⟩
Wm. Holmes, slater
Laur. Horn, shoemaker
John Blunt, junr.
Lewis Whitehead, maltr.
Thos. Waterfield, servt.
Roger Parker, gent.
John Bond, carpenter
John Crunkhorn, servt.
⟨John Wells, butcher⟩
Wm. Gilder, labr.
Thos. Adcock, hostler
⟨Roger Low, comber⟩
John Hubbard, comber
Robt. Littledyke, labr.
Thos. Warriner, gent.
⟨Arthr. Arpin, infirm⟩
Joseph Dobbs, lodger
John Bingham, mason
Wm. Dodson, baker
John Radford, comber
Jno. Bevis, upholder
Robt. Sherman, smith
John Hethrington, draper
Wm. Sharpe, barber
Jno. Garner
⟨John Garner, comber⟩
Simon Hardy, gard'ner
John Moseley, weaver
⟨Thos. Craddock, shoemakr.⟩
Jas. Beeson, smith
⟨John Patstone, sievemakr.⟩
Fell Bursnoll, mason
John Ablin, labr.
⟨Wm. Gleddall, slater⟩ 4 children
⟨Wm. Whittle, labr.⟩
⟨Chas. Burdett, baker⟩ infm.
⟨Ben. Wright, labr.⟩
⟨Henry Alderman, labr.⟩
⟨Wm. Barley, labr.⟩
Stepn. Porter, sweep
Wm. Cook, labr.
Richd. Speechly, labr.
Thos. Bolton, labr.
John Thompson, shoemr.
John Desborough, labr.
⟨John Kirk, tinker⟩
⟨John Seaton, weaver⟩
⟨Richd. Longfoot, labr.⟩
Mattw. Pattstone, labr.
⟨Gyles Bull, labr.⟩

John Cooper, butcher
Edwd. Sutton, labr.
⟨John Hunt⟩ 6 childn.
Wm. Cunnington, tanner
John Flyde, baker
Jno. Shepheard
⟨John Shepherd, farmer⟩
Ralph Wincle
Thos. Fisher, labr.
Chas. Bothway, carpenr.
⟨John Pratt, weaver⟩
⟨Jacob Baily, labr.⟩
⟨Wm. Wright, labr.⟩
⟨Thos. Denny, labr.⟩
⟨Jas. Hatfield, infirm⟩
⟨Wm. Tatman, labr.⟩
Jno. Rycraft, labr.
Thos. Andrew, labr.
Saml. Hoggart, labr.
John Bott, labr.
Isaac Baily, labr.
Thos. Deakins, labr.
⟨Geo. Bott, labr.⟩
Jas. Bursnoll, carpenr.
⟨Hen. Cunnington, shoemr.⟩
John Asdale, labr.
⟨Jos. Atkinson, gardener⟩
⟨Robt. Oliver, miller⟩
John Baxter, labr.
Edd. Laxton, grocer
⟨Robt. Young, barber⟩
Wm. Wainwright
Wm. Taylor, draper
John Berry, shoemr.
Geo. Wright, junr.
⟨Geo. Wright, organist⟩*
Thos. West, servt.
Hen. Bracken, servt.
Hen. Rodgers, sert.
Richd. Laud
Thos. Jacques
Richd. Allen, servt.
Richd. Cart, servt.
⟨Thos. Cole, labr.⟩
John Dymock, servt.
Richd. Loving, mason
⟨Geo. Ankle, mason⟩
Thos. Sharp, servt.
Robt. Gill, servt.
James Bellars, sert.
⟨James Gudge, gardner⟩
Robt. King, founder

* Organist at Peterborough Cathedral, NRO ML 869.

Chas. Wilson, pipemaker
⟨John Deboo, infirm⟩
John Draper, mercht.
Sam. Morton, weaver
Jas. Powell, heckler
⟨John Hutton, fellmonger⟩
Thos. Green, labr.
Robt. Whittmoe, lab.
Benj. Wright
⟨Benj. Wright, mercht.⟩
Wm. Wright, do.
John Stocks, labr.
Jerh. Gilbert
⟨Jere. Gilbert, whitr.⟩
Thos. Ansell, servt.
Jas. Delarue, gent.
John Porter, smith
Wm. Millington, taylor
Wm. Watt, labr.
Thos. Cassel, baker
Wm. Healy, waterman
Benj. Cole, carpr.
⟨Benj. Cole, carpenr.⟩
Benj. Cole, junr.
Robt. Allott, farmer
Wm. Shittleboro, gardr.
Geo. Nicholls, cutler
Thos. Lown
⟨Wm. English, staymr.⟩
John Hillam, thatchr.
Wm. Gibbs, taylor
⟨John Wilson, glasr.⟩
Thos. Rose, butcher
Abm. Gratrix, glover
Jas. Mahew, do.
⟨Abm. Corpe, taylor⟩
⟨Robt. Crisp, shoemr.⟩
Jno. Gibbs
⟨John Gibbs, barbr.⟩
Jno. Woodcock, junr.
⟨John Woodcock, sad.⟩
Joseph Whether
Thos. Kingston, sert.
Jere. Stamford, labr.
⟨Jos. Gates, taylor⟩
Saml. Hare, servt.
Jas. Tompson, esq.
Jona. Herrington, sert.
Waldr. Orme, esq.
Ashby Dean, servt.
Thos. Cunnington, labr.
Wm. Washington, carpenr.
⟨John Gates, taylor⟩ infm.
Wm. Elmer, taylor

Robt. Feler, taylor
Hen. Ward, taylor
Thos. Serocold, gent.
Jno. Fenn
⟨Jno. Fenn, exciseman⟩
Edwd. Biddlecomb
⟨Edd. Biddlecomb, do⟩
Jos. Bothway, grocer
⟨John Bond, watchmr.⟩ infirm
⟨John Jackson, labr.⟩
Wm. Elger
⟨Wm. Elger⟩
John Buck, servt.
Saml. Smith, servt.
James Wiffin, servt.
Robt. Nicholls, servt.
Wm. Andrew, servt.
Geo. Fotheringay, sadler
Wm. Day, glover
Wm. Fugg, glover
Wm. Gill, glover
Wm. Britain, mason
Jno. Waterfield, maltr.
Steph. Neal, mason
John Richardson, taylor
⟨Thos. Holmes, slater⟩
Jas. English, slater
⟨John Huckerby, labr.⟩
⟨Jo. Henson, comber⟩
Thos. Clarke, apothecary
Wm. Hanes, limner
⟨Saml. Richardson, smith⟩
James Hares, comber
John Batteram, labr.
⟨John Jackson, labr.⟩
Edd. Batteras, baker
Thos. Money, slater
Robt. Bull, labr.
⟨Wm. White, labr.⟩
Thos. Gervis, gard'ner
⟨*Jno. Prior*⟩
⟨John Prior, chairmaker⟩
⟨Wm. Andrew, mason⟩
Richd. Lee, labr.
⟨Danl. Stanfield, do.⟩
⟨David Holmes, heckr.⟩
Woodward
Wm. ⟨Woard⟩, gardner
Jno. Littledyke, taylor
Jno. Woods, shoemaker
Benj. Bolton
⟨Benj. Bolton, heckler⟩
House, junr., comber
John Lowder, brasier

Jas. White, slater
Wm. White, junr.
⟨Wm. White, slater⟩
Wm. Brice, carpenr.
John Kniton, shoemr.
Robt. Marshall, mason
⟨Robt. Pemberton, slater⟩
Jon. Wortlefield, labr.
Jno. Smith, carpenr.
Jas. Hine, shoemr.
⟨Fras. Washington, brewr.⟩
David Walker, hosier
⟨John Fox, heckler⟩
Jos. Fox, do.
Joseph Powell, innholder
John Loving, mason
Robt. English, brewer
⟨Wm. Freeman, 1 leg⟩
Wm. Scrimshaw, docr.
John Cox, do.
Thos. Gibbs, taylor
Robt. Young, barber
John Riddleton, labr.
Leml. Limbert, carpenr.
⟨Thos. Hasker, taylor⟩
Jno. Baker, joyner
Jno. Johnson, glover
⟨John Smith, 1 leg⟩
Jno. Bass, smith
⟨Geo. Spencer, shoemr.⟩
Thos. Rasdall, carpenr.
Thos. Thompson, labr.
Edd. Arbor, labr.
James Brookes, cooper
Hen. Chapman, carpr.
Richd. Bosworth, hostler
Thos. Alderman, do
John Gunton, do
Hugh Bull, taylor
⟨Edwd. Kingston, butcher⟩
Jas. Eaton, shoemakr.
Jno. Falkner, comber
⟨Wm. Beaver, baker⟩
Saml. Norton, butcher
⟨ *Wm. Holmes* ⟩
⟨Wm. Holmes, gard'ner⟩
Thos. Baxter, gard'ner
Jno. Jamblin, slater
⟨Jno. Colls, patinmaker⟩
⟨Robt. Sharpe, shoemr.⟩
⟨Jona. Neal, wheeler⟩
Chas. Cole, carpenr.
John Sampson, barber
Saml. Ellis, glasier

Jno. Barker, comber
Wm. Whitehead, smith
⟨Wm. Landford, barber⟩
Thos. Scarboro. tayr.
Hen. Vinter, surgeon
⟨Jas. Searl, shoemr.⟩
Jos. Fountain, nacker
Jos. Dates, butcher
Val. Deepup, barber
⟨Wm. Cliften, painter⟩
Wm. Tompson, butcher
Stepn. Wilkin
⟨Stepn. Wilkin, baker⟩
Thos. Bates, labr.
⟨Jno. Pruden, labr.⟩
⟨John Knight, smith⟩
Robt. Twiddy, do.
Saml. Dixon, pub.
Thos. Ibuit, labr.
⟨Wm. Neale, porter⟩
⟨Paul Walker, gard'ner⟩
Geo. Wright, labr.
Wm. Ashby, waterman
Wm. Pen, labr.
⟨John Eaton, waterman⟩
Wm. Meadows, do
Jas. Castle, labr.
Robt. Steel, waterman
John Leroo, gent.
⟨Thos. Vickers, carpr.⟩
Robt. Miller, fellmon.
Thos. Scaiffe, grocer
⟨Saml. Slater, shoemr.⟩
Wm. Brown, weaver
Robt. Cooper, hostler
John Flanders, waterm.
⟨Nath. Shepheard, por.⟩
John Pearcy, waterman
John Pennystone, barber
Saml. Owen, nacker
⟨Thos. Dean, maltr.⟩
⟨Geo. Weeler, pub.⟩
Saml. Slade, porter
⟨Richd. Hownslow, joyner⟩
John Eaton, cutler
Richd. Johnson, netmaker
John Dennison, boatwright
Robt. Walter, comber
Robt. Stokes, porter
⟨John Porter, cadger⟩
Robt. Simpson, porter
Geo. Palmer, waterman
⟨John Whitehead, slater⟩
Wm. Lane, slater

Richd. Thacker, grocer
Carter Sharp, musician
Hen. Hemant, matmaker
Wm. Searl, comber
Wm. Woods, boatwright
⟨Edd. Cave, shoemaker⟩
John Smith, waterman
⟨Jas. Mew, barber⟩
Jno. Russel, staymaker
Simon Rooks, schoolmr.
Ralph Whitwell, baker
Saml. Stevens, currier
⟨Richd. Speechly, butcher⟩
Robt. Clarke, joyner
John Hall, shoemaker
⟨Thos. Beaver, butcher⟩
John Goswell, cooper
Richd. Hodson, porter
⟨Wm. Noble, butcher⟩
⟨Jos. Saunders, glasier⟩
Steph. Massingarb, butr.
⟨Chas. Clarke, butcher⟩
Geo. Eaves, labr.
Robt. Mugliston, draper
John Beaver, confectioner
Jos. Fox, butcher

Saml. Noon, shoemaker
John Town, barber
⟨Wm. Bowker, grocer⟩
Edwd. Bouchier, hatter
John Griffith
⟨John Griffiths, draper⟩
Wm. Caldecott, surgeon
Brian
⟨Benj.⟩ Beetom, surgeon
Nicl. Ball, butcher
Goodman James, exciseman
John Wines, comber
Edwd. Harrison, labr.
⟨Henry Peach, labr.⟩
Thos. Hammont, miller
Wm. Fell, whitetawr.
Jno. Whitehead, smith
Robt. Bursnoll, servt.
Thos. Bromley, servt.
Nathl. Hudson,
Wm. Wade, labr.
      Coleback, labr.
Jos. Meadows, heckler
Wm. Bolton, carrier,
Jas. English, taylor
John Freear, baker

Constables
Frs. Parnell
Richard Bridges
John Wade

PETERBOROUGH

[Second list, relating probably to the extra-parochial district formed by the minster precincts.]

Peterboro.

Robt. Blake, esq.
Isa. Strong, attorney
⟨James Viel, servant⟩ inferm
John Stairs, sadler
⟨Thos. Beacher, attorney⟩ 45
⟨Wm. Wright⟩ inferm
⟨Henry Walker, glover⟩ 5 children

⟨Tho. Davis, laber⟩
Tho. Pemberton, mason
Wm. Bodgener, shoemaker
Henry Baxter, laber
Tho. Rose, bucher
Isa. Cardwell, blacksmith

DOGSTHORPE

A list of the inhabitents of Dosthorpe.

Job Johnson, farmer
Peter Smith, ditto
John King, ditto
Phill. Scatley, ditto
Frans. Hollige, ditto

Robt. Brown, ditto
Hen. Bottomley, ditto
Benjn. Hollige, ditto
Mathew Southwell, carpenter
⟨James Chapman, tayler⟩

Thos. Fever, gardener
Edwd. Woodley, weaver
Wm. Love, sarvant
John Winshley, ditto
Wm. Sissen, ditto
Wm. Smith, ditto
Robt. Boyfield, ditto
John Bayley, ditto
Anthoney Garrot, ditto
John Cole, ditto
Andrew Ridlington, ditto
Wm. Marvel, ditto
Thos. Ellise, ditto
Steven Black, ditto
John Pacy, ditto

Sam. Nuton, labouer in prison
⟨Sam. Mobry, labouer⟩
⟨Robt. Bate, ditto⟩
Jos. Church, ditto
⟨Thos. Fouller, ditto⟩
Thos. Bottom, ditto
⟨Wm. Wakefield, ditto⟩
Robt. Botherway, ditto
Thos. Werrington, ditto
⟨John Pacy, ailding⟩
⟨Charles Bull, labouer⟩
Wm. Hurst, ditto
Wm. Bishop, ditto
Thos. Nicholls, miller

Tho. Sharpe X his mark

EASTFIELD AND NEWARK

A list of ye peopels names liable to serve in ye militia for Eastfeild and Newark.

Gyles Marriott, juner
  Holmes
Saml. ⟨Holomas⟩ sarvant
John Chapman, sarvant
Wm. Baker, sarvant
Hanory Brone, laberer
Tho. Hillam, sarvant
Wm. Belley, laberer
⟨Jos. Croson, laberer⟩ 3 children
⟨Wm. Deay, laberer⟩ 3 children
James Right, laberer
⟨Adam Jones, juner⟩ disabled
Robt. Mallet, sarvent
Andr. Burton, laberer
John Burton, laberer
John Holomes, laberer

John Bensley, laberer
Jos. Lewin, laberer
John Foster, farmer
⟨Francs. Bob, laberer⟩ 3 children
Wm. Prier, farmer
⟨Tho. Bell, laberer⟩ 46 yrs
⟨Jos. Perkins, farmer⟩
⟨Larn' Eldred, shapard⟩ 3 children
Wm. Criston, farmer
Wm. Johnson, laberer
Tho. Coleson, laberer
James Jales, farmer
Georg Pank, juner
John Bosworth, sarvant
⟨John Coble, laberer⟩ 3 children

Gyles Marriott

LONGTHORPE

December the 10th 1762

A list of the inhabbetance of the hamblet of Longthorpe betwen the age of eaighteene and forty five years.

Joseph Bitting, farmers son
William Wright, labourer
James Giles, innholder
William Stimpson, labour
⟨Edward Christefer⟩ 3 children
Thomas Meadows, labour
⟨Wwilliam Lewin⟩

George Wright, labour
⟨William Barron⟩ 3 children
Thomas Wells, labourer
John Bull, farmer
William Cook, servt.
John Stricklin, servt.
⟨James Brown⟩ 3 children

⟨Francies Ayres, labour⟩ lame
Edward Kingston, butcher
William Emeney, labour
William Cave ⟨Westwood
  belonging to Peterbro'⟩
Thomas Tod, labour
James Bull, carpinter
Mr. Spence
Edward Shaw, servt.
John Hogard, servt.
John Hunt, servt.
⟨Fackony Whiman⟩ labour, 7 chil.
Henery Hichcock, farmer

⟨dito his man⟩ refusd to tell his
  name
⟨Charles Nuel⟩ labour
⟨Thomas Sharp, seaner, labr.⟩
  3 chiln.
Wiliam West, labour
Thomas Sharp, juner, labr.
⟨George Harris⟩ labour, 3 chil.
John Broton, labour
  Sherrard
Thomas ⟨Sir J. Bernards servt who
  refused to tell his name⟩

Jo. Bitting, sworn

WOTHORPE

Wothorpe. Thos. Andrew, const.

Francis Cudington, labourer

James Cotten, carpeter

THORNHAUGH

Decembr the 5th. 1762. A list of the hous diwless and servants of the parish
of Thornhaugh in the County of Northamtonshire betwen the ages of
eighteen and forty five years.

⟨John Scotney, constebell⟩

⟨Ed. *illegible*, juner, tayler⟩
Will. Deth, husbanman
Thos. Deth, husbanman
Will Reve, keeper
Will. Goodlad, husbanman
John Blads, husbanman
⟨*illegible* Cooper, laborow⟩
⟨Richard Coollins, laborow⟩ 4 chilldren
Thos, Andoro, geldor
Will Brice, laborow
Sam Ashby, laborow
⟨John Coole, cager⟩ 6 chilldren
John Peper, laborow
John Wallis, laborow
⟨Nat. Beaver, laborow⟩ 4 chilldren
Johnothon Gren, laborow
Mark Gramer, laborow
Servants ⟨Jos. Allen, gentellmans servant⟩
        Will. Hogard, gardener
        James Wats, farm. servant
        Jos. Smith, shepard
        Jos. Fitchill, farm. servant
        John Chapman, shepard

Militia meting appointed to be holden on Saturday the eleventh day of
December at the hous of Will Elger in Peterborough by nine of the clock

in the forenoon all persons think in them selves aggrived may then appeall
and no appeals will be afterwards received.

John Scotney

UFFORD

Dec. ye 11 1762

A list of the men of ye town of Ufford that is above eighteen years and
forty five.

Thos. Gee, farmer	1
John Martin, farmers sun	2
Robert Beaver, farmers sun	3
⟨John Jonson, carpinter⟩	4
⟨John Meddis, joyner⟩	5
Charles Selby, carpinter	6
John Shelton, mason	7
⟨Gorg Watson, taler⟩	8
John Hart, taler	9
John Fell, weafer	10
⟨John Riddle, showmaker⟩	11
Wm. Frear, sheperd	12
Wm. Halley, sarvant	13
John Cew, sarvant	14
John Seal, sarvant	15
Mathias Plowright, sarvant	16
Wm. Parnil, sarvant	17
⟨John Thiselton, a gardner but sinc the 4 day of this month⟩	18
Thomas Ward, a lat was out of plase biut now he is gon to his plase	19
⟨Noel Ashby, a poor man is left with three childrn⟩	20

So I hop gentlmen you will exceus these 3 men

John Burbidge, cunstable.

ASHTON

December 11th 1762. The list of ye names of ye town of Ashton.

⟨Henery Bryan, laberer⟩ five children
Richard Nottingham, laberer
Charles Garfoot, laberer
William Winslow, laberer
⟨Richard Adkin, laberer⟩ three children

Rents under forty shillings a year

William Fell, masner
⟨Robert Winslow, tayler⟩ four children
Edward Shelton, cord winder
William Munton, sarvant
William Garfoot, sarvant
William Warren, sarvant
James Rickitt, miller
Joseph Rickitt, miller

⟨Richard Popple, wever, has a lame foot⟩
⟨John Porter, lame of his nee⟩
⟨John Burle, lame of his huck bone⟩

James Stains, cunstable

WANSFORD

A list of the parish of Wansford.

Mr Pank Meadmore, merct.
John Peears, laberour
Richard Parsons, butcher
Wm. Mitchell, coardwainer
⟨John Glithorow, mason⟩
⟨Henry Glitherow, mason⟩
John Richerison, laberour
Robart Ogle, malster

John Clarkson, weaver
John Hall, malster
Edward Pauley, turnpikeeper
Robart Brown, laberour
Phillip Rose, alehouse keeper
Wm. Hopkins, sarvent man
John Deur, schoole master
John Smith, laberour

WITTERING

The parish of Wittering. A true list of the inhabetents betwen the ages of
eighteen and forty five.

James Woodward, farmer
Richd. Hule, farmer
⟨Richard Hull, farmer⟩
Hugh
⟨Huig⟩ Boor, farmer
John Irland, farmer
Thomas Irland, farmer
Paul Louth, farmer
⟨Will. Smith, laberer⟩ 3 children
Lenard Norl, laberer
Edwd. Thorpe, labourer
⟨Edwood Tarpe, laber⟩
Will. Louth, laber
Thomas Park, laber
⟨Thomas Lovday, laber⟩ 3 children

Franc.
⟨Fares Bloodwort, laber⟩ 5 children
Wm. Curtis
⟨Will. Cottes⟩ sarvent
Edwd. Lee
⟨Edwood Luee⟩ sarvent
John Colpen, sarvent
Jones
Will. ⟨Jons⟩ sarvent
Tho. Tennent
⟨Thomas Tanent⟩ sarvent
Robt. Dennis, servant
⟨Robhare Danes, sarvent⟩
⟨James Hence⟩ laber
James Hench, shepherd

The mark X of Mathw. Burnaby, constable

Note
For statistical puroses (Tables 1, 2a and 3a), '⟨James Hence⟩ laber' and
'*James Hench, shepherd*' have been counted as separate persons. It is not
clear from the Wittering list whether these entries represent two different
men, or whether the entry for Hench is a correction of the deleted entry for
Hence.

GENERAL INDEX